Passeriformes

THE
STARLING

THE
STARLING

CHRISTOPHER FEARE

OXFORD NEW YORK
OXFORD UNIVERSITY PRESS
1984

Oxford University Press, Walton Street, Oxford OX2 6DP

London Glasgow New York Toronto
Delhi Bombay Calcutta Madras Karachi
Kuala Lumpur Singapore Hong Kong Tokyo
Nairobi Dar es Salaam Cape Town
Melbourne Auckland

and associated companies in
Beirut Berlin Ibadan Mexico City Nicosia

Oxford is a trade mark of Oxford University Press

British Library Cataloguing in Publication Data

Feare Christopher
  The starling.
  1. Starlings   2. Birds–Europe
  I. Title
598.8′63′094   QL696.P278
ISBN 0-19-217705-2

Set by Oxford Publishing Services, Oxford
Printed in Great Britain by
Butler & Tanner Ltd, Frome and London

To Adam and my parents

PREFACE

I am not a fatalist, but in retrospect Starlings seem always to have been 'there' in the background of my birding life. My interest in birds began at about eight years old when my parents' garden, in Louth in Lincolnshire, was visited one winter by two bizarre birds that eventually turned out to be Waxwings *Bombycilla garrulus* (these have, in fact, been included in the Starling's family by some taxonomists but I think this is erroneous and do not regard this the start of my 'Starling days'!). The birds were identified from my description by our 'local' ornithologist, Lenton Ottaway. Presumably he sensed a latent interest in birds, for he encouraged me to go bird-watching with him and he showed me some of the Lincolnshire sights.

The first of these was a Starling winter roost at Elkington, about two miles from my home. Even before I was aware that such a thing as a roost existed, I had become accustomed to vast evening flights of birds, for each winter evening saw a flight to the coast by tens of thousands of gulls and a flight in the opposite direction, from the coastal fens of northern Lincolnshire to the edge of the Wolds where the roost lay, of hundreds of thousands of Starlings. On some evenings the flight lines stopped briefly in the fields behind our house as the birds congregated in what I now know to be 'pre-roost assemblies'. On 'good' evenings the grass fields were literally darkened by birds and constituted a spectacular entertainment for the local populace. When my tutor introduced me to the roost site itself, two aspects impressed me. One was the stench and filth and the other was a daytime roost, in the same wood, of about a dozen Long-eared Owls, *Asio otus*, which I had never seen before but which assumed must have had excellent late night restaurant facilities.

Lenton taught me most of my early bird-watching at what is now known as Saltfleetby-Theddlethorpe Dunes National Nature Reserve. There, I was introduced to many exciting 'ticks' and also to spectacular events. One of these (on 28 October 1956—I still have the notebook) was to watch the arrival over the sea of thousands of Starlings from Scandinavia. The birds arrived in flocks of 50 to 200 birds. The number of birds involved was memorable enough, but the most striking memory is of watching the odd bird fall out of the flocks into the sea, not quite having made it to land and a replenishing breakfast of Sea Buckthorn *Hippophae rhamnoides* berries.

All spare moments during my primary and secondary education were devoted to twitching (for terminology, see Oddie 1980), but University life necessitated a lull in my birding activities. Having completed a degree course in zoology at the University of Leeds, I spent three enjoyable years at the beautiful fishing village of Robin Hood's Bay, Yorkshire, completing a Ph.D in marine ecology. The basic idea of my thesis was to study the population dynamics of the Dogwhelk *Nucella lapillus*, but I found that some of the important predators of this snail were birds and devoted a lot of time to studying them. While watching Purple Sandpipers *Calidris maritima* and Oystercatchers *Haematopus ostralegus* eating Dogwhelks I was surprised to find that Starlings could also be very good shorebirds.

After Robin Hood's Bay, I went to Aberdeen to study the food of Rooks *Corvus frugilegus*, and its relation to agriculture. Thus I became a student of bird pests but when this research fellowship was over my professor, George Dunnet, offered me the prospect of two years in the Seychelles, studying the opposite of 'birds as pests'—birds as a food source for man'. The bird involved here was one of the most beautiful of seabirds, the Sooty Tern *Sterna fuscata*, whose eggs are collected by the Seychellois. But even these idyllic years, I was confronted with a starling, the Common Mynah *Acridotheres tristis*, and devoted some time to looking at its roosting behaviour (Feare 1976a).

On my return from the Seychelles (in great depression at being subjected to the British climate and an excessive human population density) I took my present post with the Ministry of Agriculture, Fisheries, and Food. Since then (1974), Starlings have dominated my life.

The European Starling inhabits a large part of the Earth's land surface, tends to be common where it does occur, and it adapts well to life in captivity. As a result, it has been the subject of a great many field and laboratory studies and of a large volume of literature. It is surprising, therefore, that an English language monograph has not been written before, although monographs in German (Schneider 1972) and Dutch (Gallagher 1978) have appeared during the last decade. (A further monograph, in Russian, is being prepared following an intensive period of research on Starlings in the USSR, under the direction of Dr S. G. Priklonskii (Priklonskii, personal communication): this volume, describing the biology of eastern populations of the Starling, is eagerly awaited.) One of the difficulties of writing such a monograph is the rate at which new literature appears—the reference list at the end of this book is by no means exhaustive and in any case it will be out of date by the time that the book appears in shops. I hope, nevertheless, that my treatment of the ecology and behaviour of the Starling will help the interested bird watcher to interpret what he sees and perhaps introduce him to a few recent concepts in animal ecology and behaviour. I also hope that people embarking on research on this beast will find the book a useful basis for their studies. If the book actually stimulates some people to undertake research aimed at answering some of the many questions that I pose, then the effort involved in writing the monograph will have been well worth while. Anyone who is so stimulated will find the task rewarding and I am sure they will be fascinated, as I have been, by aspects of the Starling's biology outside the realm of their own studies. When I began to look at the Starling in earnest I soon found that this bird had the ability to force its presence upon me: a friend has described the Starling as 'The second-hand car salesman of the bird world' and I have since found it difficult to put this comparison out of my mind! It is also a cheerful bird, for it seems to spend a lot of its 'spare' time singing.

It would not have been possible to write this book had it not been for the painstaking research of many ornithologists, past and present. Most of them I do not know, but nevertheless I thank them for making my task possible. I do have the good fortune to know some of the contemporary students of various aspects of Starling biology and this book has benefited from discussions, verbal or written, with Fadhil Al-Joborae, Chris Edwards, Peter Evans, Brian Follett, Jim Glahn, Andrew Hindmarsh, John Mackinon, Lady Stewart, Ron Summers, Jaques Tahon, Joost Tinbergen, Rudi Verheyen, and Klaas Westerterp. Many other colleagues, far too numerous to mention, have inevitably helped to consolidate my ideas through discussions of many topics. I am particularly indebted to those colleagues who devoted considerable time and effort to criticizing sections of the book in draft: Chris Edwards, Peter Evans, Brian Follett, Edward Gibson,

Derek Goodwin, Peter Greig-Smith, Andrew Hindmarsh, Ian Inglis, Ian Keymer, Ron Summers, and Ron Thearle. The text has benefited enormously from their contribution and the blame for remaining shortcomings falls entirely on my shoulders.

The drawings of Gill Wilson (open-bill probing and the wings of a primitive and an advanced Starling) and John Love (postures) have enhanced the relevant chapters and Denis Alexander, Jacqui Hogan, Robin Prytherch, Peter Purchas and Marianne Wilding have helped to make the photographic record more complete. I was permitted to take the photograph of Starlings leaving their roost as seen on the plan position indicator of a radar through the cooperation of R.A.F. Binbrook. Ian Galbraith and Derek Read allowed me to examine the Sturnidae collection in the Sub-Department of Ornithology of the British Museum (Natural History). My mother typed the manuscript and my father made initial checks for typological or phraseological errors.

I am grateful to all these people for their invaluable assistance. However, I should not have gained my absorbing interest in Starlings had the Ministry of Agriculture, Fisheries, and Food not employed me to make an economic and biological study of the species in Britain and I owe the Ministry my thanks. In writing this book I have discovered something further—that writing a book teaches one more about one's study animal than can be learned by any other means! I therefore thank Oxford University Press for inviting me to write the book. Finally, I thank all of the Starlings that have been the subject of my observations and experiments—they have been the source of ceaselessly satisfying entertainment.

C.J.F.

Ewhurst, Surrey
1982

CONTENTS

PLATES

Plates fall between pages 146 and 147.

1 INTRODUCTION

Ron Murton (1965) began his book on the Woodpigeon *Columba palumbus* by saying that it is a beautiful bird. This is precisely my feeling about the Starling, but I suspect that anyone who studies a species of animal for a long time will eventually come to regard that animal as beautiful. When one devotes many hours to watching an animal, one becomes familiar with more than just its appearance: it develops a 'character' that distinguishes it from all other animals, a character that becomes particularly meaningful to the student of the species. But if we restrict ourselves to looking at only the one species, we are likely to miss some of its less obvious characteristics. Such a narrow approach ignores the fact that that species has evolved from (probably) unknown ancestors, and that these ancestors gave rise, not only to 'our' species, but also to a wide range of other forms. These other forms also have their own particular attributes, some of which will be shared by 'our' species and others which may be quite different. Some of the attributes of the other species will be specializations which will enable them to live in their part of the world's environment, but other attributes will be part of the general make-up of the group of species concerned.

When we look at the Starling or, more correctly, the European Starling *Sturnus vulgaris*, we can gain a better insight into its 'character' and what has made it such a successful bird, if we examine it in relation to all of the other members of the starling family Sturnidae, which contains about 110 species. However, before we can begin this examination we have to ask the fundamental question: what is a starling? Here, we begin to encounter one of the dilemmas facing the biologist with interests in animal classification, for the divisions between one group of organisms and the next are seldom clear-cut. This is because what we see today is only a step in the continuing evolution of life, and from what is present now we have to attempt to piece together the past history of the starlings in order to elucidate their relationships. It is rather like looking at an old Victorian photograph of all the inhabitants of a small village (I have seen this kind of photograph in the Yorkshire fishing village of Robin Hood's Bay) and trying to work out who belongs to which family: all the faces in the photograph are human and certain facial characteristics obviously relate some individuals to others. Some faces, however, are so different from the others that it is difficult to say whether they belong to the true village families or whether they really originate from a nearby village or even farther afield.

So it is with starlings. While most of the birds included in the family are obviously starlings, other birds, on the fringe, possess some characters of starlings but others of, say, crows or other, more obscure, groups.

The basic structural characteristics of starlings can be summarized as follows. They are small- to medium-sized birds with strong legs and a bill that is generally stout and strong but not elongated. The nostrils are never covered by frontal bristles. The wings are long and always have ten primaries; however, the tenth (outer) primary is small, often lancet-shaped, and is reduced in the evolutionary history of the family. The sexes are usually similar or separated by only minor differences, for example, females may be slightly duller than males or are sometimes distinguished by the presence or absence of a coloured iris, but in some genera male and female may be quite different. Juveniles are generally similar to adults though often duller, while in a few groups they may be distinctive. The most notable characteristic of the plumage of starlings is the widespread occurrence of glossy irridescence: usually this manifests itself as oily sheens on otherwise blackish feathers but in some species at least part of the plumage is of shining orange, blue, or violet. Some genera, especially those in the Oriental region, have parts of the head devoid of feathers and the skin here is often brightly coloured.

THE STARLING FAMILY

Even when we have decided what constitutes a starling, we are still uncertain exactly how many species there are since some forms, especially those of the genus *Aplonis* on various Pacific islands, are so similar and closely related that their division into species or races becomes arbitrary. In this book I use the classification of the family that was originally suggested by Amadon (1943, 1956), although recent work by Beecher (1978) suggests that some modifications to Amadon's system might be necessary. Amadon's classification is based mainly on the study of skins that were preserved by early collectors and deposited in museums through-out the world, while Beecher examined the relationships within the family on the basis of the bone and muscle structure of the head, especially those parts concerned with the opening and clos-ing of the bill. It has now become possible to use some of the chemical constituents of birds' bodies in taxonomic studies and on this basis Sibley and Ahlquist (1974) have asserted that the two South African sugarbirds *Promerops cafer* and *P. gurneyi* should be placed in the Sturnidae. My own interests lie in the behaviour and ecology of the various genera and species. Any classification based on only one of these criteria is bound to be incomplete and when we attempt to combine those based on ecology and behaviour, jaw structure and musculature, and body form as revealed by skins, we find conflict in some areas. This is because some of the traits that are present in a species will be generalized characteristics of the family or genus, while others will be spe-cializations to the species' present mode of life. Any attempt to draw up a family tree based on all of the characteristics that happen to have been investigaed is inevitably, therefore, a com-promise. Unfortunately, as the summary in Table 1. shows, the ecology and behaviour of some of the genera of starlings are poorly known because scientists have been unable to observe them in the wild. This is due to the scarcity of some species and to the inaccessible habitats, on remote islands or in forest canopies, of others. We shall see later the various ways in which starlings have become important to man, but it is important to realize here that at least part of our knowledge of some of the more elusive species stems from man's desire to keep birds in captivity. For example, the colours of the eggs of some species are known only from the descriptions of aviculturists, and more use could be made of cap-tive birds in the study of certain aspects of behaviour that cannot be observed in the natural habitat.

It can be seen from Table 1.1 that within most of the genera of living starlings recognized by Amadon, the ecological and behavioural characters that I have examined are fairly homogeneous. Most species are gregarious and eat both animal and vegetable foods which usually consist of insects and fruit, berries, and seeds respectively. A few species also take nectar, although none is specialized for this role by the bill adaptations found in other families, e.g. the sunbirds (Nectariniidae) and hummingbirds (Trochilidae). However the peculiar crests of some

Table 1.1 Feeding and nesting characteristics of the Sturnidae. Classification follows Amadon (1943, 1956). The numbers in each column are the number of species in each genus that show the column characteristic.

Genus	No. of species	Feeding						Nesting			Spotted eggs
		Flocks	Arboreal	Ground	Fruit/Berries	Insects	Nectar	Holes in trees	Other holes	Domed	
Aplonis	20	6(12?)	14(6?)		9(11?)	2	1	8(9?)	2	1	6(14?)
Poeoptera	3	2(1?)	3		3	2		2	1		1(2?)
Grafisia	1	1	1		1			?			?
Onychognathus	10	8(1?)	2(1?)	7(1?)	8(1?)	5(1?)	1	3(2?)	7		6(4?)
Lamprotornis	16	15	11	8	16	14		13(3?)			11 usually (5?)
Cinnyricinclus	3	3	3		3	1(2?)		2(1?)			1(2?)
Speculipastor	1	1	1	1	1	1			anthill		1
Neocichla	1	1	1	occasional	?			?			?
Spreo	7	6	1(1?)	5	4(2?)	6(1?)		3	1	3	4
Cosmopsarus	2	2	2		1	2		1(1?)			1(1?)
Saroglossa	2	2	2		2	2	1	2			2
Creatophora	1	1		1	1	1			1	cups	occasional
Sturnus	16	16	8(1?)	14(2?)	12	13	4	14	9	2	0
Leucopsar	1	1			?			?			?
Acridotheres	6	6	1	6	6	6	3	5	5	1 occasional	0
Ampeliceps	1	1	1		1	1		1			0
Mino	2	2	2		2			1(1?)			1(1?)
Basilornis	4	1(3?)	1(3?)		1(3?)	?		?			?
Streptocitta	2	1(1?)	1(1?)		1(1?)	1(1?)		1(1?)			?
Sarcops	1							1			?
Gracula	2	2	2		2	1	1	2	1		2
Enodes	1	1	1		1	?		?			?
Scissirostrum	1	1	1		1			1			?
Buphagus	2	2				2		2			2

Main sources of reference: Ali and Ripley 1972; Amadon 1943, 1956; Bannerman 1953a; Brown 1965; Deignan 1945; Delacour and Mayr 1946; Dement'ev and Gladkov 1960; Henry 1971; King, Woodcock, and Dickinson 1975; Mackworth-Pread and Grant 1955, 1963; Marien 1950; Medway and Wells 1976; Meinertzhagen 1954; Meyer and Wigglesworth 1898; Rand 1936; Smythies 1953; Vaurie 1962; Whistler 1963.

of the *Acridotheres* mynahs may have evolved in association with nectar-feeding and probably play a part in pollination, and the tongue of the Brahminy Starling *Sturnus pagodarum* is brush-like, an adaptation to collecting nectar, or pollen, or both.

With respect to feeding, the main dichotomy within the family concerns arboreal or terrestrial foraging. While many species are capable of both, the more primitive forms, especially *Aplonis* and *Lamprotornis*, tend to be primarily arboreal and the starlings may well be derived from arboreal ancestors. During the evolution of the family there has been a tendency towards terrestrial feeding and specializations for this, including long toes and powerful legs, reach their peak in *Sturnus*.

This transition from an arboreal, fruit-eating existence to one of searching for insects on the ground was clearly shown by Beecher's studies of the form and function of the muscles and bones associated with feeding. In the primitive *Aplonis* and *Lamprotornis*, the muscles that pull the upper mandible downwards, the adductors, are well-developed while those that raise the upper mandible, the protractors, are less well-developed. Beecher found this arrangement to pertain in what he termed an 'island complex' of genera that inhabit islands and shores of the Indian Ocean and the Indonesian islands. These were *Ampeliceps, Mino, Basilornis, Streptocitta, Sarcops, Gracula*, and *Aplonis* and it is from this complex that the European Starling and its allies have probably evolved. The features of the 'island complex' are closely paralleled by the mainly fruit-eating and arboreal *Lamprotornis, Spreo*, and *Onychognathus* of mainland Africa.

In *Acridotheres, Creatophora*, and *Sturnus* (using Amadon's classification), the protractor muscles become more developed, associated with the penetration by these genera of drier and more temperate areas. This reaches its maximum development in *Sturnus cineraceus, S. contra*, and *S. vulgaris* and permits the feeding technique termed 'prying' by Beecher and 'open-bill probing' by others. In prying, the closed bill is pushed into the surface soil or turf and is then opened, by an upward movement of the upper mandible, to push apart the substrate to search for invertebrates within (Fig. 1.1). Associated with this ability, the anterior part of the skull has become narrower than in fruit-eating starlings; this permits the eyes to move forward during prying, enabling the bird to see where it is probing without having to tilt its head to one side to obtain a good view. Beecher attributed an ecological signifi-

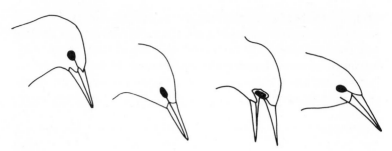

Fig. 1.1. 'Prying' or 'open-bill probing': the distinctive feeding method used by Starlings. From left to right: the starling searches for an indication of a prey item; it lowers its head and inserts the closed bill into the grass; it opens the bill, and the eyes move forward to give better forward vision; the movement is completed when the head is raised.

cance to these developments, one that is perhaps fundamental to the theme of this book—the success of the European Starling. He considered that prying was the feature that allowed this species to locate insects, often dormant, in grassland in the colder months when other insectivorous birds had been forced to migrate south.

Although the development of bone and muscle along these lines has undoubtedly contributed to the success of the evolutionarily advanced starlings, other skull modifications have been explored by some members of the family. In *Scissirostrum dubium*, the Woodpecker Starling of Sulawesi, the protractor muscles are also well-developed and help to act as a muscular shock-absorber during wood-boring activities (Beecher 1978); this adaptation is developed *par excellence* in the true woodpeckers (Picidae). A similar, but less pronounced, development has occurred in the two species of tick-bird or oxpecker, *Buphagus,* which also have long, curved, and sharp claws on their toes for gripping on to the pelts of large mammals. The tick-birds' specializations for gleaning ectoparasites have led to their being placed in a separate sub-family, the Buphaginae, from the other more typical starlings, the Sturninae.

Adaptations for breeding also show considerable uniformity within the family with the majority of species nesting in holes, especially in trees, although most of the African red-winged starlings *Onychognathus* prefer holes in cliffs, sometimes behind waterfalls. A very few species build domed nests, *Creatophora* occasionally builds cup-shaped nests and *Aplonis metallicus* builds hanging nests in colonies, reminiscent of some weaver birds. The Bank Mynah *Acridotheres ginginianus* digs its own holes in river banks and, as mentioned above, the heavy bill of the Celebesian starling *Scissirostrum dubium* is used, woodpecker fashion, to bore nest holes in dead wood. Some species, such as the Narrow-tailed Starling *Poeoptera lugubris* use holes made by other birds, especially barbets and several other starlings, including the European Starling, are notorious for usurping the holes made by woodpeckers.

A second feature of the breeding ecology of the starlings is the almost universal laying of spotted eggs, generally with a bluish background. In only *Sturnus*, *Acridotheres*, *Creatophora* and *Ampeliceps* are the eggs known to be unspotted, but in some species of even these genera spotted eggs may be occasionally laid. The spotting on eggs is usually thought to serve the function of camouflage (Lack 1966) and true hole-nesting birds like owls and woodpeckers lay white eggs: Lack suggests that the white colouration within the dark nest cavity helps the parents to see the eggs. It therefore seems strange that while the nest sites used by starlings consist mainly of holes, most of the family lay cryptic eggs. However, another difference between the typical hole-nesters and starlings is that while the former rarely take any material into the hole, starlings as a rule make bulky nests within their cavities. Perhaps starlings are derived from an ancestor which laid its eggs in a more open situation, possibly building a cup-shaped nest, and the acquisition of the hole-nesting habit has occurred during the evolution of the family, reaching its highest stage of development in the *Sturnus*-like starlings that lay unspotted eggs.

We shall see in Chapter 6 the complexities that recent research is revealing in the reproductive behaviour of the European Starling. Our knowledge of the behaviour of other species is too fragmentary to permit an analysis of the social systems within the family as a whole. It is becoming apparent, however, that in some of the tropical species a pair of nesting birds is assisted in the rearing of its young by unpaired individuals of the same species. Such co-operative breeding has so far been documented in the African genera *Buphagus*, *Spreo*, and *Cosmopsarus* (Heuls 1981) and is suspected for *Aplonis metallicus* in Australia (Rowley 1976), but future studies are likely to demonstrate a more widespread occurrence.

In Europe, we tend to think of starlings as blackish birds with glossy sheens and pale spots. The white or buff tips to feathers are restricted to the European and, to a much lesser degree, the

Spotless Starlings and while many starlings are indeed dark, the family contains species with diverse colours.

The fruit-eating and arboreal *Aplonis* and *Lamprotornis* are mostly dark, glossy green although, especially in the latter genus, several species have lesser or greater amounts of glossy purple in their plumage. In most starlings there are only slight differences between juvenile and older birds and between the sexes, but in *Aplonis* the juveniles are distinctive, being blackish-brown above with heavy streaking, especially on the breast and belly. The African genera *Spreo* and *Cosmopsarus* contain some species with dull grey and brown plumage while others have, in addition to the glossy greens and purples on the back and wings, vivid oranges and yellows on the breast and belly. Examples are the Superb Starling *Spreo superbus* and the Golden-breasted Starling *Cosmopsarus regius*. *Cinnyricinclus* similarly contains dullish forms and the females are also dull and streaked, but the back, head, and upper breast of the male Violet-backed Starling *C. leucogaster* is a brilliant glossy violet. In *Onychognathus* we encounter further sexual dimorphism, for while the males are glossy black the females have grey heads. Members of this genus, which is again African, are characterized by possessing rusty-red patches on their primaries— hence their familiar name of Red-winged Starlings. The Oxpeckers *Buphagus* are generally ash-brown.

Asia also has its predominantly dark forms, often with green or other gloss, mainly in the genera *Gracula*, *Acridotheres*, *Mino*, *Ampeliceps*, and *Basilornis*, while the large *Streptocitta* species are black and white. Many species in these genera have patches of white on them, especially on the wings, while *Mino* and *Ampeliceps* have brilliant golden feathers on the head. In the three species of *Basilornis* on Sulawesi and neighbouring islands the crown feathers are elongated into large crests. In other south-east Asian genera the predominance of glossy blacks, dark greens and blues gives way to greys, browns and pinks, although glossy black feathers are usually retained on some areas of the body. This transition to greyness is seen to some extent in the *Acridotheres* mynahs, but reaches its greatest development in the genus *Sturnus*. Grey is also the predominant colour in two of the starlings endemic to Sulawesi: the Woodpecker Starling *Scissirostrum dubium* is slaty grey but has some of the upper tail coverts, rump, and flank feathers with long stiff tips that are red and Waxwing-like (*Bombycilla garrulus*), and the Red-browed Starling *Enodes erythrophrys* is slaty grey with olive and yellow suffusions of the wings and tail and a vivid red stripe above the eye. The main departure from this colour scheme is Rothschild's Mynah *Leucopsar rothschildi*, of the island of Bali, whose plumage is pure white, except for contrasting black primaries and a patch of bright-blue bare skin around the eye.

Areas of bare skin, especially around the eye, are a feature of many Asian starlings and occur in several species of *Acridotheres* and *Sturnus*. In *Basilornis* the naked orbital skin becomes more extensive and in *Sarcops*, the Bald Starling of the Philippines, most of the top of the head is devoid of feathers save for a narrow strip down the centre of the crown. In the Hill Mynahs *Gracula* some of the bare skin is expanded into fleshy wattles. The occurrence of both a naked head and elongated wattles in breeding males of the African Wattled Starling *Creatophora cinerea* is thus a distinctly Asian character, as are other features of this peculiar species.

If we look at the geographical distribution of the various species of starling alive today (Fig.1.2) we see that the natural range (that is, excluding extensions of range caused by Man's introductions) is confined to the Old World. Within this range the main concentrations are found in Africa and south east Asia, especially east central Africa and in northern Thailand–Bangladesh. In zoogeographical terms, the main concentrations of starling species are in the Ethiopian and Oriental regions, with relatively minor incursions into the Malagasy, Australasian, and Palaearctic regions. Thus in terms of the geographical distribution of the family the European Starling, which we shall see later is a Palaearctic species, is somewhat unusual. It is in the Ethiopian and Oriental regions that the more primitive and generalized starlings, such as *Lamprotornis* and *Aplonis*, are found and it is presumably in one of these regions that the family originated, though it is by no means clear which. The generalized features of the genus *Aplonis* have presumably survived as a result of the isolation of most of the species on Pacific islands, while a primitive feature of the genus *Lamprotornis*, a long tenth primary, shows a similarity to the crows.

This brief consideration of the Family Sturnidae demonstrates that its members show considerable uniformity in many aspects of their biology and yet that some genera or species show specializations for certain ways of life. I have already indicated that birds of

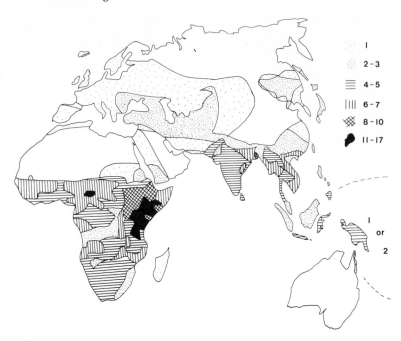

Fig. 1.2. The world distribution (excluding human introductions) of the members of the family Sturnidae. The colour-shading represents the number of species present in each area. The main concentrations are in East Africa and in south-east Asia.

the genus *Sturnus*, with spotless eggs, a very short tenth primary, and a tendency to feed on the ground, are evolutionarily advanced members of the family, but it is now time to examine the genus more closely and, in particular, to see how the European Starling conforms with or diverges from the Family characteristics.

THE GENUS STURNUS

Even within the small group of species that resemble the European Starling there is considerable controversy concerning their relationships. Amadon (1956) grouped them all in the genus *Sturnus* and this classification has been followed by the authors of most recent check-lists, giving a genus containing 16 species of starling (Table 1.2). Beecher's (1978) studies show, however, that this group of 16 species is not homogeneous in its muscle and bone structure and that there is some justification for dividing these birds into a number of genera which had been recognized by earlier workers. Thus Beecher concluded that the genera *Pastor*

Table 1.2 Some ecological characteristics of the 16 members of the genus *Sturnus*

Species	English name	Type of nest	Nest site	Breeding Sociality	Food	Feeding Area	Uses cultivated areas
burmannicus	Jerdon's Vinous-breasted	Holes	Trees, buildings	?	Insects, seeds	Ground	Yes
cineraceus	Grey, White-cheeked, Ashy	Holes	Trees, buildings	Colonial	Insects, fruit	Ground	Yes
contra	Pied	Domed	Trees	Colonial	Insects, fruit, seed	Ground, trees	Yes
erythropygius	Andaman White-headed	Holes	Trees	?	Insects, fruit, nectar	Ground	Yes
malabaricus	Grey-Headed, Chestnut-tailed, White-headed	Holes	Trees (Barbet nest or bores own)	? Solitary	Insects, fruit, nectar	Trees, ground	Yes
melanopterus	Black-winged	Holes	Rocks	Colonial	?	Ground	Yes
nigricolis	Black-collared	Domed	Trees	Colonial	Insects, fruit	Ground	Yes
pagodarum	Brahminy	Holes	Trees, buildings	Colonial	Insects, fruit	Ground, trees	Yes
philippensis	Red-cheeked, Violet-backed	Holes	Trees	? Colonial	Insects, fruit	Ground, trees	Yes
roseus	Rose-coloured	Holes	Rocks, buildings	Colonial	Insects, fruit, nectar	Ground	Yes
senex	Ceylon White-headed, White-faced	Holes	Trees	? nectar	(? Insects), fruit, nectar	Trees	No
sericeus	Silky, Red-billed	Holes	Trees, buildings	?	?	Ground	Yes
sinensis	Grey-backed, White-shouldered	Holes	Trees, rocks, buildings	Colonial	?	Ground, trees	Yes
sturninus	Daurian, Purple-backed	Holes	Trees, buildings	Solitary	Insects	Trees, ground	Yes
unicolor	Spotless, Mediterranean	Holes	Trees, buildings, rocks	Colonial	Insects, fruit	Ground, trees	Yes
vulgaris	European, Common	Holes	Trees, buildings, Other species, rocks	Colonial	Insects, fruit, seed	Ground, trees	Yes

Main sources of references: Abdulali 1947, 1964; Ali and Ripley 1972; Amadon 1943, 1956; Deignan 1945; Dement'ev and Gladkov 1960; Haneda and Ushiyama 1967; Henry 1971; Inglis 1947; King *et al.* 1975; Shi-Chun, Xi-Yuo, Yao-Kuang, and Yao-Hoa. 1975; Smythies 1953.

(for the Rose-coloured Starling *P. roseus*), *Temenuchus* (for the Brahminy Starling *T. pagodarum*), and *Sturnia* (containing eight species) should stand separately from *Sturnus* ,which he left with *cineraceus*, *contra*, and *vulgaris* (and presumably *unicolor*, but this was not stated). Furthermore, he took *nigricollis* out of this group of birds and placed it in the genus *Acridotheres*, the mynahs. While I accept that Amadon's grouping of all 16 species in *Sturnus* does not perfectly express their relationships, in the absence of considerably more information on their behaviour and ecology I prefer to maintain Amadon's simpler system and have followed it below.

Figure 1.3 shows the geographical distribution (excluding man-aided introductions) of the species of *Sturnus* that survive today. The main concentrations of species occur in the Oriental Region and in fact 14 of the 16 species spend all or part of their lives there. Their closest relatives, the *Acridotheres* mynahs, are almost

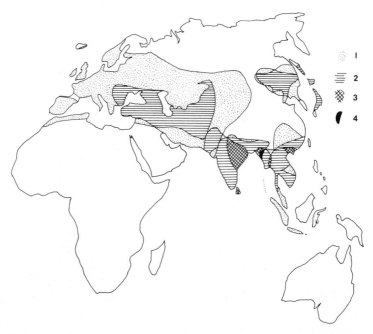

Fig. 1.3. The world distribution (excluding human introductions) of the members of the genus *Sturnus*. The colour-shading represents the number of species present in each area. The main concentration is in south-east Asia, and there are no representatives in Africa south of the Sahara.

entirely Oriental in their distribution and they, in turn, are related to the 'golden-headed' forms *Ampeliceps* and *Mino* and the Hill Mynahs *Gracula*, which are entirely Oriental. Thus it seems most likely that *Sturnus* evolved in south-east Asia and has spread to the Palaearctic, both to the north in northern China and eastern Russia, and to the west in Europe and North Africa, from there. However, the distribution that we see today appears to represent only a part of a much greater former glory of *Sturnus* starlings since Tchernov (1962) found fossil starlings in deposits of various ages in Israel. Some of these fossils were of small species, today represented only by the Red-cheeked Starling *Sturnus philippensis*, the Daurian Starling *S. sturninus*, and the Silky Starling *S. sericeus*, all of the Far East. The presence of these small starlings, and of larger forms, in the middle East indicates that the westward spread of *Sturnus* was once greater than is apparent from present-day distributions. Furthermore, at least one starling of Oriental origins penetrated Africa south of the Sahara, since the Wattled Starling, currently placed in the monotypic genus *Creatophora*, is clearly very closely related to *Sturnus*: apart from the peculiar wattles developed by the male during the breeding season, its general appearance closely resembles a *Sturnus*, and it lays spotless eggs and has the 'wing-rotating' courtship display typical of the European and Spotless starlings.

Of the *Sturnus* species that survive today, seven are residents in the Far East (Fig. 1.4). However, even some of these residents may perform local movements and Ali and Ripley (1972) record that the Brahminy Starling undertakes marked seasonal movements during the monsoons. A further three species, the Grey-headed, Grey-backed, and Silky, extend their ranges out of the breeding season, although in the Grey-headed this extension is confined to only one of the subspecies, *S. malabaricus nemoricola*. Range expansion in these species tends to be in a southerly direction and this trait is followed by the three species, Grey, Daurian, and Red-cheeked, that have colonized the eastern temperate region: all return southwards to winter in the Oriental tropics or sub-tropics (Fig. 1.5). The Rose-coloured Starling, whose breeding range lies in the central Palaearctic, also returns to the Oriental region during the winter, but to do so involves a migration from west to east (Fig. 1.6). This westward spread from the Orient is taken a step further by the European Starling which, as we shall see in Chapter 2, breeds over a vast area of the Western Palaearc-

14   *The Starling*

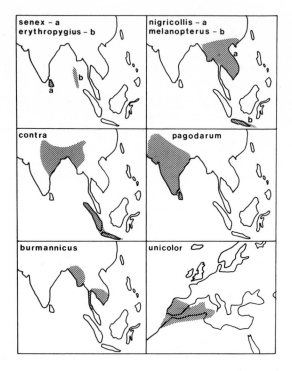

Fig. 1.4. The distribution of the eight resident *Sturnus* starlings. Seven are restricted to south-east Asia and one occurs in south-west Europe and North Africa. English names are given in Table 1.2.

tic. However, it has virtually lost all connections with the Orient, since although some birds do winter in India and there is even a resident subspecies in the north-west of the sub-continent, the vast majority of European Starlings migrate from their European or western Asian breeding grounds to the west, to winter in southern and western Europe and North Africa. In fact, the European Starling is the classic example of an east–west migrant (see Dorst 1962).

The only starling to have completely lost contact with south-east Asia is the Spotless Starling *Sturnus unicolor*, which is resident in parts of southwest Europe and north Africa although the birds that breed in Andalucia, southern Spain, migrate to North Africa in winter. It is very similar to the European Starling but adult birds in spring lack spots and they also have longer body feathers than their more widespread relative. There are also differences in social

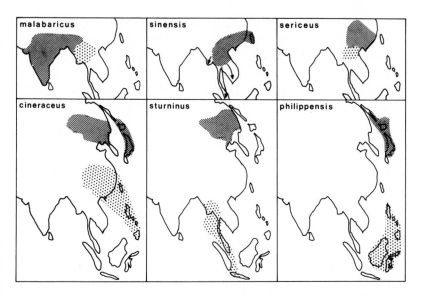

Fig. 1.5. The distribution of the migrant *Sturnus* Starlings of south-east Asia. Breeding areas are hatched, wintering areas stippled. English names are given in Table 1.2.

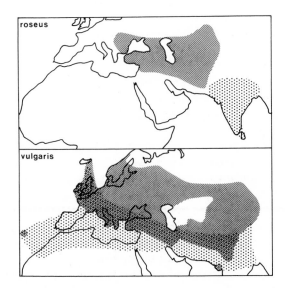

Fig. 1.6. The two most widely distributed *Sturnus* starlings, both of which breed over large areas of the Palaearctic. Breeding areas are hatched, wintering areas stippled. English names are given in Table 1.2.

behaviour, with males taking no part in incubation and possibly being regularly polygamous (my own unpublished observations), and Berthold (1971) has shown that, even in captivity, the two species do not successfully interbreed. The Spotless Starling has obviously evolved from a *vulgaris*-like ancestor and is presumably a relic of a former invasion of Europe by *Sturnus* starlings: if this occurred before the last glaciation, the present geographical distribution of this species may represent the ice free refuge in which it was able to survive.

Besides being united by the laying of spotless eggs and the possession of a short tenth primary, all the species of *Sturnus*, at some stage during the year, feed in flocks. Other features of their behaviour are summarized in Table 1.2 which shows that, although there is some variation, there is considerable uniformity within the genus. Most species nest in holes in trees, breed colonially (insofar as the distribution of available nest sites will permit this), roost communally (sometimes even with other species), feed on the ground, and eat a variety of foods including both animal and vegetable dietary components. Of particular interest with respect to the success of the European Starling is the fact that all but one (the Ceylon White-headed Starling *S. senex*) of the *Sturnus* starlings will utilize areas cultivated by man and many will feed in close association with his domestic animals.

THE STARLING FAMILY AND MAN

Throughout the geographical range of the family at least some members have held special relationships with man. Nine of the species of *Sturnus* and several members of other genera frequently nest in man-built structures, especially in houses. John Aubrey (quoted by Atkinson 1956) thought that some of the holes left in the mortice-and-tenon joints between upright stones and lintels of Stonehenge might have been left deliberately for Starlings to nest in, these birds being held sacred by the Druids who are often considered to have had connections with this monument. However, Atkinson casts some doubt on this connection and points out that Stonehenge was built over 1000 years before Druidism became a cult: perhaps it was the nesting of Starlings in religious structures like this that led to their being regarded as sacred! The Brahminy Starling and the Common Mynah have also been held as sacred by the Hindus. The peculiar Wattled Starling, in which the males periodically develop wattles on the head and subsequently re-absorb them, has been used in cancer research. The regrowth of feathers that follows this re-absorption has also stimulated people to examine the Wattled Starling for clues that might help to combat human baldness! The plumage of some of the African Glossy Starlings, notably the Purple Glossy Starling *Lamprotornis purpureus* and the Splendid Glossy Starling *L. splendidus*, has been used for human adornment, while live birds have frequently been caught and kept in captivity, again in a decorative capacity, on account of both their colourful plumage and their capacity to mimic. This has, of course, applied particularly to the Hill Mynahs (*Gracula*) but many other species are also regularly kept in captivity by aviculturists and the Coleto or Bald Starling *Sarcops calvus* is kept as a cage bird in the Philippines.

The main interaction between man and starlings has been in relation to food production. Cain and Galbraith (1956) reported that the chicks of *Aplonis brunnicephalus* are eaten by man in the Soloman Islands and the capture, for food, of the Coleto in the Philippines seems to have permitted an unusually large number of recoveries of ringed birds (McClure 1974). Doubtless many other Asian and African starlings are also eaten from time to time, and even in Britain, European starlings are shot in their winter roosts, the wings to provide feathers for fishing flies and the bodies to be exported for a Continental paté industry.

Although man's utilization, for food or adornment, of some species may have contributed to their decline, the most serious factor underlying the reductions of the endemic forms of some islands has been the destruction of natural habitats. Rothschild's Mynah and two species of *Aplonis* presently survive in very small wild populations, while a further two species of *Aplonis*, together with two starlings from Indian Ocean islands, *Fregilupus varius* of Reunion and *Necropsar rodericanus* of Rodriguez, have become extinct during the last two centuries.

However, the direct use of starlings for food is only a small part of man's interest, most of which centres around the benefit or damage that these birds cause to agriculture. We have seen that most of the species eat fruits, seeds, and insects and it appears to be generally assumed that when starlings eat cultivated fruits or seeds they are doing damage, but when they eat insects they are being beneficial. That some starlings can cause considerable agricultural damage is in no doubt and we shall see later the problems that are posed by European Starlings. Members of several genera are regarded as pests in different parts of the world: The Common Mynah *Acridotheres tristis* and the Red-winged Starling *Onychognathus morio* eat cultivated fruit, while the Blue-eared Glossy Starling *Lamprotornis chalybaeus* and the Superb Starling *Spreo superbus* damage ripening cereal crops. Even the tick-birds *Buphagus* are sometimes regarded as pests, since although they eat large numbers of ticks, some farmers complain that they keep open the sores left when ticks are removed and drink the blood that continues to exude.

The most celebrated 'beneficial' starlings are the nomadic Rose-coloured Starling *Sturnus roseus* of central Asia and eastern Europe and the Wattled Starling of Africa. Both species are great consumers of locusts and large flocks of birds will settle to establish breeding colonies wherever swarms of locusts appear. When the African swarms of 'hoppers' disappear, the Wattled Starlings desert the colony, even if this means vacating nests with eggs or young (Mackworth-Praed and Grant 1955). Rose-coloured Starlings, which winter in India and migrate back to their steppe breeding grounds in the spring, form colonies wherever locusts are abundant so that an area which has a huge breeding colony one year may be completely avoided by the birds the next (Bannerman 1953*b*). Another locust eater, the Common Mynah, was introduced from India into Mauritius in an attempt to control noxious insects and doubtless many of the introductions of this species to other parts of the world were undertaken with the same aim in mind. It is obvious that these birds devour vast numbers of locusts, but from the 'benefit' point of view the crucial question is: do the birds significantly reduce the population of locusts in plague areas or maintain populations at low levels elsewhere, thereby conferring agricultural benefit? This is a very difficult question to answer, since it necessitates detailed study of the population dynamics and feeding behaviour of the bird and also similarly detailed research into the population dynamics of the insect pest. In fact, it seems unkilely that the birds do control the insect populations: East and Pottinger (1975), studying the predation by introduced European Starlings in New Zealand on an insect larva, the grass grub *Costelytra zealandica*, found that only under critical conditions of grass grub density, starling numbers, and soil irrigation did the birds exercise any regulatory effect. Usually, these exacting conditions were not met. Nevertheless, it has been, and still is, widely held that many species of starling are beneficial to agriculture in many parts of the Old World range and it is this feature that has led to some of them being introduced into new areas (Long 1981).

The beneficial nature of the Rose-coloured Starling was highlighted by Pliny, who wrote of it as follows: 'There is a species called Birds of Seleucis for whose arrival prayers are offered to Jupiter by the inhabitants of Mount Cadmus when locusts destroy their crops; it is not known where they come from nor where they go when they depart, and they are never seen except when their protection is needed'.

The European Starling was also familiar to the Greeks and the Romans. It was kept as a cage bird in Greek houses as early as the fifth century BC (Parmelee 1959) and Aristotle used the Starling as a basis for size comparisons with other species. Pliny described the movements of birds within flocks and commented on their capacity for mimicry: he had even heard of an individual that could talk Greek and Latin 'and moreover practised diligently and spoke new phrases every day, in still longer sentences'! This is undoubtedly a gross exaggeration of their capabilities, but they can be taught to imitate words. The Romans also kept European Starlings in captivity and taught them to imitate human speech (Geikie 1912) and they were mentioned in the poetry of Priapea and Statius (Martin 1914), both of whom wrote in the first century AD. The former poet alluded to Starlings as harmful birds, but the earliest reference to their causing agricultural damage was by Babrius (*c*.200 BC), who had also observed that birds could become habituated to scaring devices: 'And a lad ran at his heels with a sling. But the Starlings from long use would listen if he ever asked for a sling, and made off before he ever had it in his hand' (Douglas 1928).

Most recent British authors have devoted few words to European Starlings. They are mentioned briefly by Shakespeare, Wordsworth, and Tennyson and even Gilbert White (1789) made only passing reference to them in his essays on the natural history of Selborne: this may reflect the European Starling's comparative scarcity in Britain in the eighteenth century. At about the time that White was writing, the composer Mozart is said to have bought a Starling and the theme of his Piano Concerto in G major is purportedly based on its whistles (Blom 1962).

The European Starling, which in subsequent chapters I shall refer to simply as 'Starling', is thus a member of an Old World Family of birds whose ancestors lived in the tropics of the Far East or Africa. These ancestors were, as are the more primitive forms today, mainly arboreal, hole-nesting birds that were mainly frugivorous but also ate insects. During the evolution of the Family there has been a tendency for a specialization towards a more ground-dwelling and omnivorous existence, accompanied by an extension of geographical range into the Palaearctic region. It was perhaps in the Middle East, where the cultivation of cereals was first begun, that the European Starling made its initial contact with agricultural man. Since then Starlings, like House Sparrows *Passer domesticus*, have led a commensal existence with man, and in this book we shall see how many features of the species' biology contribute to its outstanding success in Man's world.

2 THE SUCCESSFUL STARLING

It is readily apparent from Figs. 1.4, 1.5, and 1.6, that the European Starling occupies by far the largest geographical range of all the species of *Sturnus*—in fact it covers more of the Earth's surface than any other starling. Its range embraces many seas, mountain ranges, and even deserts, and these natural barriers to free movement have led to the evolution of several races or subspecies. The precise number is difficult to establish for, as with some of the species of starlings, subspecies are sometimes not clearly defined in terms of plumage differences or other structural features and there are often considerable zones of overlap between the areas occupied by the different forms.

The races of the Starling are separated mainly on the basis of the colours of the metallic sheens on different parts of the plumage, although there are also some size differences between some of the more extreme forms. Before considering these differences we must therefore first describe the structure and colour of what might be termed a 'typical' Starling.

It is a medium-sized bird, about 20 cm long and weighs 75–100 g. It is stockily built, as evidenced by the weights of some other birds that are about 20 cm long, such as the Little Tern *Sterna albifrons* (40 g), Sanderling *Crocethia alba* (55 g), Wood Sandpiper *Tringa glareola* (65 g), and Song Thrush *Turdus philomelos* (75 g). It spends much of its time on the ground where it walks rather than hops and as an aid to efficient walking it has powerful legs, with a tarsus about 30 mm long and its large feet span 50 mm. The toes are long and strong and each carries a sharp claw, as anyone who has handled large numbers of Starlings knows! These legs and feet help the bird to walk quickly over the ground but equally assist with movement along branches in trees when, for example, the birds are feeding on caterpillars or fruit, when they are nesting in holes or when they are roosting at night. The bill is strong and pointed and about 25 mm long: it is perfectly adapted for probing into soil but is equally adept at picking food items from the surface of the ground or from branches or leaves of trees, at catching flying insects, and at pecking holes in soft fruit.

The wings are relatively long and pointed, both of these characters being adaptations for fast flight. These features are thus those of birds of open country and contrast with relatively shorter, more rounded, wings of the arboreal starlings such as *Aplonis* and *Lamprotornis*, as shown in Fig. 2.1. The reduced powers of manoeuverability of Starlings have only been apparent to me when I have watched, from within a winter roost, the birds departing. Although the birds do not fly into the trees, collisions between birds are frequent. Nevertheless, the co-ordinated movements of the birds in flocks, especially in those flocks assembling prior to entering the roost, are spectacular and have been noted by many writers, going as far back as Pliny.

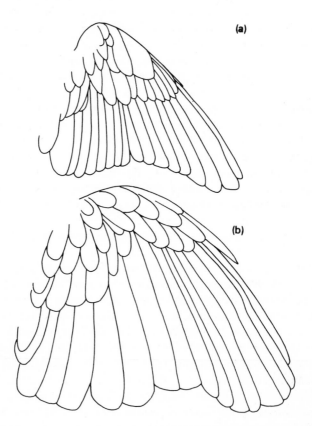

Fig. 2.1. The wings of (a) *Sturnus vulgaris* and (b) *Lamprotornis purpuropterus* showing the more pointed wing and the reduced outer primary of the former.

In possessing almost wholly dark plumage the adult European Starling differs from all other species of *Sturnus* except the Spotless Starling, to which it is obviously very closely related. The function of this dark plumage is not clearly understood. Baker and Parker (1979) have recently suggested that the dark colour of birds that regularly flock in open situations, where they are especially conspicuous, may indicate to predators that these birds may be 'unprofitable' prey. This is because in these flocks there are so many eyes that at least one of the birds is likely to see the predator as it approaches and, probably inadvertently, indicate this by its actions to other members of the flock. This may be part of the story, but the conspicuousness of dark birds, such as Starlings and many of the crow family (Corvidae), when feeding in their usual grassland situation, may also serve as an attraction to other members of the same species. Starlings and Rooks (*Corvus frugilegus*) feed more efficiently when in flocks and, therefore, there may be an advantage in attracting other members of your species to where you are feeding: however, the root of this advantage may still lie in the greater number of eyes in the larger flocks that can be employed in the perception of approaching predators.

Although all birds in a flock that is feeding in a grass field in winter may appear to be dark and equally conspicuous in that situation, there are subtle differences between individuals. In winter all Starlings have many of their body feathers tipped with white, cream, or buff. These tips are most extensive in birds in their first winter, especially in females. In adult females the amount of spotting is less pronounced and it is reduced still further in adult males. However, within each sex and even within each age group the amount of spotting is so variable that it cannot be reliably used to age and sex Starlings, even in the hand.

Rohwer (1975) has suggested that this kind of plumage variability has evolved to signal the social status of each individual in a flock in order to reduce the amount of fighting over food, fighting being the alternative mechanism for determining position in a peck order. Rohwer studied Harris' Sparrow *Zonotrichia querula* but his arguments might, if substantiated by critical experimentation, also apply to Starlings.

A useful character by which Starlings can be sexed with considerable reliability is the colour of the eyes (Plate 9). In males the iris is all dark, while in females it carries a paler ring; unfortunately this ring varies in its size and colour and in some individuals is not readily apparent. Once birds have been sexed in this way it is usually possible to determine whether they are adults or first-winter birds by the amount of iridescence on the throat feathers, adults possessing more, and by the presence or absence of iridescence on the belly. The length of the throat feathers, in particular, and the amount of gloss on them are further useful characters for sexing Starlings, for in males, especially adults, these feathers are longer and more glossy. Using this character in conjunction with eye colour, it is possible to sex Starlings in the hand with considerable accuracy.

As winter progresses, and especially when Starlings begin visiting nest holes, the spotted tips of the body feathers begin to wear away so that by the breeding season the spots may be barely noticeable. As adult males have the smallest spots during the winter they are most likely to appear unspotted during the breeding season. This lack of spotting, and consequent increase in gloss, is further enhanced since adult males have longer and more pointed feathers than females and young birds, especially on the nape, throat, and breast.

Adult females, first-year males, and first-year females appear progressively more spotted—in the first-year birds this is especially true of the belly and under tail coverts. Further changes occur as breeding approaches, with the legs becoming much redder than in winter and the bill changing from dark brown to yellow. Here a further difference between the sexes becomes apparent; in breeding season males the base of the bill is steel blue, while in females it is pale pink—blue for a boy and pink for a girl!

While breeding, Starlings do not travel far from their nests and it becomes impossible for them to form the large flocks that occur in winter, when their only tie may be a communal roost which can be 20 km or more from their feeding areas. For the efficient feeding and predator protection that feeding in flocks allows (chapter 10), the increased conspicuousness of breeding birds may assist with flock formation at a time when bird density may be lower and when there are many other duties to be performed besides feeding. But the main function of the long glossy feathers of the head, throat, and breast lies in mate attraction and in territorial defence. These feathers are used both in competition between males for nest sites and to attract females to the part-built nests of those males that have obtained nest sites.

The under-surface of the wings of both winter and breeding Starlings is browner and paler than the rest of the body. Baker and Parker (1979) suggest that the function of this paleness is to confer a certain amount of camouflage to birds that, while breeding, must repeatedly enter and leave their nest cavities. This frequent visitation of nest sites must tend to indicate their position to ground predators, probably the main threat to the nest contents, and anything that can reduce the conspicuousness of the arriving and departing adults may help to maintain the security of the nest. Alternatively, the lack of conspicuousness of the under-wings of Starlings during most of their activities may simply obviate the requirement for irridescent sheens on these feathers.

The plumage of juvenile Starlings seems to be orientated entirely to cryptic colouration. Juveniles are probably less efficient than adults at feeding and will consequently take longer to obtain the same amount of food as older birds. This will allow them less time to devote to watching for predators. Furthermore, naive juveniles may well be less able than adults to predict where and when predators are most likely to attack, they may be less efficient at taking avoiding action, and they may even be less able to recognize predators. For juveniles, therefore, the emphasis is on camouflage and in addition to being almost uniform pale brown, juvenile Starlings also seem to spend more time than adults feeding in protected situations, such as trees, in preference to open grassland. However, we shall see later that the distinct juvenile plumage may also play a part in dominance relationships with adults in feeding flocks.

The differences between the subspecies of Starling concern mainly the colours of the glossy iridescent sheens on different parts of the plumage of adults, although in some races, for example the resident forms on some of the Scottish islands and Faeroes, *zetlandicus* and *faeroensis* respectively, the juveniles are darker than in other subspecies.

Amadon (1962) and Vaurie (1959) accept that there are 11 subspecies of Starling and the names of these and their colour patterns are presented in Table 2.1. Their geographical distribution is shown in Fig. 2.2. In addition to those recognized by Amadon and Vaurie, however, I have included a twelfth form, *granti*, which is resident in the Azores, since the recognition of this race highlights some of the problems that face the taxonomist when he attempts to differentiate between races.

Table 2.1. The colours of the subspecies of *Sturnus vulgaris*. From specimens in the *British Museum (Natural History)*.

Subspecies	Crown	Nape	Mantle	Rump	Chin	Throat	Breast	Belly	Flanks
faeroensis	green	purple	bronze/green	green	green	purple	green	green	green/purple/blue
zetlandicus	purple	purple	green	green	purple	purple	green	green/purple	purple/green
vulgaris	green/purple	purple	green/purple	green	green/purple	purple	green	green	purple
granti	green	purple	bronze/green	green	green	purple	green	green	green/blue
tauricus	green	green	purple	purple	green	green	bronze	purple/green/bronze	green
purpurascens	green	green	green/purple[1]	purple	green	green	purple	purple/bronze	green/bronze
caucasicus	purple/green	purple/green	green	green	purple	purple	green	purple	purple
nobilior	purple	purple	green	green	purple	purple	green	purple	purple
poltaratskyii	purple	purple	green[2]	green	purple	purple	green	purple	purple
porphyronotus	green	green	purple	purple	green	green	purple	purple/bronze	green/bronze
humii	purple	purple	bronze	green	purple	purple	green	green	green
minor	green	green	purple	purple/green	green	green	purple	green	green

[1] *purpurascens* has a distinct bronze band across the low back.
[2] *poltaratskyii* has a distinct purple band across the lower back.

Fig. 2.2. The breeding ranges of the subspecies of *Sturnus vulgaris* and their approximate directions of autumn migration. Hatched areas indicate zones of hybridization between subspecies.

The iridescent sheens of starlings are what Thompson (1964) defined as 'structural colours'. They are not produced by pigments in the feathers, but the barbules of iridescent feathers are twisted and flattened so that a flat surface always faces an onlooker. In order for the barbules to be twisted in this way they have to lose the hooklets that normally hold the vane of a feather in place, and the loss of these hooklets reduces the strength of the feathers. Iridescent sheens are consequently not found in the flight feathers of Starlings, since these feathers must retain their mechanical strength.

Table 2.1 shows that the colour differences between the breeding males that I have examined in the skin collection of the British Museum (Natural History) are subtle and that there are considerable overlaps between subspecies. Trends in colouration are not readily apparent although eastern forms tend to be more purple than most of the western ones, which tend to be more green. In winter, when the iridescence is somewhat eclipsed by the spotting on the plumage, the races are even more difficult to separate; this can cause great confusion where the winter ranges of several subspecies overlap, as in the east of the winter range.

Figure 2.2 shows that most of the subspecies occupy fairly restricted breeding ranges, with only the Siberian form *poltaratskyi* and the European and western Asian *vulgaris* breeding in large areas of the Palaearctic region. Most of the subspecies are migratory but the breeding and wintering ranges of many overlap to a certain extent. The predominant direction of migration varies between subspecies: the general tendency is for the eastern forms to migrate to the south but to the west there is a progressive trend towards a south-westerly migration. This reaches a maximum in *vulgaris* where ringing recoveries have demonstrated an almost due west migration of birds from Scandinavia and western Russia.

Not all of the subspecies of Starling are migratory, however, and on both the eastern and western fringes of the species' geographical range occur resident races of very local distribution. In the east, *Sturnus vulgaris minor*, the smallest subspecies, is resident in Sind, while in the west there are certainly two, and possibly three or four resident subspecies, depending primarily on what criteria are used to distinguish subspecies.

S.v. faeroensis is a large form that is resident in the Faeroes where it breeds mainly in holes in sea cliffs and walls, this presumably being imposed by the absence of trees. The juvenile plumage is darker than in other races except *S.v. zetlandicus*, which breeds in similar sites and is resident in the Shetlands and in the Outer Hebrides, off western Scotland. The presence of these two resident races in the north-west of the Starling's range permits speculation about the recent history of the species in Europe. The paucity of references to Starlings by recent classical authors in Britain (e.g. Shakespeare, Wordsworth, Tennyson and, in the eighteenth century the natural historian Gilbert White) suggests that is was not a common bird in the fifteenth to eighteenth centuries. The Scottish ornithologist William MacGillivray, writing in 1840, described the Starling as 'generally distributed in Britain, but local. It is nowhere more common than in the northern and western Isles of Scotland. . . .' Thus, as recently as the middle of the nineteenth century, Starlings were not specially common in Britain and Parslow (1968) noted that this was the result of a marked decrease, with extinctions in some areas. In his recent review of the status of British birds, he notes that the great increase in the number of Starlings has occurred during the last 150 years. This increase in the population of British Starlings has been part of a general trend of population increase and westerly range extension of Starlings in Europe. This has been attributed by

Berthold (1968) to climatic amelioration which has triggered a chain of events: milder winters have reduced the distances that Starlings have to migrate to avoid inhospitable conditions; reduced migration journeys permit an earlier return to breeding areas in spring which consequently increases the chances of producing a second brood; and more birds of only one-year-old breed. Overall, therefore, these changes have resulted in a greater reproductive output that may have led to the present westerly spread. This is speculative however and an equally important factor in recent range expansion is man's modification of his environment. The northern limits of the Starling's range in eastern Europe and western Asia approximate closely to the northern boundary of temperate grassland (c.f. Harlan 1981 and Figs. 2.2 and 11.1). In western Europe, man's agricultural activities have removed vast areas of temperate forest and converted this land to grass, thereby presenting Starlings with a vastly increased area for potential colonization. In addition, man has supplied Starlings with extra food, mainly in the form of cereals, and this has encouraged a more sedentary habit and possibly allowed a higher rate of winter survival; these factors have helped the species to accomplish the colonization of new areas made available by forest clearance. But the presence of abundant Starlings on the northern and western Scottish Isles suggests that these birds had survived here when the species was less abundant in the rest of Britain. They may there-fore have remained in these treeless and grassy areas from a prior invasion of Britain by Starlings during a climatically mild period and since then have had time to evolve differences in behaviour, size, and colour to enable them to differentiate as subspecies. For various other species, Kalela (1949) postulated long-term popu-lation changes due to man's alteration of the environment and shorter-term cyclic changes for which climatic fluctuations were responsible.

P.G.H. Evans (1980) has offered an alternative explanation for the origin of *faeroensis*, having studied the genetics of European populations of Starlings using some of their blood proteins. He found that *vulgaris* and *zetlandicus* (which he accepted was a remanent of a former widespread distribution) were genetically quite variable, while *faeroensis* was more homogeneous. He con-cluded that *faeroensis* had been established by a very small number of individuals with a correspondingly small gene pool. These birds have survived and their characters had evolved into their present form by genetic drift (Ford 1964). This colonization of the Faeroes by a few Starlings need not have been associated with the earlier widespread distribution of the species in western Europe, but Evans' findings do not exclude this possibility.

The other two 'possible' subspecies, however, remain a taxonomic problem. Professor W.S. Bullough, in 1942, differentiated the bird breeding in Britain as *S.v. britannicus* from nominate *S.v. vulgaris* of continental Europe on account of the former being resident in the British Isles and also on differences that are predominantly physiological. Britain receives vast numbers of immigrants from continental Europe during the winter and Bullough suggested that these birds differed from the British residents in the timing of changes in their physiology related to breeding. In particular, he recorded differences in the times of the changes from the dark brown bills of birds in winter plumage to the yellow bills of those in breeding dress. The bills of British breeding birds began to change colour in November while those of Continental immigrants did not begin changing until January–February. These differences were associated with different rates of development of the testes and ovaries of the two races defined by Bullough, and the earlier maturation of the gonads of British birds led to behavioural traits, such as autumn singing and occupation of nest sites (and even rare breeding), winter roosting in nest holes, and lack of a tendency to migrate, that were absent in Continental counterparts wintering in the British Isles. Bullough also noted, however, that Continental Starlings which breed at lower latitudes in Europe also tend to be resident, to display autumn sexuality, and to visit nest sites during winter. Berthold (1968), as mentioned above, found that birds which migrate only a short distance return to breed earlier than birds which migrate further. These observations suggest that, even in Starlings that breed on the European Continent, birds from different geographical areas exhibit varying tendencies to migrate and with these are associated various regimes of autumn, winter, and spring sexuality. These features are under hormonal control and thus geographical variations in physiology appear to be along gradients which, in biogeographical terms are called 'clines', rather than being discontinuous. Peter Evans (1980) found, furthermore, that the Starling populations of Britain and continental Europe are genetically very similar, indicating considerable gene flow between them and suggesting that the subspecific status of British birds cannot be upheld. Interestingly, Evans' genetic studies revealed a closer affinity between the birds that have recently colonized Iceland and resident birds in northern Scotland, than with migrant populations in Scandinavia. The mechanism by which resident Scottish birds might have established themselves in Iceland, if this is indeed what happened, is unknown.

The second 'problem' subspecies is *S.v. granti*, which Ernst Hartert described as a subspecies in 1903. This form is resident in the Azores, a long way to the south and west of the nearest Continental breeding Starlings in southern France. The chief distinguishing character of this subspecies is said to be its short outer (tenth) primary, but Vaurie (1959) has doubted the validity of this in view of the extensive overlap with *S.v. vulgaris*. This is shown in Fig. 2.3. in which the outer primary and total wing length of breeding males of all the subspecies (in the British Museum (Natural History) collection) are shown. The only subspecies that can be distinguished on this character are the two smallest, *minor* and *humii*, and the largest, *faeroensis*. Although the outer primary of *granti* does tend to be relatively smaller than in most other subspe-

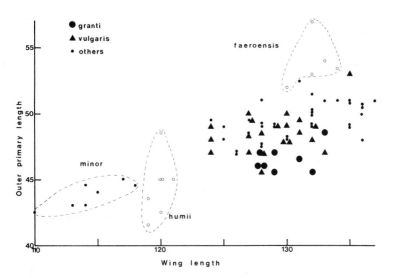

Fig. 2.3. Length of the outer primary plotted against wing length. On this basis only *S.v. minor*, *S.v. humii*, and *S.v. faeroensis* are distinct from the other subspecies; *S.v. granti* cannot be distinguished from *S.v. vulgaris* on this character. Data are from adult males that were collected during March, April, and May and deposited in the British Museum (Natural History).

cies, there is considerable overlap with *vulgaris* which, in turn, overlaps with most other subspecies. Outer primary length is not, therefore, a useful character for separating the subspecies of Starling. Table 2.1 shows that there are subtle colour differences between *granti* and *vulgaris*, however, with the former being less purple on the crown and mantle, and yet Bannerman (1966) remarked that Azores breeding birds had pronounced purple reflections on the back 'when seen under field conditions', and more purple on the flanks than *vulgaris*. Furthermore, he considered that there were behavioural differences between the Starlings of the Azores and those of Britain involving, particularly, voice and nest site. It is becoming apparent that differences in voice, that in human terms we call dialects, can occur over very short distances and they may, therefore, not be good characters on which to separate races: they do, however, seem to indicate restricted gene flow. Similarly, the habit of some of the Azores birds of nesting on the ground cannot be regarded as a character permitting subspecific identity. This habit has been recorded in several other starling populations, especially those of islands where suitable tree-cavity sites may be less abundant than on the mainland but where other cavities, in cliffs, walls, or piles of stones on the ground, may be more common.

These slight differences between the Azores and European birds, involving the length of the outer primary, colour, and behaviour differences are noteworthy, but the main point of interest is the geographical position of the resident population of the Azores. Its isolation from the remainder of the European breeding stock, whose recent westward expansion may now give a false indication of the real isolation of the Azores birds, leads me to believe that the latter may be a remnant of a former wide distribution of Starlings that subsequently contracted to the north and east. Fossil bones, whose structure and size are comparable with *Sturnus vulgaris,* have been found in pleistocene deposits in Malta, Monaco, Corsica, and Italy and Fischer and Stephan (1974) concluded that Starlings were resident in the Mediterranean region during the last ice age, whereas they are now only migrants there. If *granti* were a remnant of a former more south westerly distribution, this would place this race on an equal footing, in terms of recent historical developments, with *zetlandicus* and possibly *faeroensis*, even though morphological differences from *vulgaris* have been less developed in *granti*. This argument is speculative and resolution of the problem must await more detailed observations; these will doubtless involve investigations of the genetic composition, through analysis of protein variations, of the different populations.

The presence of two distinct races and a possible third island form at the extreme western limits of the geographical distribution of the Starling does suggest that the species has occupied a range as extensive as the present one at some period during the past. For some reason, probably climatic, this range contracted, leaving these few isolated populations, only to have begun expanding again sometime in the eigthteenth and nineteenth centuries. We know that this expansion began in the British Isles somewhere around 1830 (Parslow 1968) and the westerly spread appears to be continuing (Sharrock 1976). The species now breeds throughout most of the British Isles (Fig. 2.4) and although the Common Birds Census, organized by the British Trust for Ornithology since 1962, reveals no marked change in numbers during the last 20 years, there does seem to have been an upward trend (Fig. 2.5). During the first few years of the Common Birds Census, however, Starlings, along with many other species, did show a clear increase in numbers; the explanation usually advanced for this increase is that breeding populations were recovering from exceptional mortality caused by the severe 1962–3 winter. For the Starling, this explanation does not seem to be entirely satisfactory. In their comprehensive review of the effects of the 1962–3 winter on British bird populations, Dobinson and Richards (1964) found that although many Starlings, possibly immigrants, were found dead, no reduction in the numbers of breeding Starlings between 1962 and 1963 was evident. Thus it appears that the 1962–3 winter did not have an adverse effect on British Starlings, but it is unfortunate that annual censuses had not begun several years before in order that this suggestion could have been supported by more convincing data. The information that is available does indicate, however, that winter is not a critical time for Starlings: Dunnet (1956) thought that, in north-east Scotland, they would face their most severe food shortage in early autumn, while Coulson (1960) showed, from ringing recoveries, that winter mortality bore little relation to winter severity. The explanation for the increase in the number of Starlings in Britain in the early 1960s, therefore, remains questionable.

While this increase was taking place in the British Isles, a

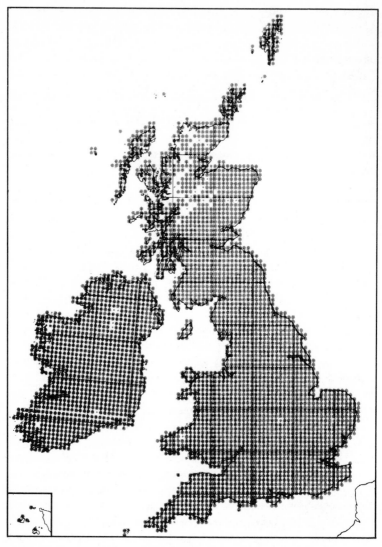

Fig. 2.4. The distribution of the Starling in the British Isles as revealed by the British Trust for Ornithology's Atlas (Sharrock 1976).

reversal of recent trends towards population expansion was beginning in parts of northern Europe and the volume of the journal *Ornis Fennica* in 1978 documented a drastic reduction in the Finnish Starling population. In six areas of Finland, Ojanen,

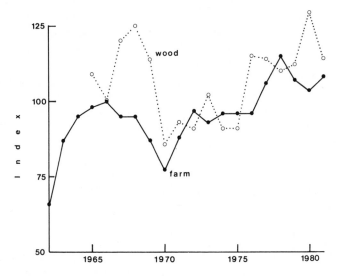

Fig. 2.5. Changes in the British population of Starlings as revealed by the British Trust for Ornithology's Common Birds Census. The index of population was arbitrarily taken as 100 in 1966 and previous and subsequent values are relative to this figure.

Orell, and Merila (1978) recorded decreases between 1963 and 1977 that ranged from 43 per cent to total extinction, but the decreases did not occur simultaneously in the different areas. Finnish authors have suggested several factors that may have been responsible: these include the extensive use of agrochemicals (Hirvelä 1977), the reversion of large areas from cultivation to forest (Ojanen *et al* 1978) and a consequent decrease in the area of land maintained for grazing (Korpimäki 1978). In addition, factors acting outside Finland, including mass-killing in an attempt to prevent damage to fruit (e.g. Steinbacher 1960) and even mortality caused by oil flares on North Sea platforms, have been postulated as causative agents in the population crash. The results of experiments on the effectiveness of mass-killing, out of the breeding season, in reducing Starling populations indicate that these populations are highly resistant to deliberate and accidental perturbations caused by man (Tahon 1980), and the modification of habitats in the breeding area seems a more plausible explanation for the decline. Unfortunately, we do not know how widespread this decrease in northern Europe is, but it is interesting that Rooks (*Corvus frugilegus*), which feed in similar places to Starlings, are also decreasing in parts of Europe, including Britain: the outcome of studies on the geographical variations in the abundance and behaviour of both Rooks and Starlings are eagerly awaited.

Despite these population decreases in a part of their range, Starlings currently inhabit an extensive area of Europe and western Asia. But the Starling's success in colonizing the Earth's surface does not stop in Eurasia, for man has aided the species' spread by introducing it to other Continents and these introductions have generally been successful (Fig. 2.6).

The introductions were made in the nineteenth or early twentieth centuries and that in Jamaica appears to have been the least successful (Taylor 1953), even though Bond (1979) found it well established. In New Zealand, where Starlings were first released in 1862, this species has become one of the commonest birds. Falla, Sibson, and Turbott (1979) state that it is abundant everywhere except in dense bush and at elevations over 1300 m. It is common on offshore islands, such as Chatham and Norfolk, and has even colonized the subantarctic islands of Macquarie and Campbell, and the tropical southern islands of Fiji, possibly via the Kermadecs (Manson-Bahr 1953). Its success in New Zealand has undoubtedly been helped by the deliberate provision of breeding sites, in the form of nest-boxes, (Coleman 1974), since it is widely believed that Starlings control the populations of a grassland insect pest (see Chapter 13). In sheep-rearing areas where natural nest sites are absent, Starlings have been encouraged to breed by placing a nest-box on almost every fence post.

In temperate and Mediterranean climatic zones of Australia and South Africa colonization has also been successful. In the latter country colonization was initially slow and Starlings were a distinctly unban bird, being confined especially to the Durban area and to a few other coastal towns. Now, they have moved inland and have ocupied areas of intense cultivation, but their spread into south-western Africa will be curtailed by the Namib and Kalahari Deserts. Expansion into cultivated parts of East Africa may be possible and it will be interesting to see how far this proceeds.

In Australia, inland extension of the present range is similarly likely to be prevented by arid conditions, but Starlings nevertheless occupy most of the intensively cultivated parts of Victoria, New South Wales, South Australia, and Tasmania. The Southwestern part of Western Australia is also intensively cultivated but currently boasts no Starlings. This cultivated area is separated

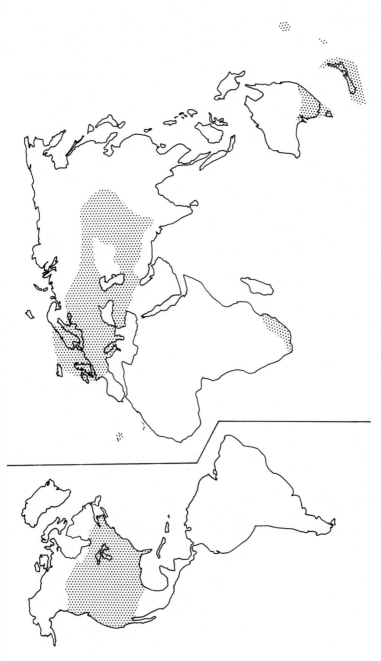

Fig. 2.6. The present world distribution of the European Starling, including its natural range in Europe and western Asia and those areas that have been successfully colonized following introductions by man.

from those of south-eastern Australia by the Great Victoria Desert, which presents an impenetrable barrier to their westward spread. The establishment of human habitations along the south coast of Australia is, however, presenting Starlings with 'leap frog' possibilities of extending their range to Western Australia. The State agricultural authorities are well aware of this and have mounted a huge publicity campaign asking people to report any sightings of Starlings. A few birds are already getting through and teams of people, armed with shotguns, are on constant alert to eliminate the invaders. So far, the birds have been unsuccessful in their attempts to colonize the agricultural areas of Western Australia, but it appears that it will only be a matter of time.

If colonization of New Zealand, Australia, and South Africa, following man's introduction, is described as successful, the population increase following a similar introduction to North America can only be described as explosive. The introductions took place in the last two decades of the nineteenth century. In 1895 Frank M. Chapman (whose Memorial Fund has provided grants for so many ornithologists to undertake work that would not otherwise have been possible) described these introductions as follows:

'This Old-World species has been introduced in Eastern North America on several occasions, but only the last importation appears to have been successful. The birds included in this lot, about sixty in number, were released in Central Park, New York city, in 1890, under the direction of Mr. Eugene Schieffelin. They seem to have left the park and have established themselves in various favourable places in the upper part of the city. They have bred for three successive years in the roof of the Museum of Natural History and at other points in the vicinity. In the suburbs about the northern end of the city they are frequently observed in flocks containing as many as fifty individuals. These birds are resident throughout the year, and as they have already endured our most severe winters, we may doubtless regard the species as thoroughly naturalized.'

By 1895 the Starling had indeed become naturalized but what was to follow was truly astonishing. The spread from the New York area was initially slow, but within 80 years of its introduction the Starling had become one of the most numerous birds in North America, with a breeding area extending from arctic Canada to the sub-tropics of Mexico (Fig. 2.6). Even though its geographical range seems to have practically stopped expanding, the density of birds is still increasing in some regions. A United States Fish and Wildlife Service report, published in 1979 by Richard Dolbeer and Robert Stehn, showed that in the south-west the number of breeding Starlings doubled between 1968 and 1976. In California, where the first individual was seen as recently as 1942, the number of breeding birds increased by 19 per cent during the same period; in less than 40 years the Starling has changed status from a rarity to an abundant bird that causes considerable agricultural damage. Dolbeer and Stehn predicted that numbers would continue to increase in the south-western United States and that conflicts with agriculture would intensify. Further increases might also be expected in other parts of the country, especially in Michigan.

This colonization of North America has been remarkable for its rapidity; the fact that the colonization occurred on a continent makes it even more remarkable. Colonization of islands by animals or plants can only occur when a pair (of sexually reproducing species) of organisms arrives on an island at the same time, finds physical features of the environment amenable, does not face intense competition for food or space from species already there, and reproduces successfully. The chance of a **pair** of organisms of a particular species meeting on a remote island decreases with its isolation, and the chances of their surviving and reproducing there depend upon the habitat diversity of the island which depends, in turn, on its surface area. These relationships have been expressed mathematically by MacArthur and Wilson (1967), but, for present purposes, the main point of this theory of island biogeography is that remote islands tend to have impoverished faunas and floras. On islands, therefore, one would expect that the introduction of an adaptable species would stand a good chance of being successful in view of the low probability, in the impoverished biome, of there being a species with similar characteristics to those of the introduced organisms. This has certainly been borne out on tropical oceanic islands by the widespread successful introductions of the Indian Mynah *Acridotheres tristis*, and also by the success of the Starling and other Eurasian birds in New Zealand.

On continents, on the other hand, remoteness is not a problem for adaptable species and the general expectation is that the niches within continental ecosystems are reasonably fully occupied. In North America, there are several species of indigenous birds with ecological attributes very similar to those of Starlings. These belong to the New World Oriole family, Icteridae, and include some of the Blackbirds *Agelaius*, Grackles *Quiscalus*, and Cow-birds *Molothurus*, which, like Starlings, are flock feeding, omni-vorous, species that inhabit open grassland habitats. That Starlings should successfully invade the areas occupied by such similar and common species is one of the most amazing features of the rapid spread over North America, but it may have been assisted in this by the early development of a trait found in the ancestral stock. In contrast with Starlings introduced elsewhere, some of the North American birds became migratory. Kessel (1953) thought that this may have developed originally from the itinerant habits of young birds but eventually true migrations with regular flight routes developed. The times of southerly autumn migration and north-erly spring migration coincide with equivalent movements in Europe and even the directions of migration are similar, with birds to the east of the Appalachian Mountains migrating to the south in autumn while birds of the west of this mountain range migrate south-west.

The extension of the geographical range in recent years has not been without sacrifice to other species, both in the areas where Starlings are indigenous and also where they have been intro-duced. In particular, the Starling has asserted itself though its ability to compete successfully with other species for nesting cavi-ties. In Eurasia woodpeckers are not uncommonly ousted from their recently excavated holes and in recent years it has been claimed that increasing Starling populations have led to a fall in some of the Hoopoe (*Upupa epops*) populations of southern Europe. Careful study would doubtless reveal that many other species lose nest holes to Starlings, especially in countries that they have colonized only recently. In the United States there is some documentation of this competition. In particular, Starlings are regarded as a pest on Wood Duck *Aix sponsa* breeding grounds since nest boxes, erected in an attempt to increase the ducks' breeding numbers and success, may often be ocupied by the for-mer species. This is of concern primarily to the hunting community but conservationists are also worried, especially about the recent decline in the national populations of the Eastern Bluebird *Sialia sialis* (Zeleny 1969) to such an extent that the species is considered by some to be 'threatened'. The decline is attributed primarily to a drastic fall in breeding success as a result of competition for nest-sites from Starlings.

In this chapter we have seen that the European Starling occupies a greater geographical range than any other species of the Sturnidae and in fact of many other birds. If the occupation of a large geographical range can be taken as a criterion of success, then there is no doubt that the European Starling is *the* successful Starling. We have also seen how the Starling can be regarded as successful in other ways; in increasing its range where it is indigenous when conditions, which we have not yet defined, permit; in competition with other species, especially for nest sites; and in its ability to rapidly colonize when introduced by man to new regions of the globe, particularly when these new regions are ecologically relatively saturated continents rather then impoverished islands. The area presently occupied by Starlings represents slightly less than 30 per cent of the Earth's land surface (Fig. 2.6) excluding Antarctica, but in Chapter 3 we shall discuss what geographical and biological attributes are particularly sought by the species within this enormous area.

3 A PLACE TO LIVE

Perhaps most people in Britain would regard the Starling as a garden bird. Those who commute to some of our cities at dawn and dusk in winter, or walk around the streets at night, might consider it a town bird. Many farmers consider it a bird of agricultural land. Bird-watchers encounter it almost everywhere and because of this often pay little attention to it. But this diversity of the layman's views of the Starling suggests that the birds' selection of habitats must itself be diverse, and this must contribute to the species' success.

The choice, insofar as it is voluntary, of a place in which a species should live depends upon the demands that the species makes upon its environment. These demands comprise a set of requirements for a variety of activities including, particularly, nesting, feeding, and roosting. The requirements may differ geographically, especially when the range occupied is large, and seasonally according to temporal changes in the animal's activities and in the availability of resources within the environment. For example, in the northern part of the Starling's range food abundance and availability drop to such an extent in the winter that the birds that breed there are forced to migrate to areas where food remains abundant. Even where Starlings are resident, however, seasonal changes in their requirements lead them to occupy different habitats at different times of year. Let us begin by defining the major requirements of a Starling during its life and then see how seasonal changes in these determine which habitats are most suitable for the different stages of the annual cycle (these will be examined in greater detail in Chapter 4). Initially, I shall consider the birds living in Britain, but shall finally discuss habitats on a wider geographical scale.

ENERGY BUDGETS

An animal's requirements for survival can best be viewed as an energy balance between the organism and its environment. Energy is expended in the metabolic processes involved in maintaining life and the energy required is obtained from food. Starlings, like all birds and mammals, are homoiothermic, or warm-blooded, which means that they can maintain a more-or-less constant body temperature over a range of environmental temperatures. The body temperature of most birds is around 39–40°C and when a bird is at rest when the environmental temperature is at about this level, the bird uses a minimal amount of energy to live. In effect, the only energy being used is that required by the chemical processes involved in the maintenance of cell activity, such as respiration and excretion. At this low level of activity, the energy requirement is described as the *basal metabolic rate* (BMR). When the bird is resting, this basal metabolic rate may, in fact, be maintained over a range of temperatures because one of the main functions of the feathers is to provide the body with a layer of insulation, the effectiveness of which can be varied by raising and lowering the feathers. The temperature range over which the feather insulation alone can maintain the bird's body temperature is called the *zone of thermo-neutrality*. In passerine birds the zone of thermoneutrality embraces ambient temperatures between about 15 and 40°C. Outside this range additional energy is required to produce heat at temperatures below the zone of thermo-neutrality, or to dissipate heat at temperatures above it. Since over much of the Starlings' geographical range the environmental temperature is considerably below that of the bird's body, energy will usually be required to produce heat to maintain the body temperature. Thus the basal metabolic rate is usually exceeded in wild Starlings, especially in winter.

In addition to basal metabolism and temperature regulation, energy is also used in the performance of physical activities such as flying and walking, both of which are necessary for feeding. Until very recently it has been very difficult to measure the energy consumption of wild birds performing these activities and the techniques that are now available (see Bryant and Westerterp 1982) have not yet been applied to Starlings, although Torre-Bueno and Larochelle (1978) estimated the Starling's energy cost of flight in a wind-tunnel. The amount of time devoted to flying, walking, and feeding varies seasonally, imposing a seasonal variation in the energy required to undertake them. Over and above this, further seasonally imposed energy demands are necessitated by reproduction and its associated behaviour, moult, migration, fat deposition and, in young birds, by growth.

These energy demands are, of course, met by the ingestion and digestion of food. Food is not eaten solely to satisfy energy requirements, however, for at different times of year specific nutrients may be required. During the breeding season Starlings need large quantities of invertebrates, presumably because of their high protein content and its easy assimilation, while in winter less dependence may be placed on protein and more on energy intake—hence in winter Starlings tend to eat more vegetable matter in the form of seeds, especially cereals. As a result of this change in diet, Starlings can quickly gather their daily food requirements in winter but, when breeding, the searching for and capture of a sufficient number of invertebrates takes longer and is probably much more energy-consuming (Feare 1980). The digestion and assimilation of the food eaten has a subsidiary effect in that these processes generate heat, called the *heat increment of feeding*. If the environmental temperature is below the zone of thermo-neutrality, this heat is used, together with heat generated by muscular activity, in body temperature maintenance. At higher environmental temperatures this heat must, however, be dissipated.

This, admittedly over-simplified, description of the energy balance of a warm-blooded animal illustrates that an individual's requirements for survival can be satisfied by two basic features of the habitat: shelter, to maintain the animal in an environment as close as possible to its zone of thermo-neutrality and to protect it from predators, and food, sufficient to meet all of the varied energy requirements, plus any specific nutrients that may be needed.

SHELTER

Communal night roost sites

Let us first examine the various kinds of shelter that a Starling is likely to need. Perhaps the most conspicuous shelter-seeking activity of Starlings is their congregation into roosts at night. These communal roosts occur throughout the year, but are most noticeable in winter when, in addition to our resident birds, Britain is host to a large number of immigrants from continental Europe. We shall discuss the behaviour involved in the formation and dispersal of these roosts later; our present interest lies in the protection that the birds derive from the roost sites that they select.

That meteorological characteristics are involved is strongly suggested by the virtual absence of roosts over 200 m above sea-level (Marples 1934; Delvingt 1961) but the conclusions reached by researchers on the physical characters of roost sites and their significance are conflicting. They may indicate that a complex of factors, rather than one simple over-riding factor, is involved. The two climatic factors that have received most attention from students of communal roosting in birds are temperature and wind, but Kelty and Lustick (1977), who have undertaken what is perhaps the most comprehensive investigation to date, also looked at differences in relative humidity in a Starling roost. They found, however, that both temperature and humidity were similar inside and outside the roost, whereas in the parts of the wood where Starlings roosted wind velocity was almost always zero, irrespective of the wind velocities outside and above the wood. Furthermore, the position of the roosting birds within the wood changed according to the wind direction, suggesting that they selected the most sheltered parts each night. Kelty and Lustick also examined the metabolic responses of roosting Starlings to different temperatures and wind velocities and found that the birds' metabolic rates increased linearly with the square root of increasing wind velocities, except that at the highest wind velocity, 15.1 km h^{-1}, the metabolic rate increased markedly (Fig. 3.1).

Walsberg and King (1980), working in a small roost (24–39 birds) of American Robins *Turdus migratorius* in a fir plantation, found no temperature difference between roosting and non-roosting areas, but although they recorded a 28 per cent reduction in wind speed among the trees they concluded that this would allow only a very small saving of energy by the Robins. In Israel Yom-Tov, Imber, and Otterman (1977) found that the temperature within a Starling roost was 5.0–8.5°C higher than in the surrounding area, the difference being greatest on a rainy, windy evening. This difference was not, however, due to the metabolic heat production of the birds but was a climatological feature of the site itself. In a combined field and laboratory study of the roosting behaviour of Rooks *Corvus frugilegus*, Swingland (1977) found that individuals would change their positions according to the prevailing weather in order to minimize overnight energy losses; he further recorded that older birds maintained the 'best' positions, i.e. those that afforded the most protection against heat loss, while young birds were relegated to poorer places. As in the

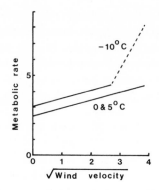

Fig. 3.1. The increase in metabolic rate (ml oxygen g^{-1} min^{-1}) by roosting Starlings as wind velocity (km h^{-1}) increases. From Kelty and Lustick 1977.

studies of Starlings and American Robins mentioned above, the 'goodness' or 'badness' of the roosting sites used by the birds were conferred by the physical properties of the sites themselves, particularly the shelter from the prevailing wind, and were not related to heat loss from neighbouring individuals. This knowledge that birds utilize the protection afforded from wind in their roost sites has been put to practical use: Good and Johnson (1976) found that Brown-headed Cowbirds *Molothurus ater*, Starlings, and a variety of other species could be prevented from roosting in their preferred sites by thinning the tree canopy.

Although the investigations mentioned above detected no elevation of temperature due to heat production by roosting birds, Francis (1976), working in a mixed roost of Starlings and several species of American blackbirds (Icteridae), thought that under calm conditions birds raised the roost temperature by about 0.5°C. Brenner (1965) went even further by claiming that roosting Starlings huddled together, with bodily contact, in a Pennsylvania conifer plantation. He thought that this behaviour was essential for the survival of Starlings in cold weather. Other workers, on the other hand, have remarked on the regular spacing of birds within roosts (Kalmbach 1932; Kelty and Lustick 1977; Yom-Tov *et al.* 1977). Certainly urban roosting Starlings in Britain space themselves out on the ledges of buildings and even on very cold nights the birds in rural roosts that I have seen in conifers and laurels have always been spaced. (Plate 1).

It seems, therefore, that night roosting sites are selected on the basis of their meteorological characteristics, especially the protection afforded from wind and the consequent saving of energy expenditure. But avian energetics must be considered on a longer term than simply during the night, for the energy expended in temperature regulation during the night must be made up by energy gain from food intake during the day, and this energy gain must also be sufficient to allow for all of the daytime activities of the birds; this includes, of course, the energy required for the twice-daily flights between the communal roost and the feeding grounds. As already mentioned, there is no estimate of the energy cost of flight of wild Starlings but Torre-Bueno and Larochelle (1978) measured the metabolic rates of unrestrained Starlings flying at a variety of speeds in a wind tunnel. They found the metabolic rate, measured in terms of carbon dioxide production, to be relatively constant with wind speeds between 8 and 18 m s^{-1} (the range over which they worked) at just under 20 ml carbon dioxide per minute. At a flight speed of around 60 km h^{-1}, which Eastwood (1967) found to be an average speed for Starlings leaving their roost in the morning, the energy consumption is about 0.63 kJ/km^{-1}: this value was also obtained by Yom-Tov *et al.* (1977), for Starlings weighing 80 g using Tucker's (1970) formula. Thus if energy conservation were the sole reason for communal roosting in Starlings, a bird flying 10 km from its feeding grounds to the roost (i.e. 20 km day^{-1}) would need to save at least 12.6 kJ per night that would otherwise have been lost. Yom-Tov *et al.* (1977) concluded that for many individuals the energetic cost of the flight would not be compensated for by an adequate saving of energy overnight, and therefore that communal roosting must confer other advantages. Gyllin, Källander, and Sylven (1977) reached a similar conclusion in their discussion of communal roosting in Jackdaws *Corvus monedula*.

One of these advantages could be protection from predators, since some sites, for example reed beds, are inaccessible to certain land-based predators. The large concentrations of birds that are involved, however, certainly attract avian predators and reed-bed roosts might even attract aquatic animals such as mink *Mustela vison*. The behaviour of Starlings, and other birds, when entering a large communal roost demonstrates adaptations to this potential concentration of predators (Chapter 10) and a reduction of predation pressure at the sites selected for roosting is an obvious advantage. Roost sites are undoubtedly selected with deference to energy conservation, and to a lesser extent, predation risk, and while other aspects of behaviour may have over-riding importance in the evolution of communal roosting (Chapter 10) these two factors seem to be the principal determinants of the habitats chosen for nocturnal roosting. So what kind of habitats provide the essential requirements outlined above?

Table 3.1 shows the seasonal changes in the kinds of communal roosting site used in summer and winter in Britain and Belgium. While deciduous trees are widely used for the usually small summer roosts, the emphasis in winter turns to conifers and evergreens which provide more shelter from wind at this time of year. Reeds (*Phragmites* and *Typha*) are used during both summer and winter but their importance, relative to the number of roosts in other situations, declines in winter. Reed beds can be flattened by winter storms but perhaps more important in the loss of their ability to provide shelter is the destruction that can be caused by the Starlings themselves. Yom-Tov *et al.* (1977) estimated that the reed-bed roost that they studied contained up to 530 birds per cubic metre: this is equivalent to over 40 kg of Starlings per square metre of reed bed, a weight that the reeds cannot support indefinitely. Similar destruction by sheer weight can also occur in roosts in trees and this, together with the adverse effects of large deposits of guano, has aroused the concern of foresters. A survey of the kinds of roost used by Starlings in plantations managed by the Forestry Commission was undertaken by Bevan (1962); he found that most roosts were in conifers but that even within this broad category of trees the birds demonstrated some selection. Spruce (*Picea*) trees, with their dense foliage, were used in preference to other species, and woods in relatively sheltered south-facing situations were

Table 3.1 The roost sites used by Starlings in summer and winter in Britain and Belgium showing a greater use of conifers and evergreens in winter in both countries. Data (from Marples (1934) and Delvingt (1961)) represent the number of roosts reported during surveys within the two countries

Roost site	Summer		Winter	
	Britain	Belgium	Britain	Belgium
Reeds	8	4	10	7
Deciduous	10	12	9	18
Conifers	1	2	22	14
Evergreens	1	0	16	36

selected in favour of more exposed situations. High altitudes were also eschewed, but even with this selection many apparently suitable sites are flown over on journeys to roosts in the evening. The Starlings involved are obviously seeking advantages additional to the protection from weather afforded by their selected sites and while this will be discussed later, it is relevant to note that many roosts are traditionally occupied year after year. Marples (1934), in his comprehensive study of winter roosts in Britain, found that 20 per cent had been in use for over 10 years, and a few had been used for over 100 years, but these long-term roosts tended to be either in sites that the birds could not destroy, e.g. cliffs, or in sites that could regenerate each year: Marples' example of the latter was the reed bed at Slapton Ley, Devon, which (at his time of writing) had been in use for 135 years: it is still used! A similar picture was found by Delvingt (1961) in Belgium. Seventy per cent of the roosts that he recorded had been in use for over five years and 12 per cent for over 50 years.

Urban roosts

In recent years a new form of roosting habit has developed. Although there has been no evidence of a decline on the number of reed bed or woodland roosts used by the Starlings, there has undoubtedly been an increase in their tendency to roost in warm or sheltered sites unwittingly provided by man. Roosting on buildings in towns or on other industrial structures is presumably an extension of the cliff-roosting habit that is seen in the Starlings of barren islands, especially the races *S.v. zetlandicus* and *S.v. faeroensis*. But while the shelter provided by their cliff-roosting sites has not been measured, there is no doubt that birds roosting in cities experience higher temperatures than their rural counterparts (Gyllin *et al.* 1977) and some industrial sites may be even warmer. There appear to have been no attempts to measure the protection from wind provided by these sites on city buildings or other structures.

The roosting of Starlings in cities seems to be relatively uncommon in continental Europe, although urban roosts occur in introduced populations in Australia and America and possibly elsewhere. In Britain, town roosting is now common and Potts (1967) traced the history of its development. The earliest recorded urban roost was in Dublin in the 1840s. Like the first roosts recorded in most cities, this was found in trees in the city centre. Once roosts have become established on trees, or on other structures, there seems to be a natural progression to roosting on buildings. In some cities Potts found that this change occurred when the leaves fell from deciduous trees in the parks, suggesting that shelter was the main requirement of the birds, but in other towns the Starlings continued to roost in trees after leaf-fall. In the latter case, perhaps the trees themselves were in situations that were relatively sheltered owing to their positions in relation to buildings.

Potts considered several hypotheses to explain the evolution of urban roosting over the last 140 years. Part of the increase in this behaviour might have been due to the expansion of the British Starling population over this period, although he concluded that only about 5 per cent of the resident population resorted to city roosts (immigrants seemed hardly to use them at all). Another possibility was that increasing urbanization had led to the destruction of some of the rural sites that might otherwise have been used. Potts did not consider, however, the part that increasing numbers of tall buildings might play in providing shelter from wind, and the part that the use of electricity, gas, oil, and motor vehicles might play in the raising of temperatures in urban areas. Since we have already seen that protection from two factors (wind and low temperature), which both reduce the energy that must be expended in temperature regulation, seem to be of prime importance in the selection of roost sites, it would be of particular interest to compare the shelter provided by a variety of urban sites. In addition, however, urban roost sites are unquestionably freer from both avian and terrestrial predators than their rural counterparts but since such a small proportion of Starlings use urban roosts, this is probably a relatively unimportant factor.

Day roost sites

I have dealt at length with the selection of nocturnal roosting areas because they have been the subject of more research than have the other habitat requirements of Starlings. But when food is plentiful these birds will also spend a considerable proportion of the daytime in non-feeding situations that may also be described as roosting. There have been no studies of the protection afforded by the sites chosen but my own observations indicate that shelter is again involved, although predation probably plays a greater part than it does in the selection of nocturnal roost areas.

Bridget's Experimental Husbandry Farm, near Winchester,

Hampshire, plays host to up to 2000 Starlings, mainly immigrants, during the winter. These birds have an abundant supply of food in the cattle yards and surrounding fields (Feare 1980) and they are consequently able to spend a large proportion of most days sitting and preening in daytime roosts. Two kinds of roost site are involved, one being extremely sheltered and the other extremely exposed. The sheltered sites are in farm buildings, in dense Ivy *Hedera helix* that covers many of the trees in the farm yard and in a few Spruce and Holly *Ilex aquifolium*. These sites confer considerable protection from wind and also allow the birds involved to be practically invisible from most potential predators: the main ones on the farm are domestic cats and Sparrow Hawks *Accipter nisus*. The exposed sites, which are used by most of the resting birds, are the tops of tall trees (Plate 2), mainly Ash *Fraxinus excelsior*. Here the birds preen, or sit facing into the wind apparently oblivious to any requirement for shelter from it. The chief advantage of this kind of site seems to be the good all-round visibility and the many pairs of eyes that are available to watch for predators. These flocks periodically indulge in what appear to be panic flights, similar to the 'dreads' of terns. All calling by the roosting birds suddenly stops and the birds take off and wheel around: what stimulates these flights is rarely apparent but the appearance of a Sparrow Hawk has this effect, suggesting that anti-predator behaviour may be at least a part of the explanation. The Starlings that roost in these tree-tops are sensitive to wind, however, since in strong winds, especially when accompanied by driving rain, the birds transfer their roosting to the ground in the lee of buildings, hedges, or any other suitable wind breaks.

I have said little about the significance of rain to roosting birds because little is known about it. When the birds' plumage is in good condition it is water repellent and rain will then present them with little additional metabolic stress. When the birds are moulting and feathers may be badly abraded or missing, rain could potentially impose greater stress but in Starlings the feathers are in poorest condition and are moulted at what is generally the warmest time of year, July to September. Besides simple wear and tear, other factors may damage the water-proofing of feathers and in an ingenious experiment Yoram Yom-Tov (1979) has shown that communal roosting could be hazardous from this point of view. He kept Starlings in cages that were stacked one above the other so that birds in the lower cages accumulated increasing amounts of faeces on their feathers. The birds from the different cages were then subjected to simulated rainfall and Yom-Tov found, by weighing the birds, that those that had experienced the greatest faecal deposition increased most in weight as a result of their poorly proofed feathers absorbing water. In this way the lower birds in a roost might be at a disadvantage and have to expend more energy to combat the cooling effect of the loss of insulation, but this has not been demonstrated in wild Starlings, which would have more freedom to seek sheltered positions, both from droppings and from rain, than did Yom-Tov's birds.

Nest sites

We shall see below that shelter may be important to feeding birds, but the main period of the year during which shelter plays an important role is the breeding season, for the nest site is not simply a hole, but a place in which many features are combined to produce the maximum economy of energy utilization and protection from predators. For Starlings, the major investigation of the thermal processes involved is that of Westerterp (1973), although the energetics of other hole-nesting birds, especially the Great Tit *Parus major* (Royama 1966; Mertens 1969), have also received detailed study.

During incubation, eggs are warmer than their surroundings (except, perhaps, in some tropical species) and therefore tend to lose heat. In order that the eggs are maintained at the more or less constant temperature required for their development, heat must be provided by the incubating bird: in Starlings this is usually the female and the heat is transferred through her highly vascularized and featherless incubation patch (Plate 9). Biebach (1979) found that in the zone of thermo-neutrality Starlings did not require extra energy during incubation, but at $-10°C$ the energy consumption of incubating birds increased 35 per cent. In order that the female does not waste energy, which might entail her leaving the nest to feed for long periods each day of incubation, the nest site is selected and the nest is constructed with energy conservation as an important consideration. The thermal insulation provided by the material of a Starling's nest has not been measured but the bulky mass of dried grasses from which it is made no doubt reduces the conductive heat loss that would otherwise occur if the eggs were simply laid on the floor of a cavity. The siting of a nest in a cavity itself affords protection from heat loss, both for the eggs and nest and for the incubating bird. Verheyen (1980) found, in addition, that Starlings that built in nestboxes preferred those with entrances that faced south or east; the significance of this, in energetic terms, has not been assessed but some energetic gain may be derived from the heat of the early morning sun. Verheyen also found that his population of Starlings preferred the higher nest boxes that he erected in his study area. While this may be a reflection of the heights at which suitable nest holes may be naturally available in trees, it does suggest that the cavities selected may be those that reduce accessibility to ground predators. This is difficult to establish using nestboxes, however, because unlike natural cavities, which are all different, nestboxes are similar and once a predator has learned that such a box contains potential food, this predator can then identify the birds' nest sites at a distance and this may lead to higher levels of nest predation than occurs in natural sites. A predator's ability to locate nest sites may also increase after hatching since the chicks call, especially when hungry, and the frequent visits to the nest sites by the adults when feeding young may provide potential predators with a cue as to the whereabouts of the nest. Thus during the later stages of breeding the nest site may confer little protection from predation, except that the size of the entrance to the cavity will prevent larger birds and mammals from entering. The nest does, nevertheless, continue to cater for the Starlings' requirement for energy conservation.

Even towards the end of incubation, the embryos developing within the eggs produce heat as a by-product of their metabolism. This continues after hatching but as the young chicks are not protected by an insulatory covering of feathers much of this heat is lost to the surroundings. The surroundings include, of course, the other chicks in the nest and both Royama (1966) and Mertens (1969) have found that, in Great Tits, chicks in larger broods require less food than do those in small broods. This is because with the larger brood sizes the chicks, huddled in the nest cup, together have a lower surface area, from which heat can be lost in relation to their total volume than do the chicks of smaller broods; as a result the latter lose more heat. As a consequence of their greater heat loss, Royama found that small broods had to be brooded for longer periods of the day than did larger broods. These aspects have not been studied experimentally in Starlings but, given that Starling clutches are generally smaller than those of tits, similar principles may apply.

The energy demands and energy expenditure of nestlings

change as they develop, with different proportions of the total energy intake being devoted to growth, temperature regulation, activity, and basal metabolism at different stages of the chick's life. Westerterp (1973) obtained an overall energy budget for a Starling chick during its life in the nest and this is shown diagrammatically in Fig. 3.2. With respect to this discussion of habitat requirements, the important point is the low proportion (3.4 per cent) of the energy intake that is required for temperature maintenance. Westerterp concluded that this low cost of temperature was made possible by three factors: brooding by the parents, huddling of the chicks, and the insulation provided by the nest. The insulation provided by the nest itself appears to vary, however, during the nestling period. During the chicks' early life, faeces and urine are excreted in a 'faecal sac' that the parents are able to pick up and carry out of the nest. In this they are diligent during the early days of their chicks' life and, while this behaviour may be important from a sanitary point of view, it is also vital if the nest material is to be kept dry to maintain its insulatory properties. That nest insulation is the more important factor at this time is suggested by the fact that, after 10–12 days, when the chicks are feathered and able to regulate their own temperatures, nest cleaning by the adults decreases: by the time the chicks fledge, at 20–22 days old, the nest material is little more than a damp, faeces-impregnated mat which can be of little value in providing insulation against heat loss.

Temperature maintenance and protection from predators are the two features of cavity nesting that have helped the Starling to be so successful in comparison with many species that nest in open cups. Cup-nesting birds are more susceptible to predation (Lack

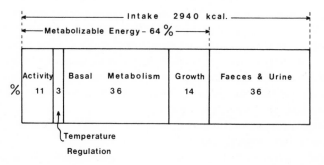

Fig. 3.2. The energy budget of a nestling Starling for the 19 days that it remains in the nest. From Westerterp 1973.

1968) but, perhaps more important as far as reproductive output is concerned, they tend to lay smaller clutches. Royama (1966) has suggested that this is because the greater heat losses from chicks in cup nests, compared with those in well insulated nests in holes, lead to a greater food requirement. Conversely, the lower food requirement per chick in hole-nesting birds means that the adults can, for the same energy expenditure on their part, feed more chicks and are thus able to rear more young per breeding season.

Since so many of the benefits of hole-nesting are provided by the nest built within the cavity, by the comparatively large number of chicks in the brood, and by the reduced amount of energy demanded of the incubating or brooding bird, the physical features of the cavity itself appear to be relatively unimportant. This allows the Starling a high degree of adaptability in its choice of sites, with the size of the entrance and its orientation being the chief physical attributes; the size of the cavity within can vary from a space large enough to house only the nest and the incubating bird to a huge area like a house roof space, in which the birds will construct their nest in a corner not too far from the entrance hole. This adaptability enables the Starling to occupy a wide range of breeding sites. While the most commonly occupied sites are holes in trees (Plate 3), the spectrum includes holes in cliffs, walls or even on the ground and a variety of man-made buildings from garden sheds, farm buildings, and houses to factories, aircraft hangers (and even aircraft themselves), and electricity cable pylons.

FEEDING SITES

So far we have been concerned only with the kinds of habitat that allow Starlings to reduce their energy expenditure to a minimum, and we must now examine those habitats which provide the birds with their energy needs. For example, a suitable cavity is no good for breeding unless it is surrounded by the kind of habitat from which the birds can obtain sufficient nutritionally adequate food. Similarly, an excellent feeding area cannot support a breeding population if there are no nest sites (Plate 4). Thus, for successful colonization a habitat must contain both the energy saving and energy providing features required by the birds. So what constitutes a good feeding area?

No attempts have been made to assess the quality in terms of the energy gained per unit time, of the different feeding areas used by Starlings. We shall see later (Chapter 9) that the profitability of, for example, a grass field can vary considerably on a very fine scale even within the field, and the exploitation of these feeding sites therefore requires subtle behavioural characteristics involving memory and the use of a wide range of cues. But for the present we shall consider habitats on only a crude scale.

Starlings are essentially grassland feeders; they take invertebrates (and, to a lesser extent, seeds) from the foliage, from the surface of the ground, and from the upper few centimetres of the soil. They are selective in the kind of grassland in which they like to feed, however, and show a marked preference for short grass. There seem to be several reasons for this. For example, short grass is easy for a small bird to walk through; it is easier to locate items of prey or, for prey that live beneath the soil surface, to identify the cues by which these animals are discovered; and in short grass Starlings have a good all-round visibility which enables them to watch for approaching predators and also to see what other Starlings are doing. Short grass is made available by die-back during the winter, which renders most grass fields, or at least parts of them, suitable for feeding. In addition, man creates suitable feeding sites by his mowing activities: this involves domestic lawns, playing fields, park-lands, and even those agricultural areas that are cut for hay or silage. But perhaps the most important creator of short grass is the cow or sheep, and as well as keeping grazed areas short, these animals deposit droppings which are rapidly invaded by a variety of invertebrates which are also eaten by Starlings. Starlings also feed in close association with domestic stock and they may derive some benefit from the disturbance of insects that the animals cause as they move through the grassland, in an association similar to that of Cattle Egrets *Bubulcus ibis* and wild ungulates in Africa. The energetic benefit that Starlings derive from feeding amongst grazing animals, or in fields recently grazed and where dung is abundant, has not, however, been measured. Starlings are also known, of course, to feed 'oxpecker-fashion' by searching for external parasites on the backs of sheep (Plate 5).

Figure 3.3 shows that Starlings spend most of their time feeding in grassland throughout the year. During the breeding season, and especially when feeding young in May and June, their diet consists almost entirely of invertebrates obtained from the surface or from the upper few centimetres of the soil of grass fields. Should this source of invertebrate food disappear for some reason, for

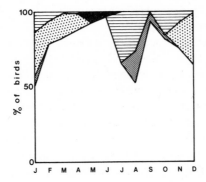

Fig. 3.3. The proportion of Starlings using different feeding areas at Bridgets Experimental Husbandry Farm in each month of 1975. The unshaded area represents grass; diagonal hatching, plough; horizontal hatching, stubble grain, spilled grain in the farmyard, and pea waste in July; stippled, feedlots; block, trees.

example during a particularly dry spell, the chances of survival of the chicks are much reduced when they are given alternatives such as bread, cereals, and cattle food. This happened in 1975 at Worplesdon and it resulted in the total failure of all of the late broods. In addition to being presented with plant proteins, which are less readily assimilated than animal proteins, the absence of invertebrates in the diet deprived these late chicks of practically their only source of water.

Outside the breeding season Starlings are less dependent on animal foods, but even towards the end of breeding another rich source of animal protein becomes available in most years, at least in many parts of Britain. Shortly after bud-burst in the Spring the young leaves of trees, especially oaks *Quercus spp.* constitute a highly nutritious source of food for vast numbers of defoliating caterpillars. These form the main items of the diets of many woodland birds, for example the tits (Perrins 1979), at this time of year but some of these caterpillars are also fed to Starling nestlings. Caterpillars seem to become even more important to recently fledged young, which spend much of their time in trees; here they wait for their parents to return with food but also begin to feed themselves to an increasing extent until they become independent of their parents a few days after leaving the nest. The juveniles then have a tendency to remain more arboreal than their parents (Feare 1980), a factor which, when the requirements for an invertebrate diet relaxes, predisposes these young birds to switch to summer-ripening fruit.

Thus seasonal changes in the kinds of food eaten by Starlings, and therefore in the habitats that can be exploited by them, are imposed not only by the nutritional requirements of the birds but also by the presence of foods alternative to those available in grassland. The birds' ability to digest plant foods, such as fruit in summer and seeds in winter, out of the breeding season involves both physiological and morphological changes in the alimentary system: these changes, which include an increase in the length of the intestine (Plate 6), enable the birds to make the best use of these nutritionally less-adequate foods. This, in turn, allows Starlings to be more catholic in their selection feeding sites, especially in autumn and winter. Many species of bird range more widely in autumn and winter than at other times of year and can be seen feeding in atypical habitats, for example, several species of thrush feed on the sea-shore in winter (Simms 1978). Starlings feed in such large numbers in such a wide variety of habitats in winter that few of them can be called atypical. Some of the feeding areas that are exploited provide the birds with invertebrates and the utilization of these areas probably represents an extension of grassland feeding. Examples of frequently used habitats of this kind are the sea-shore, the banks of rivers, estuaries, lakes and man-made reservoirs, and sewage farms.

Feeding sites that provide Starlings with vegetable foods are even more diverse. In urban areas, gardens and their bird-tables and also parks, provide an enormous variety of household waste that attracts Starlings, sometimes, to the annoyance of the bird-table owners, at the expense of other species considered to be more desirable. Further household waste is eaten, both by Starlings and many other birds such as gulls and crows, at refuse tips, while in dockyards, around warehouses, and in farmyards the large quantities of grain that are spilled daily provide a rich source of food for Starlings, Feral Pigeons, House Sparrows, and a variety of other species. Once Starlings had learned to exploit the accidental spillages in farmyards, it was only to be expected that they would find the 'deliberate' spillages, in the form of cattle food in open troughs, equally attractive. Greater emphasis is placed on these resources when grassland food supplies are rendered unavailable by hard frost and snow (Dunnet 1956, Bailey 1966).

A characteristic of all of the sites discussed so far is that they, like grassland, represent open areas, providing the birds with good all-round visibility. Shelter does not appear to be of great importance to feeding flocks, although in strong winds and driving rain Starlings do tend to feed in the lee of woods, hedges, buildings, or any other structures that give some protection. I have already said that in the summer some Starlings, especially juveniles, tend to be arboreal and in winter some less-open habitats are used for feeding; thick woodland is usually avoided but Starlings feed readily inside buildings. Waste fruit in orchards attracts Starlings and thrushes and although there are currently few vineyards in Britain, some of them are experiencing Starling damage; on continental Europe autumn and early winter flocks of Starlings are regarded as serious pests in vineyards, as they are in olive groves in North Africa and elsewhere around the Mediterranean.

Finally, another major habitat, the air, is also exploited by Starlings from time to time. The moderately long and pointed Starling's wings are adapted for speed rather than manoeuverability but nevertheless the birds are adept at flycatching, like hirundines, when aerial insects are abundant. The nuptial flights of ants, mainly in July and August (Imms 1947) provides such an abundance and aerial feeding by Starlings (Plate 5), often in association with Swallows *Hirundo rustica*, House Martins *Delichon urbica*, and Swifts *Apus apus*, is commonly seen. Starlings also frequently hawk insects in the spring, just before the breeding season, though what they are eating then has not been established.

Starlings are thus extremely adaptable in their use of feeding sites, especially in winter, but even at this time of year there are indications that, over and above the basic concept that the birds must obtain sufficient energy to allow them to perform all their daily activities, some other nutritional constraints are imposed. During my study of the birds that fed at Bridgets Experimental Husbandry Farm in Hampshire I found that, while over half of the Starlings were found feeding in grassland throughout the winter, the birds that were eating cattle food were predominantly males. While males can presumably concentrate on high-energy foods like the barley given to cattle, females may have to devote more time to feeding on invertebrates throughout the winter in order to maintain high protein reserves (Feare 1980) since Jones and Ward (1976) have suggested that a high protein reserve could be essential for early breeding and to enable the female to lay a large clutch.

We have now discussed the demands that Starlings make of their environment in order that they can minimize their susceptibility to energy loss and predation and maximize their energy and other necessary nutritional intake. We have also established that the features that constitute 'protection' must occur hand in hand with those that permit optimum nutritional gain. With this background we can now consider what habitats are 'good' for Starlings, that is, which habitats are likely to support a high density of birds. Since both the birds' requirements and food availability vary seasonally, I shall describe what appear to be ideal habitats for the breeding season and winter.

While breeding, Starlings need a suitable cavity for the nest and a feeding area that will provide them with sufficient food, mainly invertebrates, for the adults and their young. We shall see later that the adults rarely forage more than 500 m from the nest and spend most of their time within 200 m. Most of the feeding is done in short grassland, so that a 'good' breeding area should be provided by a nest cavity, surrounded by 12 ha of grassland. Starlings are not territorial on their feeding areas, however, and this area could support many feeding birds. More important is the fact that they breed colonially with extensive interactions between the pairs in the colony. A good breeding habitat should therefore consist of a number of nest cavities within the required area of grassland to enable the establishment of a colony of breeding birds and sufficient feeding area to allow the birds to feed in loose flocks. Such areas are found where clumps of old trees, which provide an abundance of nest sites are surrounded by or adjoin grassland, in the form of extensive lawns, parks, or grass fields (Plate 4). In urban areas the clumps of trees may be replaced by buildings that provide suitable nest holes, as long as there is sufficient grassland in the vicinity.

Not all habitats are equally satisfactory for breeding Starlings and therefore bird densities vary between different areas. Table 3.2 gives densities that have been estimated for a range of habitats. Even though these are from a wide geographic area, the figures show that open agricultural land and park land, both habitats which have been created by man in many parts of the world, support the highest densities of Starlings.

In winter, feeding flocks tend to be more compact than during the breeding season and they are also considerably larger. The resulting higher density of birds on a feeding area, which can, as

Table 3.2 Breeding densities (number of pairs per km^2) of Starlings in different habitats

Habitat	Density (No. pairs/km^2)	Source
Specific habitats		
Park land (Poland)	782–809	Tomaliojc and Profus (1977)
Park land (Poland)	666	Tomaliojc (1974)
Park land (Poland)	170–220	Luniak (1977)
Beech forest (Poland)	598	Jakubiec (1972)
Beech forest (England)	>200	Williamson, K. (1968)
Built-up area (Warsaw, Poland)	6–70	Luniak (1977)
Built-up area, < 10% grass (Warsaw, Poland)	6–20	Luniak (1977)
Larger areas of farmland including woodland and villages		
Britain	c.10	Sharrock (1976)
Poland (mainland)	7–9	Jablonski (1976)
Poland (Sobieszewska Island)	12.1	Gromadzki (1978)
West Germany	12.4	Oelke (1967)

Data from small areas of a particular habitat illustrate the range of variability in breeding density that can occur, while the censusing of larger areas, incorporating the various habitats available in agricultural land, show a greater constancy of density

we have seen, include a variety of sites apart from grassland, needs suitable sites for the formation of daytime roosts. These day roosts are generally in exposed situations: in rural areas they tend to be in the tops of tall deciduous trees while in urban districts television aerials may be used. In addition to the day roost a suitable site for roosting at night must also be available, generally within 20 km of the feeding area. Thus a good winter habitat for Starlings consists of an area of short grass (or in urban areas other feeding sites, such as sewage farms, where invertebrates are abundant), probably together with other food sources that can supply the birds with easily obtainable high-energy foods, tall trees or other suitable day roosts, and a reed bed, wood, or thicket, or even a town centre, within easy reach for the communal nocturnal roost. Unfortunately, we do not yet have reasonable estimates of the densities of Starlings in Britain in winter, but the habitats that fulfil these requirements, and also appear to have high densities of Starlings, seem to be most commonly found in eastern and southern Britain, although this picture may be complicated by the proximity of these

areas to continental Europe, whence Britain receives around
35 000 000 immigrants for the winter (Potts 1967).

POPULATION ESTIMATES

Table 3.2 shows that breeding densities of Starlings can be
extremely variable and the difficulties involved in obtaining estimates have led few people to attempt them. Any estimate of a
population of a large geographical area must take into account the
high densities found in urban and wooded areas and also the low
densities found in marginal habitats; such an estimate is inevitably
a very rough approximation.

Sharrock (1976) used a value of 10–20 pairs of Starlings per
square kilometre as an average density for the British Isles. This
gave an estimate for the British Starling population of between
four and seven million pairs. Potts (1967) had earlier arrived at a
figure of around 3 500 000 pairs. If we assume a density of 10 pairs
per square kilometre to calculate the population of Starlings
throughout the geographical range, using the distribution shown in
Fig. 2.6, we arrive at a world population of about 600 000 000
birds. On the same basis, the Starling population of north America
is something over 200 000 000 birds. Although these figures must
be treated with considerable reservation, the comparison between
those of north America and the 'natural' Old World range probably has some validity. In other words, over one third of the
world's Starlings live in North America. When we remember that
all of these birds originated from about 100 birds introduced into
Central Park, New York, only 90 years ago, we perhaps get the
best indication of what a successful bird the Starling is!

4 THE CALENDAR

Most animals and plants are subjected to fluctuations in their environment. Many of these, for example variations in temperature or in food supply, cannot be accurately predicted. Environmental fluctuations that are based on astronomical features, on the other hand, can be predicted in terms of both their periodicity and their amplitude. Thus the tides, day-length, lunar and annual cycles all exhibit specific periodicities to which living organisms can and do adjust. Most birds demonstrate diurnal and annual rhythms in many of their physiological processes and behavioural activities and this is especially true in temperate regions, where daily and seasonal cycles are pronounced. In some cases the cycles are imposed directly by the environmental variation but in others the cycles continue even in constant conditions; in this case the environmental changes synchronize, but do not drive, the cycles within the animal. Perhaps the best demonstration of this mechanism can be seen in the daily occurrence of locomotor activity.

If Starlings are kept in an experimental aviary with the lighting controlled so that their daily light–dark cycle consists of 12 h light and 12 h dark, their activity is confined mainly to the period when the light is on: this is precisely what we observe in free-living birds. But if the light is then turned off so that the birds are kept in constant darkness, activity does not cease but continues at regular intervals. Gwinner (1975a) found that these intervals were slightly longer than 24 h so that the Starlings steadily drifted out of phase with the normal 24 h light–dark cycle. If Starlings were kept in constant light, however, their 'daily' cycle was slightly less than 24 h. Thus these birds demonstrated that even in the absence of their normal environmental stimuli, they could maintain regular cycles of activity and rest. Biological rhythms like this that continue without the influence of external stimuli and operate on an approximately daily routine are called *circadian* rhythms. Besides locomotor activity, various other activities in birds, such as body temperature, are repeated with a circadian periodicity and some of the physiological processes that operate on this frequency are incorporated into the 'circadian clock': this forms an essential part of the sun-compass used by some species as a navigational aid in migration (Emlen 1975; Keeton 1981) and also forms the basis of the photoperiod (the proportion of the day that is light) measuring system whereby Starlings can detect the lengthening days of spring and begin preparations for breeding.

Gwinner's experiment, outlined above, demonstrated that when his Starlings were subjected to a 'normal' daily light–dark cycle, their circadian rhythm of activity was synchronized by this photoperiodic cycle so that their activity accorded with that which would be useful to them during the 'normal' day. In the language of the physiologist, this process of synchronization of an internal rhythm with an environmental stimulus, in this case the daily cycle of light and dark, is called *entrainment*, and the entraining stimulus is called a *Zeitgeber*.

It is, of course, much more difficult to demonstrate the existence of internal rhythms that operate on an annual basis, simply because this means that birds must be kept under controlled conditions for periods well in excess of a year. Nevertheless, such *circannual* rhythms have been shown to exist in birds and Gwinner (1977) demonstrated that changes in the daily photoperiod constituted an important Zeitgeber that entrained the rhythm of moult to the yearly cycle. Gwinner also suggested that testis size showed a circannual rhythm of development and regression, but here the effects of changing the photoperiod may be more direct. By modifying the periodicity of the photoperiodic cycle so that the number of hours of light in a day changed from nine hours to 15 and back to nine every 73 days, instead of every 365 days, Gwinner stimulated Starlings to undergo five cycles of testis growth and moult in one year. Further difficulties of interpretation arise from Murton and Westwood's (1977) discovery that Starlings that were subjected to different photoperiods ate different amounts of food, even when the food was available to them for one six-hour interval during the period of light; here, photoperiod may have acted in conjunction with, or by stimulating, other factors besides having a direct effect on testis growth. The main criticism of the hypothesis of a circannual rhythm of testis growth stems from the work of Schwab (1971). He found that Starlings only exhibited an annual cycle of testis development when they were subjected to a constant schedule of 12-h light and 12-h dark (LD 12:12). If the daily light period was less than 11 h or more than 13 h, they showed no such annual cycle. Similar results have been found in the more recent investigations of Ebling, Goldsmith, and Follett (1982). These authors found that in Starlings maintained on a LD 11:13 schedule, testis growth was slow but once growth had occurred the testes remained large. With 13 or more hours of light per day, the Starlings' testes grew rapidly and then regressed and remained small. Only under LD 12:12 did testis development become cyclic and show the features typical of wild Starlings under natural photoperiods, with a period of testis growth followed by their collapse, a period of refractoriness (lack of sensitivity of photoperiodic stimulation), and then renewed growth.

The factors that control the annual cycles of birds are thus highly complex and our understanding of the interplay between them is relatively poor. The evidence that does exist nevertheless suggests that changes in the daily photoperiod play an important role in determining what happens when. Even within the Starlings' breeding geographical range, however, latitudinal differences between the northern and southern extremities indicate that the birds living in different regions are subjected to widely different seasonal photoperiodic regimes. The responses of Starlings from differing geographical areas to various photoperiods have not been investigated and we can only assume that birds from different latitudinal populations are stimulated to breed, moult, migrate etc. by different photoperiodic thresholds, meanwhile accepting that other, hitherto unknown or unsuspected, environmental stimuli may also be important. We do know that the Starling populations present in Britain in winter, consisting of British residents and immigrants from the Continent, behave differently in late winter and spring, under identical environmental conditions, though it has not been established to which factors the birds respond: increasing photoperiod, however, does seem a likely candidate. While British resident Starlings in winter spend much time in their breeding areas, frequently visiting potential nest sites, singing (even females sing in autumn), and defending song posts, their continental counterparts, who cannot, of course, visit their nest sites, do not show these tendencies. They live in larger flocks but, when not feeding, they do periodically sing in day-time roosts; they also sing in the night roost after arrival in the evening and before morning departure. But the intensity of this behaviour, in terms of the amount of time spent singing and the aggression towards other Starlings, is far less marked in the immigrant birds. The difference between the two populations may also be apparent in some morphological features. For example, Bullough (1942) thought that the bills of British Starlings begin to change from dark brown to yellow, their colour in 'breeding condition', in November–December while the bills of continental birds do not change until January–February. Evans (1980), however, suggested that the difference may not be so clear cut. Similarly, British residents, especially males, tend to attain their glossy iridescent feathers earlier than continental birds. The acquisition of this iridescence is, however, due to the abrasion of the buff/white feather tips that appear after the post-nuptial (late summer) moult, rather than to a change of feathers, and this abrasion is enhanced by the tendency of British birds, in autumn and winter, to visit nest holes. The change in bill colour and the tendency to sing and visit nest holes are probably, on the other hand, a response to changed hormone levels, showing that although the British and continental birds are subjected to the same photoperiod and climatic conditions, their physiological responses to these conditions vary.

We now come to the important question: how do the relevant environmental factors or Zeitgebers, the most important of which seems to be the photoperiod, modify the internal rhythms of the bird? Our understanding of the processes involved is very limited; in fact it is not even clear which sensory organs are involved in the reception of the environmental stimuli, the evidence from recent experiments on different species being conflicting. It does seem, however, that the pineal organ, situated on the top of the brain, may play a role in the reception of photoperiod stimuli and the transmission of information derived from them, probably by chemical means, to other parts of the brain. When Gwinner (1978) removed the pineal organ of Starlings, he found that their circadian rhythms persisted when the birds were kept under constant environmental conditions. The rhythms were, however, drastically altered and lost stability, so that sequences of movement around the cage could begin and end apparently spontaneously. Other workers have also obtained data that implicate the pineal organ in the reception and transmission of photoperiodic information (e.g. Turek, McMillan, and Menaker 1976: Simpson and Follett 1981) but the mechanisms involved need considerable clarification.

We have obviously still much to learn about the synchronization of body activities with environmental factors but the brief outline above, summarizing what we know so far for Starlings, provides some illustration of the complexity of the systems involved. We know even less about how the body's perception of seasonal changes in the daily photoperiod becomes translated into the physiological and behavioural attributes that allow the bird to reproduce, moult, and undergo other essential activities that enable it to survive the various phases of the seasonally changing environment. We do know, however, that the physiological events in the Starling's calendar are influenced by hormones secreted by the pituitary, an organ situated in the lower surface of the brain, even though it is not understood how the pituitary receives information about daylength or other factors.

We know of half a dozen or so hormones that are produced by the pituitary—there may be others as yet undiscovered but all of those identified so far are proteins. Some of these hormones are called *trophic* hormones, which means that they act upon other glands in the body to either stimulate or retard the secretion of hormones produced by these glands. For example, the pituitary secretes thyroid stimulating hormone (TSH), the trophic hormone that acts on the thyroid; this stimulates the thyroid gland to secrete its own hormone, thyroxine, which controls a range of body functions including moult. The other pituitary hormones of special interest in our consideration of the Starling's annual cycle are the gonadotrophic hormones, that is, those hormones that act directly on the ovary (birds have only one) or testes. These hormones are luteinizing hormone (LH), follicle stimulating hormone (FSH), and prolactin. These hormones are the same or very similar to those of the same name that are found in mammals, including man, although the mechanisms involved in the release of the hormone from the pituitary and in the action of the hormone when it reaches its target organ via the blood stream, may differ in birds and mammals. For example, in birds the release of prolactin from the pituitary is stimulated by a chemical produced by the hypothalamus—a protuberance of the brain that enters the pituitary: in mammals this same chemical acts in the opposite way by inhibiting the release of prolactin. Similarly, the action of prolactin itself differs in the two groups of animals: in mammals one of its main functions is to stimulate the release of milk from the mammary glands. Birds do not possess mammary glands but prolactin*

---

*It is interesting to note, however, that in one group of birds, the pigeons, the female does produce a secetion with which to feed its young; this material, produced by cells in the wall of the crop, is called 'pigeon milk' and its secretion is controlled by prolactin.

nevertheless has several important roles in the breeding cycle and in migration. Our knowledge of these is undoubtedly incomplete but new techniques for measuring the concentrations of hormones in the blood are helping to elucidate the functions of prolactin, along with those of LH and FSH.

Dawson and Goldsmith (1982) measured the concentrations of these three pituitary hormones in Starlings collected throughout the year and their results are summarized in Fig. 4.1. In both sexes there was a clear annual cycle, with peak concentrations of the hormones occurring during the breeding season; Dawson and Goldsmith thought that the rise in hormone concentration in the plasma was most likely a response to the increasing photoperiod at this time of year.

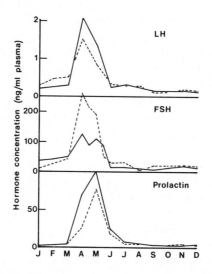

Fig. 4.1. Annual variation in the plasma concentrations of the pituitary hormones LH, FSH and prolactin in female (————) and male (- - - -) Starlings. Redrawn and simplified (LH and prolactin) or data compiled (FSH) from Dawson and Goldsmith (1982). Note that LH and FSH reach their peak concentrations earlier than prolactin.

FSH and LH reach their maximum concentrations in April while prolactin does not peak until May. FSH is responsible for the initiation of gonad development in both sexes while high concentrations are associated with gonad maturation and stimulate the gonads to secrete some of their own hormones. In the male, LH stimulates the Leydig cells in the testis (Ebling *et al.* 1982). These produce the male hormone testosterone, although, as we shall see below, Temple (1974) found that testosterone levels in the blood of male Starlings were high for a much longer period than Dawson and Goldsmith's LH concentrations and also longer than Temple's own measurements of high Leydig cell number and size. In females, LH stimulates mature ovarian follicles to secrete progesterone, testosterone, and several other oestrogens and Follett and Davies (1979) consider that ovulation, the release from the ovary of an ovum ready for fertilization, is caused by combined action of LH and progesterone. A rise in plasma LH causes the ovary to secrete progesterone, but this hormone acts on the pituitary, stimulating the production of yet more LH. This continuing interaction between the pituitary and ovarian hormones ultimately produces a surge of LH, which is followed about four hours later by ovulation; this LH surge is believed to be the trigger for ovulation.

FSH and LH are thus concerned with the onset of the reproductive period. Dawson and Goldsmith (1982) found that peak plasma concentrations of prolactin occurred somewhat later and this has been confirmed experimentally by Ebling *et al.* (1982), using male Starlings subjected to different photoperiods. Under natural conditions, prolactin reaches its maximum concentration during incubation and remains high during the feeding of the young. This pattern occurs in both sexes and, despite the smaller contribution of the male to incubation of the eggs (see Chapter 6), it appears that prolactin may be involved in promoting parental behaviour, although the mechanism for this has not been elucidated. Prolactin does appear to suppress the secretion of LH and Ebling *et al.* (1982) have suggested further that prolactin may be involved in gonadal regression and in driving the birds into a photorefractory state at the end of the breeding season. There is clearly much interesting work ahead for endocrinologists studying the pituitary hormones of Starlings and other birds.

One of the earliest studies of the concentration of gonadal hormones circulating in the blood plasma was that of Temple (1974), who measured the titre of testosterone in the blood of male Starlings. The seasonal changes in circulating testosterone are shown diagrammatically in Fig. 4.2. In males, testosterone tends to be the dominant sex hormone that circulates in the blood but in females its action can be overridden by the so-called 'female hormones', oestrogen and progesterone. Oestrogen and pro-

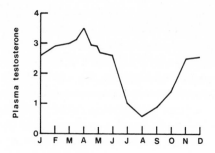

Fig. 4.2. Seasonal variation in the gonadal hormone testosterone circulating in the blood of male Strarlings. Testosterone titres are in ng 10 ml^{-1} of plasma. The graph is simplified from data in Temple (1974).

gesterone are produced during the breeding season but in the autumn the main sex hormone circulating in the blood of female Starlings is in fact testosterone. This hormone is responsible for the female's change in bill colour, as it is in the male, but the high level of testosterone in females in autumn also stimulates them to sing at this time—they do not sing in spring when the other steroid hormones predominate.

Figure 4.2 shows that there is an obvious annual cycle with high concentrations from November to June which reach a peak in April and with a sharp fall in July with levels remaining low until September–October. Hilton (1961) had earlier measured the total concentration of cholesterol in the testes of Starlings and he found peak concentrations in July and August, which represents an inverse relationship with Temple's data. However, since cholesterol is the chemical precursor of testosterone, Temple interpreted this as indicating that when testosterone production and secretion by the testis were at a low ebb, there was an accumulation of the steroid from which the hormone would eventually be produced. In addition, Temple found that the annual cycle of testosterone concentration in the blood of Starlings closely parallelled the seasonal cycle of size of several components of the testis. There is undoubtedly, therefore, a close relation between the annual gonad cycle of Starlings and the hormones produced by the gonads, and these cycles are controlled by the hormones secreted by the pituitary. However, although it is known that the pituitary hormone LH stimulates testosterone secretion (see above), other factors must be responsible for the high levels of testosterone production in autumn and winter when LH secretion is at a low ebb (Dawson and Goldsmith 1982).

I have already suggested that the secretion of gonadotrophic hormones from the pituitary is influenced by changes in the daily photoperiod which thus affect the annual cycle of the Starling. In experiments on the effects of other individual birds on the circannual cycle of Starlings Gwinner (1975*b*) has found, however, that the circannual rhythm of testis size can be altered by the presence or absence of females. In particular, he found that the presence of females prevented the regression of the testes after the resurgence of their growth in the autumn. Similarly, J.A. Lloyd (1965) showed that although the development of the Starling's incubation patch could be stimulated by implants or injections of oestrogen, prolactin, and testosterone, environmental factors including photoperiod and the presence of a mate were important in allowing the maximum development of the incubation patch. Thus although the Starling's annual cycle appears to be ultimately governed by seasonal changes in the photoperiod, other modifying factors, such as the time during the 24-h cycle when food is available, the presence or absence of other birds of the same or opposite sex, and probably factors yet to be discovered, may also play a part in determining precisely what happens at a particular time of year.

In the remainder of this chapter I shall discuss three events of the Starling's annual cycle, weight changes, moult, and migration, while the other major event, breeding and its associated activities, forms the subject of Chapters 6 and 7.

WEIGHT CHANGE

In common with most birds, Starlings do not maintain a constant weight and when we say that a Starling weighs 75–90 g (Chapter 2) we attempt to embrace the range of weights that a healthy, full grown bird may experience during its life. Variation in weight can be due to a number of factors, however, including where a bird is feeding and the kind of food it is eating. For example, I have caught a male in winter, just after it had completed a feed on barley, that weighed 121 g but a considerable proportion of this 'excess' weight must have consisted of the barley it had just eaten. A bird that fed in grassland, eating invertebrates, could probably never attain such a weight. The emptying of the gut overnight is one component of diurnal weight changes in Starlings: this is especially true during long winter nights when a Starling can lose 10 g (Taitt 1973), but fat may also be metabolized overnight (Jones 1980*a*) and this contributes further to weight loss. This weight, is, of course, made up the following day. There may well be other components of the daily cycle of weight change, involving especially protein (Jones 1980*b*) and water metabolism, but these aspects have not been studied in Starlings.

Seasonal changes in weight have received much more attention, largely because the changes are greater and easier to measure. There are, however, considerable difficulties in obtaining what might be regarded as a realistic picture of the annual weight cycle since ideally all of the birds involved in the analysis should be collected at the same place and at the same time of day: in practice, this is rarely possible. The seasonal pattern of weight change shown in Fig. 4.3 (from data collected near Oxford by Al-Joborae, 1979) nevertheless reveals the major features of minimum weight in summer and maximum weight in winter. The range of weight over the year is greater in males than in females, as found also by Coleman and Robson (1975), due mainly to the greater weight attained by males in winter. Some, probably the

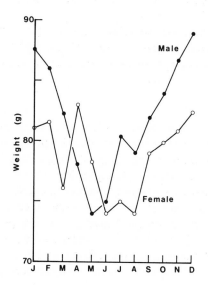

Fig. 4.3. Seasonal changes in the weights of Starlings caught near Oxford. From Al-Joborae (1979).

main, components of this weight cycle have been identified but others will doubtless emerge with more intensive study.

One of the main contributors to winter weight increase is the deposition of fat. This can be clearly seen on dissecting a Starling in winter, when the abdomen and neck, in particular, house large deposits of fat which are absent in birds that have been collected in summer. Coleman and Robson (1975) found that in winter Starlings had about 7.5 g of fat in their bodies, almost twice as much as in summer. Winter fat provides birds with a certain amount of insurance against unpredictable food shortage since the fat can be used as an energy reserve, and Taitt (1973) thought that additional fat in birds that she considered to be continental immigrants had been accumulated as an energy store for migration. Westerterp, Gortmaker, and Wigngaarden (1982) have also shown that fat reserves can be depleted during the breeding season, especially in adults feeding larger broods.

Coleman and Robson (1975) found that the liver was heavier in winter than at other times of year and, as with fat, they attributed the high winter weight to storage, in this case of glycogen, fat, protein, and water. The winter increase in the liver weight only amounted to about 0.5 g, however, and so this contributed little to the overall greater weight of Starlings in winter.

Of greater importance is the food processing machinery, the gizzard and intestine. We shall see in Chapter 9 that the gut undergoes dramatic changes in association with the switch from a predominantly insectivorous diet in spring and summer to a more vegetarian diet in winter. In particular, the wall of the gizzard increases in thickness and the intestine increases in length in winter, both of these changes leading to an increase in weight of the digestive system amounting to around 4 g. Clearly, this is a major contribution to the Starling's winter increase in weight.

Figure 4.3 shows that males lose weight steadily in the spring while females attain a peak weight in April. This spring increase in weight is due to the growth of the reproductive system, especially of the oviduct and associated structures, and it becomes most pronounced during yolk deposition and, of course, the maturation of fertilized eggs just prior to laying.

These seasonal weight changes, especially the winter increase, reflect certain needs of the birds but they also influence the birds' activities. For while the Starling's weight alters, its wing area remains the same, so that there is a modification of the bird's aerodynamic capabilities. Other things being equal, it is more efficient for a heavier bird to fly faster than a lighter one (Pennycuik 1975) and Eastwood (1967) found that Starlings departing from their roost in the morning flew faster in winter than in summer. Although our knowledge of the components and functions of seasonal weight changes is still fairly basic, we may well find that these changes have far-reaching repercussions with respect to many of the Starling's activities.

MOULT

Starlings undergo one complete moult each year and the sequence of feather replacement has been studied by Williamson (1961) and Bährmann (1964). The process begins and ends a little earlier in adults than in juveniles and moulting birds can be found from late June to mid October or rarely, early November. There is almost certainly some variation in the timing of moult between years, but this has yet to be investigated. In 1978 and 1979 in my study area at Worplesdon, Surrey, Starlings laid their first clutches late and did not attempt to lay second clutches (Chapter 6); very soon after the chicks of the first broods had fledged the bills of the adults began to turn dark. This was in late May, whereas in years when second broods have been raised this change in bill colour did not occur until June. We have seen above that both bill colour and moult are under hormonal control although different hormones, testosterone and thyroid hormone respectively, are involved. Despite this difference, the completion of parental duties may signal the onset of moult in which case moult, as well as the change in bill colour, might occur early when no second broods are reared. According to Bährman (1964) moult is influenced by the weather, with dry and warm conditions accelerating and cold wet weather delaying it; the basis for this conclusion is not given.

Moult begins with the shedding of the innermost primary. In adults this usually occurs at the end of June while in juveniles moult commences in early July, or later in birds from second broods. The primaries are shed in sequence from inner to outer (i.e. descendantly) and during primary moult there are usually two feathers growing at the same time and during their growth a third may be shed. Each feather takes 20–30 days to grow to its full extent, depending upon its final length, and the completion of the replacement of the primaries takes about 100 days (R.W. Summers, personal communication). The moult of the inner wing feathers begins about half-way through the moult of the primaries, with the tertials being shed just before the moult of the secondaries commences. Secondary moult is ascendant, working inwards from the first (outer) to the sixth (inner). Moult of the secondaries is more rapid than that of the primaries so that the two sets of feather replacement are completed at about the same time. During the moult of the remiges the wing coverts are replaced, the moult of the primary coverts coinciding with the replacement of the feathers to which they are related.

The moult of the tail feathers begins after primary moult has commenced and, according to Williamson (1961), not until August. Tail moult does not appear to follow an invariable sequence but it usually begins with the shedding of the inner pair of feathers. Then, either the next innermost or the outer feathers may be shed and the remaining feathers can be moulted almost simultaneously. The moult of the tail feathers is rapid and Williamson found some adults with complete new rectrices by the end of August, at which stage the ninth primary was about half-grown.

The occurrence of wing and tail moult is readily visible only in flying birds, but body moult is conspicuous in Starlings at rest or feeding for the new feathers are conspicuously different from the old, especially in juveniles. Moult of the contour feathers begins at centres on the sides of the breast and belly and on the rump. The new feathers, with their white or buff tips, contrast with the older iridescent feathers of adults while in juveniles the new feathers, being blackish with broad pale tips, are totally different from the grey-brown juvenile feathers. Replacement of the body feathers spreads from the moult centres to the remainder of the breast and belly; the moult of these areas is almost complete before the mantle and scapular feathers begin to be lost and the feathers of the head are the last to be moulted.

Moult of the contour feathers begins in late June or early July, at the same time as the primaries, but is not normally completed until late August or even September. In October, young birds may be seen with bleached brown juvenile feathers still present on the head. In total, therefore, the moult takes about three months for completion.

After the moult the extensive pale tips to most of the body feathers, especially in birds entering their first winter, gives Starlings a distinctly spotty appearance and yet during the following breeding season much of this spottiness is replaced by a sleeker, more iridescent appearance. This is not achieved by a pre-nuptial moult in the spring but by the gradual wearing away of the pale tips of the feathers as the winter progresses. This abrasion is accelerated, especially in males, as the birds visit nest holes, initially while prospecting for suitable nest sites but later when incubating eggs and feeding young.

I began this discussion of the annual moult by remarking that it commenced in adults when their breeding activities were completed. Bährmann (1964) noted that while the two longest (8th and 9th) primaries were being moulted the wing was shortened by almost 7 per cent. He considered that this would have little influence on the flying abilities of the birds, but this may be a contributory factor to the slower flight of Starlings on leaving their night roosts in summer (Eastwood 1967 and Chapter 10). As Bährmann suggests, the rapidity of the moult of the rectrices may well be an adaptation to minimize the period during which manoeuvrability is impaired. On the grounds of both the more limited flying capabilities and the presumed different food demands of moulting birds, the lack of overlap between breeding and moult is to be expected. We might also expect moult and migration to be mutually exclusive and this indeed appears to be the case in migratory populations, though some migrating birds have been found to be completing the moult. We saw earlier that while the thyroid hormone, thyroxine, plays a role in controlling moult, migration is under the influence of prolactin. How the secretion of these hormones interacts to maintain the separation of moult and migration is not known.

SEASONAL MOVEMENTS

At certain times of year some populations of Starlings partake in large-scale movements. Most notable of these movements are those that take the more northerly populations south or south-west in autumn to winter in more equable regions, only to return to the northern breeding grounds the following spring. The birds that undergo these seasonal movements are true migrants and the extent of the wholly migrant populations and their wintering grounds can be judged from Fig. 2.2. The extensive ringing of Starlings in western Europe over the last 50 years or so has led to the accumulation of a considerable volume of information about these migrations; the migrations of the Asian populations are less well known. Towards the south of the Starling's breeding range, especially in the west, the populations are mainly resident while in some regions both residents and migrants breed side by side. In some areas it has even been found that an individual may migrate in one year but not in another.

During their migration Starlings do not, of course, respect international boundaries and as a result Starlings enter the political arena. The Starlings that are regarded as beneficial, on account of their consumption of insect pests in fields and forests, in northern and eastern Europe are precisely the same birds that cause damage in cattle feedlots, vineyards, and olive groves in southern and western Europe in winter. Thus while farmers of the former countries encourage Starlings by erecting nestboxes, people in the wintering areas call for the cessation of these endeavours and the destruction of the overwintering birds (Bernis 1960).

In addition to autumn and spring migration, some Starlings undertake another seasonal movement called a 'summer migration' by some authors (e.g. Gromadzki and Kania 1976). In ornithological terminology the word 'migration' implies a return movement between two areas (usually the breeding and non-breeding areas) (Thompson 1964). Since the summer movements observed in some regions take place in one direction only, they are more correctly termed a post-breeding dispersal, especially as in most places the summer movement seems to have no marked directional tendency.

Post-breeding dispersal

Ring recoveries have shown that within a few weeks of leaving the nest, juvenile Starlings may move some distance from their place of birth. In Belgium, Tahon (1980) found that 20 per cent of recoveries of juveniles in July were 100 km or more from their natal colony, while a further 20 per cent had moved less than 10 km. Thus there was no marked shift of the population as a whole and Tahon did not discover any inclination for these birds to move in any particular direction. In terms of the Starlings' capabilities, however, these movements of even 100 km are not great—in winter, distances of 20 km or more may be travelled daily to and from a night roost (Chapter 10). Similar local dispersals occur in the resident British birds and were recorded by Gromadzki and Kania (1976) in southern Poland. In northern Poland, however, different movements were observed, these being more directional and involving greater distances. In summer, northern Polish juveniles moved westwards, occasionally reaching The Netherlands, while at the same time northern Poland received birds which had been reared to the northeast in Lithuania, Latvia, and possibly Estonia. Nankinov (1978) recorded southerly dispersal of Starlings from the Leningrad region in summer and Saurola (1978) recorded a southerly movement from Finland into Estonia and Latvia at this time of year. Dement'ev and Gladkov (1960) also record southerly and south-westerly movements of the northern populations of the USSR as soon as breeding had ceased. These movements were by *S.v. vulgaris* and it is interesting that Dement'ev and Gladkov did not mention similar dispersal by northern populations of *S.v. poltaratskyii*, although this may simply reflect lack of knowledge. These summer journeys are made mainly by juveniles but some older birds may be involved. The important point about summer movements is that they occur some time before autumn migration to the wintering grounds commences.

   The directions of the movements discussed so far might be regarded as an initial step in taking the birds south for the winter, although if this were true it is rather surprising that birds from northern Poland undertake a directional summer movement while those from southern Poland do not. Beklova (1978) did not report directional summer movements of birds bred in Czechoslovakia, which may imply that these birds do not undertake them, and yet Studer-Thiersch (1969) found that Swiss Starlings did undergo a directional summer movement. Surprisingly, the movement of these birds took them north or north-west, as far as the North Sea coasts of the Low Countries, and in a direction almost opposite to that which they took later in the year on their autumn migration. Summer dispersal and autumn migration seem, therefore, to be unrelated and although we need to know much more about the summer movements of Starlings, especially juveniles, over Europe as a whole, the pattern that has so far emerged suggests that those birds that undertake these movements tend to concentrate near the coastal areas of the southern North Sea (Fig. 4.4). Studer-Thiersch (1969) thought that the unusual northerly summer move-ment of Swiss Starlings resulted from the geographical location of Switzerland in south-western Europe and also the alpine aspect of this country. Unfortunately, we know nothing of the summer dispersal of Starlings that breed in neighbouring countries. In Chapter 9 I shall discuss the ecological separation of adults and juveniles, suggesting that this is an adaptation to reduce compe-

Fig. 4.4. The summer movements of populations of Starlings that undertake a directional post-breeding dispersal.

tition between experienced adults and naive juveniles for scarce summer food supplies. The movement of northern European and central European juveniles towards the cooler and more humid climate bordering the North Sea could take them to areas where soil invertebrates remain more abundant in summer and be another adaptation aimed at maximizing the survival of juveniles, but this suggestion is highly speculative. Although some first-year birds and even some adults partake in the northerly movement of the Swiss birds, this journey is undertaken primarily by juveniles and yet by no means all of the Swiss juveniles reach the Low Countries. We have obviously much to learn about the extent of these movements by different populations in Europe before we can understand their function. For the present, it is important to realize that in those birds that undertake a directional post-breeding dispersal that is followed by an autumn migration, the autumn migration commences at the point reached by the summer dispersal and not necessarily at the breeding area of the population in question.

Migration

In those parts of the geographical range where the Starling is a summer visitor it is one of the earliest migrants to arrive in the spring. In the south and west of the range, Starlings arrive on their breeding grounds by late February, while in the north-east they do not reach their nesting areas until the middle of April (Fig. 4.5) and arrivals may continue there until the middle of May (Dement'ev and Gladkov 1960). Adults are usually the first to arrive with birds in their first year reaching the breeding area some days or even weeks later. The Siberian populations that arrive latest at their breeding colonies are also the earliest to depart, with most of the birds vacating their nesting areas by the end of September or the first week in October (Dement'ev and Gladkov 1960). The early departure of north-eastern populations is made possible by their early completion of moult; this, in turn, is permitted by the commencement of moult soon after the early broods have fledged, there being no second broods in these birds. As a result, the moult of some individuals of *S. v. poltaratskyi* begins as early as late May and can be completed by mid August. More southerly populations have moult schedules more similar to that of British birds, described earlier, and the southern birds delay the start of their autumn migration until October or even November. Over most of

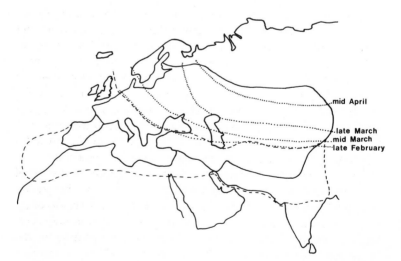

Fig. 4.5. Approximate times of arrival of migrant Starlings on their breeding grounds. The dashed line encloses the winter range.

their wintering areas, therefore, the Starlings' sojourn lasts only about four months, from early November to late February, but during this period the vast numbers of birds can consume large quantities of man's resources.

The impression that the above description gives of the Starling's autumn migration is of a simple movement of populations from northern breeding areas to southern wintering areas. The movements involved can, however, be complex. Figure 4.6 shows the autumn migration of Swiss Starlings described by Studer-Thiersch (1969). Juveniles begin their migration from the areas reached after their post-breeding dispersal; they move from the Low Countries, south across France and the Mediterranean to Algeria. During the winter they move westwards in North Africa to converge on areas reached by adults after their own migration. The adults move from Switzerland across southern France, south through Spain to winter in Iberia and Morocco. A smaller number of Swiss birds migrate through northern Italy and across the Mediterranean to Tunisia.

Rydzewski (1960), in a preliminary analysis of recoveries of Starlings ringed in Poland, indicated that birds from different parts of the country undertook distinct migrations; Rydzewski's conclusions have since been verified by Gromadski and Kania (1976). The latter authors identified three 'populations' of Polish Starlings

Fig. 4.6. Schematic representation of the autumn migration of Swiss Starlings described by Studer-Thiersch (1969). Some adults migrate south but most migrate south-west to Iberia and north-west Africa. Juveniles migrate south from northern France and the Low Countries (that they reached during summer dispersal) to North Africa, followed by a westerly movement during the winter.

on account of their wintering areas. Birds from the north of the country migrate along the southern North Sea coasts to winter in the southern third of Britain and in western France; birds from central Poland migrate through southern Germany and the Rhone valley to winter in south-western France and Iberia, and birds from southern Poland migrate through northern Italy to winter in Tunisia and northern Algeria (Fig. 4.7). We have no idea how such different migratory pathways, from a relatively small geographical area, could have evolved but these Swiss and Polish studies do illustrate the complexity of Starling migration. Over most of the species range, however, the wintering areas of birds from particular breeding areas are far less precisely known.

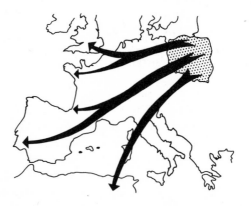

Fig. 4.7. The autumn migration of Starlings from north, central, and southern Poland to their separate wintering areas.

Ali and Ripley (1972) reported that four subspecies, *poltaratskyi*, *porphyronotus*, *nobilior*, and *humii* winter in the plains of northern India. This suggests that the predominant direction of autumn migration of these birds is south, while *nobilior* must travel south-east to reach India and Pakistan. *S.v. poltaratskyi* also winters in Caucasia (Kazakov 1979) and even reaches Israel, indicating a more westerly component in the migration of some members of this subspecies and *caucasicus* and *tauricus* must also travel west of south to reach Israel (Fig. 2.2). Thus the more western populations tend to migrate in a more westerly direction in the autumn and this reaches its extreme in *vulgaris*, where we have seen that Polish birds must travel almost due west to reach England.

Saurola (1978) found that Starlings from Finland also reached England after a migration that took them through the Low Countries and birds that breed in Holland are themselves known to winter in England. Although Starlings do reach Britain by a direct crossing of the North Sea, there is obviously a highly concentrated migration through the Low Countries and this has been documented by Perdeck (1967a) who analysed recoveries of birds trapped and ringed on migration near The Hague, The Netherlands in September, October, and November. From these data Perdeck was able to establish that birds from different breeding areas passed through Holland at different times. In September and early October the migrants were mainly Dutch birds; in the middle of October German and Scandinavian birds migrated through while those migrants that occurred in late October and in November were of Polish, Finnish, and Russian origin. Perdeck also found a change in the ultimate destination of the passage migrants with the earlier birds tending to winter in England and the later ones remaining on the continent, especially in Belgium and France. This suggestion that Finnish birds would tend to winter in continental Europe, rather than in England, is contrary to the findings of Saurola (1978), who thought that Finnish Starlings were much more likely to winter in England than were birds from northern Poland. These apparently conflicting ideas can be resolved only by more detailed studies of the migrations of the various populations involved. It would be particularly interesting to know whether the wintering areas and migration routes of any of the populations have changed since intensive ringing of Starlings began; Berthold (1968) thought that a reduction in the distance travelled to winter quarters and the resulting earlier arrival on the breeding grounds in the spring could have been an important factor in raising the fecundity of the European Starling population, permitting its recent expansion and westward spread. The present decline in the Finnish breeding population of Starlings could ultimately reduce the number of birds that winter in Britain, but since this country receives Starlings from many sources, this reduction could be difficult to detect. Goodacre (1959) found, however, that birds from different breeding populations tended to winter in different parts of the British Isles. Starlings from Norway and northern Sweden concentrated in Scotland, Ireland, and northern and eastern England; birds from southern Sweden wintered mainly in Scotland and eastern England; Danish birds concentrated in northern England and Ireland; Dutch birds ocurred mainly in southern England, as did Starlings from Germany and northern Poland, while birds from Finland and European Russia predominated in eastern England.

These findings suggest that Starlings must return to the same wintering area each year and yet Spaans (1977) found this to be untrue for birds that were ringed in winter in Holland; in the years following ringing, these birds were found up to 1000 km from the ringing site. Spaans did find, however, that the mean distance between the site of first capture (and ringing) and capture in subsequent winters decreased, from 236 km in the first winter to 68 km in the fourth winter after ringing. He surmised that the lack of fidelity to a wintering site could have been due to Holland representing a poorer winter area than, say, southern England where birds suffered a lower mortality than those that remained on the continent (Perdeck 1967a). But at my own study area in southern England, a farm near Winchester, I have been surprised by the rarity of returns of ringed birds in successive winters, again suggesting a lack of fidelity to a wintering area from one year to another. This is in sharp contrast to the fidelity to a winter feeding site that Starlings show during a particular winter and which is described in Chapter 9. Unfortunately, my own observations are not supported by recoveries of my ringed birds away from the study site in later winters, but this is not really surprising because I had ringed only about 400 birds. This apparent lack of fidelity to a wintering area obviously deserves further study; we should expect birds to return to areas where they had experienced good conditions in one winter since they would have learned much about their food supplies, susceptibility to predators, and protection from weather—information that could benefit them in succeeding winters. We would only expect Starlings to derive advantage from visiting new areas each winter if the food reserves of each site were totally unpredictable, a situation that does not prevail in most of the species' wintering areas.

Orientation

The many cues that may be available to the birds as navigational aids have recently been reviewed by the late W.T. Keeton (1981). They include astronomical features, geographical features, magnetic fields, olfaction and infrasound. To what extent these cues are actually used by Starlings is unknown although experiments, particularly those by Kramer (1952) and Perdeck (1964) and observations by Gruys-Casimir (1965) have given us some idea of the navigational aids used by Starlings.

Starlings usually migrate by day. Gruys-Casimir (1965) found that Starling migration was most intensive within the first few hours of dawn but that the volume of migration was not constant from day to day. On successive days of 'good' weather the volume of migration gradually decreased while after a period of 'bad' weather migration recommenced with a big rush. Thus weather plays a part in determining whether Starlings will migrate on a particular day and Gruys-Casimir found that the amount of migration increased with low temperatures, tail winds, and clear skies. Following winds and cloudless skies seem to be particularly important features of 'good' weather for migration, presumably because they offer the birds the best flight and navigation opportunities.

Even following winds can present migrating birds with problems, however, for if the air currents are too strong migration will cease. Within the range of acceptable speeds we can see effects on the birds, for in light winds Starlings fly higher than in stronger winds. Here, the birds are doubtless taking advantage of the reduced wind speeds close to the ground. We do not know what is the 'optimum' speed of following winds for Starling migration but we do have some idea of the heights at which they fly under apparently good conditions. From his radar observations, Lack (1960) found that Starlings that flew in the early morning from Holland across the North Sea to East Anglia migrated, in light winds, at heights up to about 1000 m; birds that left Holland in the evening flew somewhat higher, up to about 1300 m. Gruys-Casimir (1965) noted that Starlings flew higher over the sea than over land and flocks that I have watched arriving on the Lincolnshire coast have all done so below 300 m.

When migrating into head winds Starlings fly much lower, even just a few metres above the sea. Head winds necessitate a greater energy expenditure by the flying bird but cross winds harbour other dangers. Despite the range of navigational aids that Starlings have at their disposal they can be blown off course. This may be how some of our rarer bird visitors, including Rose-coloured Starlings from the east, arrive on British shores. Gruys-Casimir (1965) noted, however, that while Starlings were drifted off course by the wind over the sea, they remained on their correct heading over land, despite unfavourable winds. This indicates, of course, that over land these birds are able to use some environmental cue that is absent at sea and the geography of the land itself presents many features that the birds can follow. Coastlines, rivers, valleys, mountain ranges, and even roads all present readily identifiable features that can be used to keep the birds on their correct course. The use of such physiographical features presupposes, of course, that the Starlings are familiar with these landmarks. Remarkable though this may seem, we shall see (below) that Starlings do have a good geographical memory that can be used in navigation.

In the absence of unfavourable winds, Starlings can nevertheless navigate accurately over featureless areas such as the sea, and young birds can achieve similar accuracy over unfamiliar territory. Gruys-Casimir (1965) found that migration out to sea was inhibited by rain and she noticed, further, that flight directions were more dispersed when the sky was overcast. These observations strongly suggest that Starlings made use of the sun in their orientation. We now know, of course, that many species of bird, and even other animals such as insects, are capable of using the sun as an aid to navigation but we owe much of our basic knowledge of the principles to the classic experiments of Gustav Kramer, who used Starlings as subjects in many of his tests (Kramer 1951, 1952).

Kramer had noticed that in the autumn caged Starlings remained in the south-west corner of their enclosures and were restive. This 'migratory restlessness' is typical of captive birds during their normal migration season. Kramer used this orientation within cages to examine various features of migratory behaviour. By altering the magnetic field around the cage using electric currents, he found that the birds' orientation in the cage was unaffected by magnetic changes. (In the light of more recent findings, using very weak magnetic fields that do influence orientation in pigeons, this aspect of Starling navigation should be re-examined.) Having eliminated geomagnetism as an environmental cue used by his birds, Kramer concentrated his attentions on light since he had gained the impression that the Starlings were receiving their information from the sky.

In accord with Gruys-Casimir's (1965) finding of less precise orientation on overcast mornings, Kramer (1951) had found that his caged Starlings failed to restrict their migratory restlessness to any particular sector of the cage when the sky was obscured by cloud. When the sky cleared, however, the birds resumed their concentration of activity in that part of the cage that coincided with the direction of their normal migration. Clear skies were therefore important in permitting accurate navigation, but what feature of the sky was involved?

Kramer's cage was housed inside a specially constructed building with six windows through which light could enter. Under natural conditions the Starlings positioned themselves in the 'correct' position in the cage according to their direction of migration. Each window had a mirror whose position could be altered to change the direction of the light entering the cage. When the mirrors were angled so that the incident light entered the cage at 90° to its true direction, the Starlings adjusted their orientation accordingly. They were therefore using sunlight as their navigational aid but, by using filters, Kramer found that the birds did not have to see the sun directly: the area of the sky from which the sunlight originated was sufficient. Thus they could orientate correctly when the sun was obscured by light cloud, which allowed some property of sunlight to penetrate, but not, as we have seen, in heavy overcast. In addition, Kramer (1952) found that Starlings could compensate for the changing position of the sun during the day. In other words, besides being able to utilize the sun's light, the birds have some sort of internal 'clock' that enables them to predict where the sun should be at a particular time of day and adjust their direction of travel accordingly. Hoffmann (1959) even showed that Starlings could orientate using the midnight sun!

As any sailor or aviator knows, however, it is not sufficient to be able to determine one's direction from the sun. A knowledge of position in terms of latitude and longitude, a navigational fix, is also essential and the computation of this position requires further information about the movement of the sun, for the arc described by the sun through the sky varies daily. Despite attempts to interpret Kramer's findings in ways that would provide the birds with an accurate fix (Matthews 1953), recent opinion (Keeton 1981) tends to the view that the sun's azimuth, coupled with the time determined by the bird's internal clock, provides the bird with a compass bearing and little more. This 'sun-compass' must, therefore, be used along with other cues in navigation.

Where juvenile and adult Starlings begin their autumn migrations from different areas or migrate to different wintering areas, as do the populations of Switzerland, the navigational cues used by the two age groups might well differ. In these cases the juveniles are unable to derive benefit from the adults' previous experience of migration; the juveniles must possess some innate sense of direction for their first autumn migration. Perdeck (1958, 1964, 1967*b*, 1974) attempted to discover the navigation aids used by the age groups by displacing birds, caught on migration in Holland, to Switzerland and north-eastern Spain. The birds were transported by aeroplane and were usually released in the latter countries with 24 hours of their capture in Holland. They were, of course, individually marked before release and a control group of birds was released at the site of capture.

The results of these experiments are summarized diagrammatically in Fig. 4.8. Juveniles that were displaced to Switzerland continued to migrate in a south-westerly direction, while adults that were released in Switzerland eventually headed towards their normal wintering area, although there was an indication that they initially also continued migrating to the south-west. The juveniles that were displaced to Barcelona exhibited two kinds of behaviour. Most of those that were released early, in the first three weeks of October, continued their south-westerly migration and provided recoveries in southern Spain, while those that were released in the last week of October and the first week of November remained in the Barcelona area. Adults that were transported to Barcelona provided recoveries to the north-west and north of their point of release, in the direction of their 'normal' wintering area.

Perdeck interpreted these experiments as follows. After displacement, adults were able to head for their usual wintering area. In other words, they were able to identify the location of their point of release, relate it to where their normal wintering area should be, and then set off on the correct course for that wintering area. These birds were truly navigating towards a goal. Juveniles, on the other hand, appeared to make no attempt to orientate towards their normal wintering area. Instead, when they were released they continued in the direction that they had been following when captured in Holland. They were not, therefore, navigating but were flying in a particular direction: Perdeck called this 'one-direction orientation'. Perdeck (1967*b*) thought that the failure of late migrant juveniles to migrate further after displacement to Barcelona, in contrast to the earlier migrants that flew on to southern Spain, indicated that the cessation of the one-direction migration of juveniles had a time basis. Towards the end of the 'normal' migration period, juvenile Starlings would settle in the

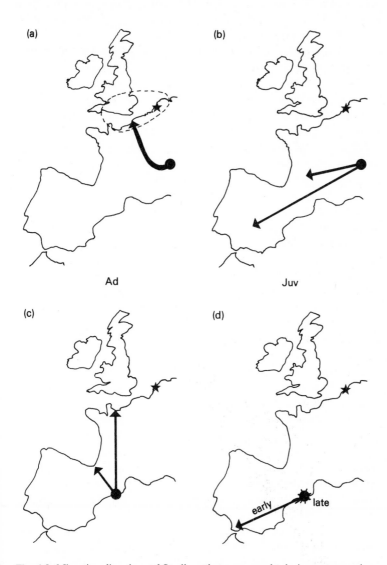

Fig. 4.8. Migration directions of Starlings that were caught during autumn migration at The Hague (The Netherlands), indicated by *, and released following displacement to Switzerland (a) and (b) or Barcelona (Spain — (c) and (d)). On release, adults tended to migrate towards their normal wintering area (enclosed by the dashed line in (a)) while juveniles continued in the direction in which they were migrating in Holland. From Perdeck (1964, 1967).

closest suitable habitat, while during the course of the migration juveniles would continue to fly until their internal clock told them they had flown long enough: then they would seek suitable habitat in which to spend the winter.

Perdeck (1974) then displaced juvenile Starlings on their return migration in the spring. Migrants were again caught in Holland and released in Switzerland. Some juveniles from this group were recovered in the area in which they had been born, indicating an ability to navigate back to this area, although a smaller sample was recovered near the point of release. There are, nevertheless, indications from this experiment that juveniles can navigate back to their natal area by a process of 'goal-orientatation' similar to that used by adults on their autumn migration.

The one-direction orientation demonstrated by Starlings on their first autumn migration suggests that they are using some sort of innate guidance to take them in the direction of their wintering area. Precisely what form this guidance takes, and what cues are used to keep the birds on track, are not known but Baker (1978) regarded this phase of a juvenile's life as exploratory. During this exploration an individual commits to a 'spatial memory' a wide variety of features of its surroundings. All of the area that it traverses becomes a part of its 'familiar area' within which it will find subsequent orientation relatively simple owing to its ability to recognize these features.

It remains to be seen whether Baker's hypothesis will be substantiated by further experiments but there is no doubt that after their first autumn migration Starlings are able to locate both their breeding and wintering areas during subsequent migrations. The autumn migration of juveniles, sometimes following a marked post-breeding dispersal, clearly sets a pattern that the birds can follow for the rest of their lives (should they choose to migrate every year), but there is one factor, rarely considered, that could provide juveniles with an important directional cue. Starlings migrate in flocks. Those that I have watched arriving on the Lincolnshire coast have usually consisted of between 50 and 200 birds although Gruys-Casimir (1965) recorded migrating flocks of up to 100 000 individuals. If these flocks contain both juveniles and adults (this seems likely although it has yet to be demonstrated), the juveniles could fly in the correct direction to locate the wintering area of their breeding population simply by flying in company with experienced adults, thereby relying on the navigation abilities of their elders. In Perdeck's (1958, 1967) experiments, the displaced juveniles might have followed the adult birds migrating from or through the areas to which the juveniles were displaced, since there is little difference in the direction of birds migrating through Holland, Switzerland, and north-eastern Spain. A more critical test might be provided by the displacement of juveniles from northern Poland to the south of that country (Fig. 4.8) or to Czechoslovakia, since the destinations of birds from these two areas (north-western Europe and north Africa) are quite different.

In subsequent chapters we shall see the extent to which Starlings derive information from or are stimulated by their neighbours: it would be surprising if juveniles on their first migration could not profit from the previous experiences of older birds.

5 OSTENTATION

MEDIA OF COMMUNICATION

When we wish to draw attention to ourselves we have a variety of senses upon which we can draw at our disposal. The first stages of human courtship usually do not involve physical contact, so that the sense of touch is not involved. But in man sight, hearing, and smell are all important. Both men and women dress in a way that they hope will attract the opposite sex, and although, in music-hall comedy, the women are supposed to be the good talkers, it seems to be the teenage boys who talk more loudly and flamboyantly in attempts to attract the attention of potential mates through their auditory senses. In western man, it is usually the females who endeavour to attract males using olfactory senses. Man's sense of smell is, however, rather poor compared with many mammals and humans are consequently not endowed with the wide variety of scent-producing glands that, for example, dogs possess. For this reason, women tend to rely on perfumes and men on after-shaves in attempts to increase their standing in sexual competition. Birds seem to have an even poorer sense of smell than man, although it has recently been suggested that olfaction may sometimes be involved in migratory orientation (Wallraff and Hund 1982). Smell does not, nevertheless, appear to be involved in communication between individual birds but future research may reveal that we are underestimating their capabilities.

We are left with sight and hearing as the main senses through which Starlings might be able to attract the attention of their neighbours. In my analogy using humans I concentrated on sexual attraction, because this is where communication between individuals tends to be most overt, but we must remember that communication with one's fellows, and with other species, is a vital aspect of everyday life and is not restricted to sexual contests. In birds, the most obvious forms of visual communication are those provided by the colour patterns evident in their plumage. The role of the red breast of the Robin *Erithacus rubecula* in conflicts between individuals was established by David Lack (1943) and

Niko Tinbergen (1953) showed that the red spot on the lower mandible of the Herring Gull *Larus argentatus* served to stimulate chicks to beg to their parents for food, and the prodding of the red bill spot by the chick's bill served, in turn, to stimulate the adult to regurgitate food. Thus these different colour patterns could be used to signal to other individuals, be it competitors or parents, a particular state of mind or need. Starlings do not possess conspicuous colour contrasts like Robins and Herring Gulls, even though a wide range of colours may be apparent in their plumage when viewed at close quarters. These colour variations, involving variations in purple and green sheens when seen in different lights, and, as we have already seen, seasonal variations in the number and extent of pale tips to some feathers, leading to spottiness, are subtle in comparison with many species. Starlings do possess, however, other morphological features that can be used to accentuate these subtle colour patterns. For example, the highly iridescent throat feathers, particularly of males, (generally referred to by students of Starling biology as the 'hackle' feathers) are longer than surrounding feathers and can be 'puffed out' to accentuate their appearance. This represents a particular posture that Starlings can adopt in certain contexts to transmit particular information—for example that 'this is my nest site and if you come near I shall attack'. We shall see that the use of postures or movements is one of the main forms of communication used by Starlings.

The other main medium used for transmitting information is, of course, sound and sounds are frequently used in combination with postures or movements. Starlings do not possess a song that can be described as aesthetically pleasing, like that of the Blackbird *Turdus merula* or Nightingale *Luscinia megarhyncha*, but its song does possess qualities that are remarkable and which have attracted the attention of classical authors. Many of them, for example Pliny and Shakespeare, referred to the Starling largely on account of its ability to mimic the sounds of other animals that it encountered in its surroundings. I doubt, however, that it has produced sentences of human speech, as has been claimed by some romantics. Mimicked calls are, nevertheless, frequently incorporated into Starling song, and the male that has nested in a box in my garden for three years regularly reproduces one of the calls of the family cat, together with that of a lamb that used to live in a field close to the house. In addition to its song, the Starling has a wide variety of other calls that are used in particular situations and the aim of this chapter is to attempt to relate the various calls and postures to particular contexts in the life of the bird. Many of the calls and postures are used in association with one another and their effects may sometimes be amplified by certain structural features of the bird. But, as with all aspects of Starling biology, we shall find that we do not understand the functions of many aspects of behaviour and that much further research is needed to elucidate a number of problems.

Let us begin by considering the behaviour of Starlings going about their day to day activities: these are concerned primarily with obtaining an adequate food supply.

AGGRESSION AND SUBMISSION

As we have seen before and as will become apparent in subsequent chapters, Starlings are primarily grassland feeding birds and they generally feed in flocks. People often ask how, when food is thrown out on a lawn, so many Starlings assemble so quickly to exploit the new source. This rapid formation of a flock is facilitated by the birds that are already feeding on the ground, following the chance discovery of the food by the first bird. For while a Starling that is simply standing on the ground presents no particular attraction to other birds that may be around, a bird that is feeding definitely provides an attraction for birds in the vicinity.

The bird that simply stands adopts what might be described as a 'neutral' posture; this posture does not signal 'attraction' information to other birds that may be looking on. The bird with its beak down in the grass, especially if it is rapidly probing or pecking, on the other hand, indicates quite inadvertently that it has found a good food source simply by the actions it makes while obtaining its food. Frenzied activity is attractive to other individuals and in a laboratory experiment my colleague, Ian Inglis, and I (Feare and Inglis 1979) showed that when feeding in a flock an individual's pecking rate was related to the peck rate of its nearest neighbour. This kind of observation can have practical applications: Inglis and Isaacson (1978) found that plastic models of Brent Geese *Branta leucopsis* could attract or deter flocks above from landing, depending whether the 'flocks' of models were in feeding postures, with their heads down, or in alert postures, with their heads pointing up into the air. Similarly, I have used groups of plastic models of Starlings to attract Starlings to areas where they can be caught and Evans (1980) and Clergeau (1982) found that Starlings stuffed in a feeding posture proved attractive to wild birds. It must be emphasized that the feeding birds are not deliberately signalling to other birds; the latter simply recognize that a standing bird suggests 'no food' while a group of feeding birds suggests 'plenty of food'. Similarly, a Starling that is preparing to take off by crouching on the ground and looking up, ready to push itself into the air (this posture is sometimes called a flight intention movement) may signify to watching birds either that there is no food in that area, and therefore that it is not worth landing there, or that there is danger due to a predator of some sort and thus it would be safer to stay away. It also seems likely that with these inadvertent postures, the more individuals that are involved the stronger is the signal that is transmitted to other birds. This suggestion is supported by Inglis and Isaacson's (1978) work with geese and may well apply to most species of birds that feed in flocks.

In this account of the Starling's postures and calls, it is when the bird takes off that we encounter the first vocalization. As soon as it takes flight, a Starling frequently utters a faint purring 'prurrp'. The call is often given when birds take off from a feeding site and it can also be heard by many birds as they leave their roost in the morning. They almost invariably give the call when they are released after being handled, for example after being ringed. The function of the call is not known: Eva Hartby (1969), in her analysis of Starling vocalizations, called this the flight call but did not ascribe to it a function. The utterance of this call on release from a human hand almost suggests the anthropomorphic sensation of relief, while the frequency with which birds departing from a roost give the call may indicate that it reflects insecurity. When taking flight Starlings enter a three-dimensional medium, the air, in which a predator such as a Sparrowhawk *Accipiter nisus* can attack from any direction. When a Starling is at rest, either on the ground or in a tree (especially within a roost), a predator's approach is more restricted and this may confer a greater sense of security to the Starling. If the flight call does express anxiety or insecurity, its function may be to stimulate other individuals within the flock to perform the same activity in order to 'swamp' the danger. This is based on the assumption that if you are the only bird in flight you are the only one that a predator can aim at, whereas if you take off with 99 others there is, all else being equal, only a one-per-cent chance that the predator will direct its attack at you.

What I have termed the 'inadvertent' postures, and also possibly the flight call, seem to promote flocking. On a feeding-area, proximity to another flock member can, however, lead to conflict. This may be a contest over a particular food item or, where space is limiting as at a bird table or a cattle feeding trough, the contest may well be over space in which to manoeuvre while feeding. The conflict generally necessitates a combination of aggression and submission in the interacting birds, for if the submission of one member of a contesting pair is delayed an out-and-out fight may ensue: this does not usually occur. What determines the status of individuals in these contests is quite unknown, but a range of aggressive and submissive postures, sometimes accompanied by calls, is used. Many of these postures, and the sequences in which they usually occur, have been described in detail by Van der Mueren (1980) from a study of captive birds. Although I shall now describe several categories of these behaviour patterns, it must be realized that the degrees of aggression and submission vary from contest to contest and some of the postures involved also vary in the intensity of their expression.

Perhaps the simplest threat display shown by a Starling is to 'stare' at the opponent. This is often done with the head held higher than in a resting posture and the height at which the head is held may indicate the intensity of aggression. In this posture, the impression of height may be accentuated by raising the crown feathers (Fig. 5.1). In a conflict situation a 'stare' is often sufficient to induce submission in the opponent. Here, submission may be

Fig. 5.1. The 'stare' and 'open-bill threat' postures. The bird on the left has adopted an upright stance with crown feathers raised and stares at his opponent. The bird on the right has a higher level of apprehension, with head held higher and with the bill open.

signalled by the 'loser' moving away or by adopting a posture that is in essence the opposite of the stare; the submissive bird may lower its head, sleek its feathers and crouch (Fig. 5.2), in which case the victor may allow its opponent to hold its ground.

Fig. 5.2. 'Submissive crouch'. The submitting bird lowers its body and sleeks its feathers.

If the stare fails to produce a submissive response in the bird to be vanquished, a more extreme form of aggressive posture may be adopted but both the kinds of aggression and submission depend to some extent on the situation in which the protagonists find themselves. For example, within a flock in a grass field an aggressor may lower his head and run towards the opponent with his bill pointing directly at the latter. To heighten the impression of ferocity the bill of the aggressor may be opened during the encounter. In this situation the submissive bird is able to hop (Starlings usually walk), run, or fly away. Where space is more restricted, as at a cattle trough, this movement is impeded and displays that require less movement are used. Here, an aggressor can adopt an even more exaggerated upright stance and threaten with a deliberate, but fairly slow, opening of the bill, thereby displaying the gape to the opponent (Fig. 5.1). In confined spaces a submitting bird may be unable to retreat, and if lowering the body fails to appease the attacking bird the subordinate bird may indulge in a spell of intense bill-wiping (Fig. 5.3)—a piece of behaviour derived from a quite different context.

Starlings do not feed all day but feed in bouts interspersed with other activities, such as bathing, preening, or resting. The end of a feeding bout is usually followed by a spell of bill-wiping: both sides of the bill are wiped on a twig, on the side of a cattle trough, or on any other suitable structure. It seems that bill-wiping is recognized by other Starlings as an indication that a bird has stopped feeding. Thus, if a bird is seen to be bill-wiping, it indicates to a feeding

Fig. 5.3. 'Submissive bill-wiping'. Submission may be indicated to an opponent by a bout of bill-wiping, during which the body is held low and the feathers are sleeked.

bird that that individual no longer represents a competitor for food items, and it is therefore not worth expending time and energy in attempting to drive that individual from the feeding area. This indication that a feeding bout has finished has been ritualized as a signal that can be used in non-feeding situations. Bill-wiping has evolved, in fact, into a submissive act that can indicate to an aggressor that that bird is not longer interested in competing for the resource in question. Thus a feeding bird that is threatened by another feeding individual can indicate by a spell of intense bill-wiping that it is prepared to back down from the conflict and the same behaviour is used to submit in contests over nest sites.

Although threat by one individual is usually followed by submission by the threatened bird, the latter may sometimes attempt to defend its position. Should this happen, the intensity of conflict is often heightened leading to the use of more extreme postures.

When discussing the stare I commented that the head is usually held somewhat higher than in a more 'normal' standing or resting posture. This is achieved by both extending the neck and straightening the legs. If two contesting individuals are evenly matched, for whatever reason (we do not know what determines the dominance status of birds in these conflicts), the stare posture may be exaggerated by a further extension of the neck and legs, so that both individuals adopt an extremely upright stance (the 'tall posture' of Ellis (1960)) while still staring at each other. This kind of conflict appears more common where feeding space is limited, suggesting that a factor in the apparent determination of a subordinate not to give way may simply be the restriction of its ability to escape. If neither of the birds facing each other in the upright posture shows signs of submission, then simulated attack can occur.

The simplest form of attack is where one of the upright birds stabs its bill at the opponent. As with all of the threatening or submissive behaviour that I have so far described, even this stab does not generally involve any form of vocalization. If, however, the stab does not produce submission in the target Starling, actual fighting, accompanied by calling, may follow.

Fighting usually takes the form of a 'fly-up' (Fig. 5.4) and this is the fight most commonly seen in flocks feeding in fields, at cattle troughs, and at bird tables. The two birds fly up together from the feeding site to a height of one or two metres, stabbing at each other with their bills and kicking their feet. This is accompanied by loud squawks and chattering which Hartby (1969) called the attack call. Van der Mueren called this behaviour 'dance-fighting' and termed the accompanying vocalizations 'screams'. In fact, this attack call incorporates a variety of different sounds but its main component is a harsh rapidly repeated 'chackerchackerchacker'. The fly-up, although the most intense form of fighting over food or feeding-space, may be repeated several times before one of the pair submits. Submission may take the form of a hurried departure from the flock or simply landing after a fly-up a few centimetres further away from the victor. In densely crowded flocks, as we see frequently at bird tables or at food scraps thrown on to lawns, three or four individuals may be involved in a fly-up.

Three other behaviour patterns are used in aggressive encounters. Van der Mueren (1980) considered that the ruffling of the feathers of the throat, breast, and back was one of the actions that could initiate an act of aggression. The effect of raising the feathers in this way is to make the bird appear larger and this posture is often used by a bird that is chasing an opponent, but Van der

Fig. 5.4. A 'fly-up'. After an unresolved aggressive encounter on the ground, two birds fly up calling at each other and threaten with stabs and kicks.

Mueren (1980) found that birds demonstrating their aggression by adopting the upright posture did not simultaneously ruffle their body feathers. Body feathers can be erected in another context, however, since at the end of an aggressive encounter the ruffling of feathers like this often precedes a vigorous shaking of the body. I have not attempted to quantify these behaviour patterns but I have the impression that body shaking is performed more by the victorious than by a vanquished bird. To revert to an anthropomorphic interpretation, body shaking seems to lower tension.

The other two postures seen in aggressive situations involve wing movements, but Van der Mueren (1980) found these postures to be infrequently used by his captive birds. In 'wing-flicking' the wings are slightly raised from the body and then returned rapidly to the resting position; several flicks may be made in rapid succession and these actions may be used in association with a series of 'chip' calls, to be described below. Van der Mueren found that wing-flicking occurred only in birds that were lowering their bodies, a posture that usually indicates submission, and wing-flicking may be derived from flight intention movements. In some situations the wings may be lifted from the body and rotated in a peculiar action that resembles slow-motion flying movements with the wings only half extended. This behaviour is most commonly performed by males during the breeding season (see below) but in agonistic encounters it can be used by both sexes and Ellis (1966) and Van der Mueren (1980) termed it 'aggressive wing waving'. He found that aggressive wing waving occurred in combination with a variety of other aggressive postures and it may therefore represent an intense state of aggression.

The postures and calls that we have discussed so far are those used by birds in an established flock in which conflict has arisen. When a bird joins a flock, it may give calls itself and may also stimulate other flock members to respond to its arrival.

Arriving birds do not always call but when they do the call they give is usually a short, metallic 'chip' which may be repeated. Hartby (1969) referred to this call as a 'warning or mobbing' call but it is difficult to see its function in this light when a bird lands amongst birds already in a flock. The same call is, however, given in other contexts. Repeated 'chip' calls are given by birds that rise in a dense flock to mob an aerial predator such as a Kestrel *Falco tinnunculus* or Sparrowhawk—hence Hartby's use of the term mobbing call. But 'chip' calls are also given by some birds as they enter a roost, by birds leaving a roost after most others have gone, and by many birds as they arrive at a feeding area from the roost first thing in the morning. These arriving birds fly at heights of up to 100 m depending on wind speed and direction. They do not usually make a gradual descent to their first feeding, resting, or preening area of the day; instead, flock cohesion breaks down and individuals tumble erratically down to their landing place. This erratic behaviour, often also seen by birds descending into a roost site, is the kind of behaviour associated with anti-predator man-oeuvres: unpredictable movements that a potential predator would find difficult to intercept. Both the feeding areas that are used by large flocks and the night roost sites are, to a greater or lesser extent, traditional and therefore a Starling might anticipate that predators will learn their whereabouts. This certainly happens and large winter Starling roosts can be good places to see a variety of raptors and owls congregating around the roost at dusk and dawn. That the Starlings' erratic movements are accompanied by 'chip' calls might suggest that they are anti-predator calls, es-pecially when the call is also used by birds mobbing a predator. This explanation does not seem to apply to birds alighting in a feeding flock, however, but a state that may exist in a Starling in all of these situations is that of anxiety and the 'chip' call may reflect this state. This does not explain the function of the call to the Starling, since a simple expression of anxiety seems insufficient reason for producing a call. In birds tumbling down to a roost or feeding area, the call may indeed have an anti-predator role, with the uttering of 'chip' calls periodically by different members of the flock serving to increase the confusing effects of erratic flight to the predator. There may be a component of this in an individual landing in an established flock since the only flying individual in an area may be the most vulnerable to a Sparrowhawk, but the expression of anxiety by the landing bird may also signify submis-sion to the already feeding fellows. This submissive behaviour of an arriving bird may help it to establish a place in the flock by reducing the tendency of surrounding birds to threaten or attack it. There is obviously considerable scope for testing these ideas experimentally.

That a landing bird is a frequent target for attack by neighbours is readily apparent to anyone who feeds birds in his garden. The response by birds already feeding can range from a mild threat, such as the stare, to an attack that may involve a fly-up, but one kind of response seems to be used predominantly in these situations. This involves a bird raising its head from the feeding position and threatening the new arrival with the bill open and giving what Hartby (1969) described as a 'rattle' call, a rapid chattering 'chacker-chacker', as in the attack call mentioned above, with a slight variation in pitch. Both the posture and the call serve an aggressive function, presumably aimed at maintaining the aggressor's limited amount of space within the flock. The resolution of this conflict situation is frequently the adoption of a crouched submissive posture, with very little body movement, by the recently arrived bird. At this the aggressor usually accepts the presence of the new neighbour and both commence feeding while maintaining a mutually acceptable distance between each other. In this kind of aggressive encounter, and, as we shall see, in contests over mates and nest sites, the bird that begins the threat or attack is almost always victorious. Ian Inglis and I (Feare and Inglis 1979) verified this in caged Starlings that fought over feeding space, but it has also been demonstrated previously in many different species of animal, including mammals, reptiles, fish, and insects. Precisely what confers dominance on these individuals at that time is not known. In feeding flocks that may number several hundred individuals it would not be possible for one bird to recognize and know the social status of all others in the flock, although Rohwer (1975) has suggested from studies of a New World Sparrow, Harris' Sparrow *Zonotrichia querula*, that variations in plumage may be related to position of any dominance hierarchy. In Starlings the main plumage variable, especially in winter, is the amount and extent of spotting but at present no attempt has been made to relate this to social status within a group. Such plumage characteristics may help birds to determine the status of a possible opponent but this does not alter the fact that, in aggressive encounters, the assessment of status must depend upon an 'on the spot' decision of whether to attack or not, rather than on a personal knowledge of all individuals in the flock.

DISTRESS CALLS

In most situations we do not know whether the decision to fight or flee, to threat or submit, or to call or remain silent is related to the age or sex of the competing birds. This is because it is usually impossible to distinguish the ages and sexes of contestants in field flocks. A Starling call that has been examined in relation to these characteristics is a repeated high-pitched, raucous and penetrating scream, often referred to as a 'distress' call. This kind of call is given by many species of bird and Starlings may use it when they are held or cornered by a predator or even when one Starling grasps another in a fight—this kind of extreme form of fighting I have only seen close to nest sites, and not on feeding grounds. The distress call is, however, given by some birds when they are caught in and being recovered from mist nets and this is what renders it more amenable to study than many of the other calls. Table 5.1 shows the kind of variation in the tendency to give distress calls that we have found in Starlings caught in mist nets during the course of our work. The incidence varies seasonally as well as with the age and sex of the birds. More juveniles give distress calls than do adults and, although samples should ideally be larger, there is a suggestion, in the adults, that more birds give distress calls during the period of moult than at other times of year. Furthermore, in winter females tend to call much more than males.

Various hypotheses have been proposed regarding the functions of distress calls in birds and other animals. Some people suggest that the sudden emission of a high-intensity call is designed to startle a predator which, in a moment of panic, might then release its prey. Others have argued that if this were the case all captured birds should give distress calls—this, however, would lead a predator to expect a distress call from its prey on capture and the anticipation of the call would remove its surprise value.

Another explanation is that, by giving a distress call, a bird alerts its neighbours of the presence and whereabouts of a predator. This could serve two functions. The bird might be altruistic, that is, it might simply be indicating to its fellows that a predator is around and that they should therefore be more vigilant. Alternatively, the bird giving the call could be indicating the whereabouts

Table 5.1. Variations, according to age, sex, and season, in the frequency of giving distress calls by Starlings when being extracted from mist nets.[1]

Age and sex	Breeding March–June	Moult July–September	Winter October–February
Adult ♂	27.7 (18)	25.0 (28)	9.8 (108)
Adult ♀	16.6 (18)	32.0 (25)	30.8 (130)
Juvenile	77.8 (9)	33.1 (156)	—

[1]Figures are percentages with the sample size in parentheses.

of the predator in the hope that its fellows will come and mob the predator, thereby confusing the animal and possibly making it release the bird it has caught.

A third explanation of the function of a distress call is that such a call, given just before the predator actually strikes, means 'I have seen you and am therefore going to take defensive action. You cannot, therefore, surprise me and you are wasting your time if you try to press your attack home'.

Do the data that I have presented for Starlings (Table 5.1) give credence to any of these theories? The ability to avoid predation depends to some extent on luck, but once this factor is eliminated two further factors remain important: knowledge, gained by experience, of how, when, and where a predator is likely to strike; and exposure to possible predation simply by living in vulnerable situations. Juvenile birds are naive in many respects because they have not learned, through experience, how best to cope with many of the problems that life presents. As a result juveniles, rather than adults, figure prominently in the diets of predators such as Sparrowhawks (Newton and Marquiss 1982). Moulting birds do not have their full complement of wing and tail feathers and are probably less agile and manoeuverable than non-moulting birds. We shall see later that in winter females are subordinate to males in feeding flocks which may require that they feed for longer each day and also, in certain situations, in more exposed situations than males. The higher incidences of distress calls given by juveniles (and possibly by moulting birds and by females in winter) suggests that birds that are more vulnerable to predation may be more prone to give distress calls. This could be taken as evidence for each of the three theories and the data from Starlings do not help us to elucidate the functions of distress calls, except that the higher incidence in the groups more susceptible to predation does suggest that predation has been a factor in the evolution of these calls. Whether the anthropomorphic term 'distress' should be used in relation to these high-intensity calls is moot, and more research on their nature and causation is required. Despite this lack of knowledge, the responses that these calls elicit in the birds can be of use to man: the broadcasting of tape-recorded distress calls is widely used on airfields to scare birds, including Starlings, away and this technique is still the best we have for dispersing winter roosts of Starlings.

The calls and postures that have been considered so far are not concerned with reproduction although they are used throughout the year, including during the breeding season. Most of them are not very noticeable to the casual observer, but the behaviour associated with the acquisition of mates and nest sites is usually much more readily seen. As we saw in Chapter 4, testosterone concentrations circulating in the blood begin to rise again towards the end of moult, with the most dramatic rises in September, October, and November. We also saw that singing is stimulated by high testosterone concentrations. In southern England, however, Starlings sing in most months and after a brief cessation after breeding, song recommences in mid July. This is the autumn song in which both sexes partake and it is less intense than that given by males in the spring. There are, however, many common features.

SONG AND MIMICRY

The Starling's song, not as aesthetically pleasing to the human ear as that of, say, a Blackbird, is nevertheless remarkable for the variety of sounds that is incorporated. This variety is such that it is virtually impossible to describe using the written word, but whistles, clicks, rattles, squeaks, and screeches are all involved. Many of the calls that I have already described in relation to feeding and fighting may also be included.

All individuals (even females in the autumn) seem to have the capacity for this variety of sounds but when one listens closely and over a period of several days to a few singing in their territories in the spring, it soon becomes apparent that the song of each bird possesses its own particular quality that confers a degree of individuality. This was most noticeable when I watched a female Spotless Starling (*Sturnus unicolor*) during her courtship and incubation. (Spotless Starlings in towns in southern Spain nest at a low density, so that it is easy to observe the response of a female to different males.) When her mate arrived, after a short absence, back at his song post in a tree a few metres from the nest in a hotel wall, he began to sing with a distinctive whistle. On hearing this the female emerged from the nest, flew to his side and solicited copulation. Occasionally, both during the presence and absence of her mate, other males came to the tree and began singing, and although I only saw this happen three or four times, the female never emerged from her nest hole. In other words, the female seemed to be able to recognize her mate by his own individual song.

Hausberger and Guyomarc'h (1981) have examined these whistled calls in singing male European Starlings. Individual birds were found to have a repertoire of whistles, some of which were unique to the individual while others were characteristic of the breeding colony. These authors thought that this combination of individual- and colony-specific whistles could facilitate the individual recognition of birds within the colony.

This kind of recognition must be very important to birds that live colonially since it avoids waste of time and energy in approaching the wrong bird, which in any case could be dangerous if it involved fighting.

Besides the range of notes that we can regard as 'typically Starling', however, singing males further diversify their songs by incorporating sounds that they learn from their surroundings. This increase in their repertoire through their ability to mimic, not only bird or mammal sounds but also odd noises produced by man's machines, is one of the features that brought the Starling to the attention of early classical writers. The quality of the imitations is revealed by comparing sonograms of the Starling's copy with the genuine call (Fig. 5.5). But why should a Starling want to increase its repertoire in this way, and at what age, or at what time of year, does it learn the mimicked components of the song or, for that matter, the other parts of the 'normal' Starling song? I have the impression, from casual observation rather than from critical experiments, that the noises mimicked by adult males are those heard in the immediate surroundings of the singing bird. This suggests that these are learned either when the bird is very young, before it disperses, or after the male has established his territory, that is, after he has returned from his juvenile dispersal. Studies on other birds, especially Chaffinches *Fringilla coelebs*, have shown that song is learned by chicks while they are still in the nest and before they can even practice the component calls themselves, and this may be true of Starlings also. My casual observations have convinced me that once a particular mimicked call has been learned, the male will reproduce this call as part of his song each breeding season that he survives, but new mimicked calls can be incorporated into the song in succeeding years. Experimental work is obviously required to substantiate these views.

As described above in the Spotless Starling, individuality of song almost certainly plays a part in recognition between the sexes in the European Starling, and we shall see later that the calls of the

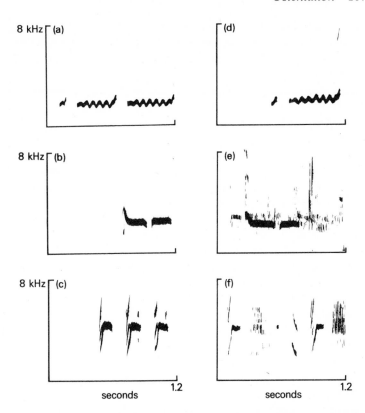

Fig. 5.5. Sonograms of the calls of (a) Curlew, (b) Redshank, and (c) Chaffinch, and sonograms of the Starling's attempts to mimic these calls (d), (e), and (f) respectively. (Recordings and sonograms by Andrew Hindmarsh.)

adults may also be recognized by begging young. Although Etche-copar and Hue (1962) stated that Spotless Starlings mimicked other calls, I have found no reference to this elsewhere in the literature on this species, and while closely watching the courtship behaviour of the species at Marbella, on the south coast of Spain, I was struck by the absence of mimicry in their song. I think that mimicry is not the norm in Spotless Starlings and, if this is the case, why should European Starlings resort to this tactic for increasing their song repertoires? The simple answer is that we do not know.

I began this discussion of song by highlighting the importance of individual recognition to a colonial bird like the Starling, and the subsequent consideration of song repertoires and mimicry has perhaps carried the implication that more complex songs assist the birds in a colony to recognize each other. However, the calls that Hausberger and Guyomarc'h (1981) found to be important in individual recognition were what might be regarded as the simpler elements of the song, namely the whistles. In studies with other species Falls (1969), Harris and Lemon (1976), and Searcy, McArthur, Peters, and Marler (1981) have shown that species with large song repertoires tend, in fact, to show rather poor individual recognition. If Starlings can recognize their partners and neighbours on the basis of the whistles, as my observations on *S. unicolor* and Hausberger and Guyomarc'h's (1981) study suggest, we are still left with the problem of why Starlings go to such lengths to increase the complexity of their song.

I stated above that new mimicked calls can be incorporated into a male's song in successive years, leading to the possibility that older birds have greater song repertoires. This has been demonstrated in a number of species (e.g. Howard 1974 for the Mocking bird *Mimus polyglottis*), and a large song repertoire might therefore provide an indication of the age and, more important, the experience of a singing male. A female that hears a male with a complex song might therefore think: 'he sings well and must therefore be experienced and high in the social order; this means he will have a well-defended territory, good access to food, and may provide help in rearing the young; I would be well advised to pair with him in order to maximize my own breeding success.' McGregor, Krebs, and Perrins (1981) have shown than male Great Tits with larger repertoires tend to have a higher reproductive success that males with simpler songs.

A large song repertoire might also convey a message to other males, however, again relating to the age and experience of the singer. The information perceived by a potential competitor might be: 'he sings well and must therefore be experienced and therefore a more dominant individual; if I attempt to oust him from his territory I shall simply be wasting my time and energy because I know that he will win; I shall therefore be well-advised to leave him alone and seek a nest-site elsewhere.' Krebs (1977) performed an ingenious experiment, again with Great Tits, whose results supported this idea. He caught some male Great Tits and removed them from their territories; normally they would be quickly replaced by other birds but Krebs 'defended' the vacated territories by broadcasting tape-recorded songs. The larger the repertoire in the song, the longer was he able to keep the territory free from intruders. The song of the Starling certainly warrants examination with respect to variations in complexity with age; in fact, I find it remarkable that the song of a bird with such a reputation for mimicry has not already been the subject of extensive research.

Another possible function for song complexity stems from the finding that male song can stimulate the female in various ways, and the larger the repertoire the greater the stimulation. We saw in Chapter 4 that the circannual rhythm of testis size in Starlings differed according to whether females were present or absent. Kroodsma (1976), using Canaries *Serinus canarius* as his subjects, has found that male song can influence the behaviour of females, presumably again through some hormonal mechanism. He found that females exposed to tape-recorded songs with large repertoires built nests earlier and with greater determination, and also laid more eggs, than females exposed to less complex songs. This could provide a clue to the mechanism underlying the social stimulation that synchronizes egg-laying, which is discussed in Chapter 6.

In other species therefore, there seem to be good reasons for a male to increase his song repertoire as much as possible and future research may well show that Starlings derive similar advantages from complex songs. This does not explain, however, why Starlings have resorted to mimicry in attempts to diversify their song, rather than rely on the development of a song typical of its own species, as the familier Blackbird, Song Thrush *T. philomelos*, and Nightingale have done. I do not know why Starlings have opted for mimicry but a step in the evolution of mimicry of other species' sounds could well have been the copying of particular parts of their neighbouring Starlings songs, especially the various whistles. This copying has been called 'song matching' by students of bird song and seems to be a family common phenomenon: in Britain, neighbouring territorial male Song Thrushes can be frequently heard indulging in what sounds like a song duel. Starlings do the same. When one male starts his song with a whistle, his neighbour may quite often immediately imitate the same whistle. Although I did not hear Spotless Starlings imitate the calls of any other species, they frequently indulged in song matching, their louder and more distinctive whistles, that almost invariably initiate a bout of singing, perhaps rendering this form of mimicry more apparent than it is in the European Starling. If we listen carefully to our Starlings singing in a colony, we can nevertheless hear that neighbouring pairs do indulge in this kind of behaviour.

We now come to another aspect of song, and probably also of other calls, which stems from the learning of sounds heard in the immediate surroundings. We are well aware of the existence of dialects in human language and dialects are now known to occur in the songs of many birds, there being slight differences in the songs of birds from different geographical areas. In Starlings I know mainly through mimcry that regional variations occur for while the male in my present Surrey garden incorporates calls of the Bullfinch *Pyrrhula pyrrhula*, Tawny Owl *Strix aluco*, Pheasant *Phasianus colchicus*, (and my cat!), birds that are heard fairly regularly, though it should be pointed out that these are far from the commonest calls heard in the vicinity, the Starling that occupied my former garden in Aberdeenshire imitated the Oystercatcher *Haematopus ostralegus*, Curlew *Numenius arquata*, and Grey-lag Goose *Anser anser* among others. This kind of variability will almost certainly be found to apply to other aspects of the Starlings' song and perhaps also to other calls, but confirmation of this must await further research, as must our understanding of the meaning to an individual of the acquisition of one dialect rather than another.

There is one further aspect of song that must be mentioned. When Starlings enter their communal roost at dusk, and again before the dawn departure, they sing and some individuals can even be heard singing all night. Spencer (1966) found that only in May and June, in roosts with high proportions of juveniles or moulting adults, did they remain relatively quiet. It has been suggested that singing in the roost is restricted to males but this requires substantiation, especially in the autumn when females sing when away from the roost. The function of this roost singing is obscure but its volume is striking—the birds that roost in Trafalgar Square and, more appropriately, on the facade of the nearby English National Opera House can be heard above the noise of London's rush-hour traffic on winter evenings. Roost-singing in the mornings could conceivably have a role in synchronising departure because the volume of singing gradually increases until eventually a sudden silence precedes the exodus of a wave (see Chapter 10). Singing then increases again until another cessation precedes the departure of the next wave about three minutes after the earlier exodus. The volume of the singing, the number of birds involved in the singing, or even some other factor associated with it could provide an indication of the birds' readiness to depart, thereby synchronizing the departures into the wave structure that can be readily observed. This is, however, conjecture.

POSTURES DURING SONG

Voice and posture act together to influence a mate or competitor and a singing Starling adopts a characteristic posture that varies with the intensity of the song. The lowest intensity of singing is probably that heard in the autumn, when small groups of Starlings, both male and female, sit together in exposed positions and utter soft songs, consisting mainly of high-pitched whistles, rattles, and clicks that are audible only at fairly close range. These birds adopt an upright stance, with the bill slightly above horizontal and with throat having a somewhat swollen appearance (Fig. 5.6). In more intense singing, when the song becomes louder, the upright stance is maintained but is exaggerated by the tail being pointed downwards, giving a 'hunch-back' appearance. In addition, the throat and upper breast feathers are erected so that they appear fluffed out. Although I have described these as two postures associated with low key and slightly more intense singing, there is no clear division between them—rather, they are part of a continuum of gradually increasing intensity. Ever more extreme postures are adopted by males as the breeding season approaches, and especially during the acquisition of a mate and maintenance of a territory around the nest site.

The song becomes louder and more variable and it is at this time that the incorporation of mimicked sounds becomes most notice-

Fig. 5.6. Low intensity singing with throat feathers ruffled and wings held slightly away from body.

able. In addition to the hunchback and the fluffed out throat, the wings are periodically flicked (Plate 7). This occurs commonly during a frequently used piece of song that involves sharp 'chweer' calls interspersed with 'chack' calls and much longer rattles. At each 'chack' the wings are flicked and as the series of 'chacks' and rattles progresses the wing-flicking often becomes more exaggerated. This behaviour may be a precursor to the climax of song display which usually occurs at the end of a bout of singing.

It involves a further development of wing flicking into what might best be described as wing-flailing (the wing-waving of Ellis 1966), for the wings, half extended, are rotated by continuing the flicking movement so that they are raised above the horizontal, pass forward, become extended in front of the body; then they are moved down and backwards and the movement is repeated (Fig. 5.7 and Plate 7). This peculiar wing movement—it is, in fact, not unlike an exaggerated but slowed-down flap used in flying—is not used by any other British bird and it seems to be characteristic of some of the *Sturnus* Starlings, although it is a display also used by the Wattled Starling *Creatophora cinerea*. In the European Starling it appears to be associated mainly with the spring period of sexual activity since I have seen it primarily between mid-January and mid-May, and rarely during the autumn. Ellis (1966), however, recorded it in autumn in North America. As mentioned above, Hartby (1969) and Van der Mueren (1980), who called the same wing movements 'aggressive wing waving', found that this kind of display could be used in agonistic encounters, but it is undoubtedly primarily a movement associated with the breeding season.

Fig. 5.7. 'Wing flailing'. High intensity singing with tail pointing down, giving a hunch-back appearance, and wings being vigorously waved.

The main function of wing-flailing seems to be mate attraction, though it may also be used in other situations. It is usually performed by a male on his song post close to his nest site. Wing-flailing is frequently stimulated by another Starling flying nearby, in which case the displaying male may or may not be singing at the time, but it is difficult here to ascertain whether the territory owner is trying to attract a mate or repel a potential intruder. Usually, however, wing-flailing occurs towards the end of a bout of singing and appears to represent a climax to intense song. But song is not restricted to the territory and we shall see (Chapter 6) that during the few days before laying commences the male accompanies his mate wherever she goes. During this period of mate-guarding, the male stays close to his mate even when she is feeding but the male, instead of feeding, often sits nearby and sings; this song on the feeding grounds is often accompanied by wing-flailing, even though the male is sitting on the ground. The occurrence of wing-flailing in these two situations suggests that this behaviour is related to mate attraction, both in the initial stages of courtship and in the subsequent maintenance of the pair bond during mate-guarding, and also to the expression of ownership of nest site and mate. That the former is probably the main function of wing-flailing is suggested by the context from which the behaviour may have been derived.

Various pre-copulatory actions have been described, including singing by the female, sexual chases, mutual bill-wiping, and courtship feeding (Kessel 1957; Hailman 1958; Schneider 1972; Verheyen 1970), but usually there seems to be little preamble with the female simply presenting herself in a submissive posture close to the male. When mounting, the male frequently holds the female's nape feathers with his bill and waves his wings in a manner reminiscent of wing-flailing (Plate 7). Both of these acitivities may be attempts by the male to keep his balance but this waving of the wings during copulation may provide a clue to the derivation of wing-flailing. Some copulations occur on the feeding grounds after a bout of singing and wing-flailing by the male during mate-guarding, but most coitions take place near the nest. Here, apart from comparatively rare instances of rape, the copulating male is the territory owner. The use of a form of behaviour, associated with copulation, in mate attraction and territorial defence, would be a logical expression of ownership and it may therefore be that wing-flailing represents a ritualized form of the male's movements while maintaining balance during copulation.

CALLS OF THE YOUNG

Once pairing, egg-laying, and incubation have been completed we hear two more calls that must be described in this chapter. The first of these is the array of begging calls given by the hungry chicks—calls that people who have Starlings nesting in their roof spaces will recognize only too well.

Nestlings begin calling when one or two days old. The call is given, as described by Hartby (1969), with the neck stretched and the bill wide open and pointing upwards, in other words ready to receive food. At this stage this begging call is little more than a weak 'tzee' that is given when the nest hole is disturbed. This is usually by the adults returning with food and the begging stimulates them to feed the chicks, but when chicks are hungry they may give this call between feeds. As the chicks grow their calling 'matures' into two calls that Hartby named the 'close begging call' and the 'distant begging call'. They are both used in the nest and for a time after the youngsters have fledged.

The close begging call is the raucous 'cheer cheer cheer' call is given when the adults approach the chicks, in or out of the nest, with food. This is the loud call that is continuously heard in late April and May wherever there is a colony of Starlings, and the call that can promote an early wakening of people whose houses are also homes for the birds.

The distant begging call is a quieter and more mellow 'churrrr' which is given in the parents' absence. When the chicks are still in the nest the call gives me the impression of being one of satiation and contentment, but I suspect that its function extends beyond this anthropomorphic interpretation. Once the chicks have fledged this is the call that is frequently heard from groups of youngsters sitting in bushes and trees awaiting their parents' return with food. The call continues when these fledglings fly off and it may help to maintain flock cohesion as well as aiding the parents to locate the young Starlings after a change of position.

I have no evidence that adult Starlings recognize the calls of their own chicks but I think it highly likely. On many occasions, however, I have seen recently fledged birds sitting in bushes giving the quiet 'churrrr' call. At times, this has gradually changed to a more rapid and higher pitched 'cheer' close begging call and shortly after this the adult has arrived with food. On one occasion, when few Starlings were in the vicinity, two fledglings that I had been watching began increasing their pitch and rate of calling; I looked in the direction where a parent had last departed and saw an approaching Starling about 200 m away. This bird was indeed the adult bringing food. I did not hear it call, but there is no doubt that the youngsters had recognized their parent, by voice or sight, at a considerable range. The individual recognition that I mentioned earlier in relation to a pair of adults can obviously be extended to parent and offspring, though the mechanism remains to be determined.

The final call to be considered here is the one given by adults close to their nests when the latter contain young, usually at the approach of a potential predator such as a scientist visiting nest-boxes! Hartby (1969) titled this the 'snarl', perhaps an appropriate name for a low pitched 'caaar' call. The adult producing the call generally holds its ground or even approaches the predator with intense wing-flicking movements, but I think it unlikely that the call is intended to drive the predator away. It does sometimes promote stares, snarling, or even mobbing from neighbouring birds, though this by no means always happens since neighbours may well be away foraging. The invariable reaction is that the chicks become silent and the call may therefore be intended to silence the chicks in order that the nest-site should not be detected by the predator. The 'snarl' is, however, used very occasionally at other times of year and may even be incorporated into phases of song so that a precise definition of its functions awaits resolution.

FREQUENCY RANGE

I have now described and attempted to interpret the main displays, incorporating both voice and posture, that are used by Starlings. Apart from occasional references to high or low pitch, I have said nothing about the frequency ranges of the Starling's vocabulary. Reference to Hartby's paper shows that most calls fall within 1 and 6 kHz which is well within the human range of hearing. Within this range there is, nevertheless, a tendency for a division between high- and low-frequency calls. This division is functional, for high-frequency calls tend to be detectable at a long distance but without much precision, whereas low frequencies permit more accurate location of the source but have a lower carrying power. Thus calls whose function is to relay information at a distance, such as the distress call, or without betraying their source, as in the distant begging call, are high frequency, or high-pitched, calls, while calls that have been evolved to identify location or to be used only over a short transmission range, such as the snarl or the flight call, are of low frequency. Song contains both components, with high-pitched whistles which can be heard over long distances and lower frequency warbles, rattles, and other sounds that can be detected only at close range, and this illustrates the versatility of messages that are transmitted by song.

The Starling's freqency range of auditory perception might be expected to correspond to the frequencies that it transmits, but Starlings, like all other animals, must perceive the sounds produced by other organisms in their environment, especially the

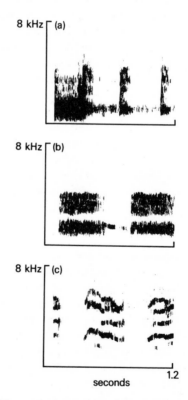

Fig. 5.8. Calls of different frequency ranges. (a) Low frequency 'chip' calls, (b) broader spectrum 'snarl', (c) broad spectrum 'distress' calls with emphasis on higher frequencies.

sounds of predators or food. Frings and Cook (1964) found that Starlings responded to frequencies up to 16 kHz for most of the year but in July and August this was increased to 28 kHz. The upper limit of human hearing is about 16 kHz, so that Starlings can hear some sounds above the range of human detection. The Starling's perception of high frequencies is insufficient, however, to warrant the assumption that ultrasonic emissions will have an adverse effect upon them and ultrasonic frequencies cannot, therefore, be expected to be useful as scaring devices against Starlings.

Brand and Kellogg (1939) found the lower limit of hearing in Starlings to be about 700 Hz, compared with a lower limit in humans of about 20 Hz. Thus the Starling is unable to hear middle C (259 Hz) on the piano or even the C an octave higher! Most of the Starling's calls, however, fall between 1 and 5 kHz (Fig 5.8).

In this chapter I have described a variety of postures and calls that are used by Starlings throughout the year. The description of these is relatively easy, but their interpretation, in terms of their meaningfulness to the bird, is much more difficult. This is an area where a great deal of valuable research remains to be undertaken.

6 A NEW GENERATION

PAIR FORMATION AND NEST BUILDING

The singing by the male described in Chapter 5 plays a large part in territory acquisition and pair formation, both of which are prerequisites for successful breeding. I have referred to territories before and should explain what a Starling's territory consists of, since it is unlike that of other garden birds such as the Robin *Erithacus rubecula* and Blackbird. A territory is, by definition, an area defended by a bird and in Robins and Blackbirds the territory contains the nest site and the feeding area. A Starling's territory, on the other hand, is a small area, which Kessel (1957) considered to extend no more than 0.5 m from the nest-hole, that the male defends against other colony members or intruders from outside the colony. In my experience, however, males defend an area larger than 0.5 m in the few days preceding egg laying and will chase off another male that lands within about 10 m. The feeding areas used by the colony are shared by its members who usually feed in flocks, although the males do not necessarily feed in the same flocks as their mates. Individuals do not defend parts of the feeding area for themselves and there is no evidence that colony members defend any part of the feeding area against non-members. Thus although the defended area around the nest is a territory, the area covered by the birds while foraging is called a home range and the home ranges of the pairs within the colony overlap. While the territory of a Starling, which has a nest and a mate (the reason for this qualification will become apparent below) rarely extends more than 10 m from the nest, the home range can comprise suitable feeding areas within 500 m.

Verheyen (1969, and 1980) has provided detailed accounts of nest site occupation and pair formation in Starlings. There are geographical variations in territorial behaviour, for where Starlings are resident, as in Britain and parts of North America, nest holes may be visited in most months of the year but where the birds are migrants they occupy holes only in the breeding season and for a brief period in September and October, before they depart for their winter quarters.

In Britain, some older males occupy nest sites and territories in the autumn but, although nest building and even egg-laying have been recorded at this time, colder weather generally leads these birds to vacate the territories for varying periods during the winter. Territorial behaviour can be truly associated with breeding which begins in late January or February, when males and, later, females may roost in suitable holes at night, leaving a high preponderance of first-year birds in the communal roosts (Wynne-Edwards 1929; Marples 1934).

Verheyen's work in Belgium showed that the oldest males were the first to establish territories and occupy nest cavities. At first, an old male's territory usually contains several nest holes and he attempts to defend most of these. As more males begin to search for nest sites the early incumbents find themselves unable to defend all of those that they had previously occupied and their territories therefore contract. They continue to defend one of the nest holes, presumably the one that appears to them to be the best, with the displays described in Chapter 5. The male also embarks, of course, on the process of attracting a mate.

This process also depends on song and posture but other aspects of behaviour are added to increase the attractiveness of the male, his territory, and particularly his nest site. Verheyen found that when a female landed near to a singing male who had not yet acquired a mate, the male immediately stopped singing and flew into his nest hole where he began singing once more as an invitation to the female to enter the nest. Sometimes, however, the prenuptial displays of the male culminate in a sexual chase when the courtship tends to move away from, rather than be centred upon, the nest site. In Belgium this behaviour began in February but in Britain it can occur earlier and Morley (1941) recorded a pair being together in October. This seems to be common and males will take nest material into holes in the autumn and in winter single birds and even pairs (or occasionally more birds) may roost in nest sites. Whether these autumn and winter pairs are of the same individuals as in spring is not known, although it seems highly likely since some pairs re-mate in consecutive years. Kessel (1957) nevertheless found birds changing partners in these nest roosts. Pair formation behaviour in resident British birds, and presumably in non-migrant populations elsewhere, can occur in mild weather throughout the winter and in these circumstances pair formation can be a very protracted process. However, birds that arrive late at British and North American colonies, such as young birds breeding for the first time, can nevertheless accomplish the necessary rituals in a very short time, just as Belgian birds do.

The building of a rough nest by a male is a part of his incitement to a female to become his mate. In my own study area at Worplesdon, Surrey, some nest boxes have nest material in them periodically during the winter, but by March most boxes have at least some material inside, even though it may not be recognizable as an incipient nest. In late March and early April an added attraction is brought to the nest in the form of petals of flowers or fresh green leaves. At Worplesdon, leaves of Ivy *Hedera helix*, Nettle *Urtica dioica*, Bramble *Rubus fruticesus*, Bluebell *Endymion nonscriptus*, and Rhododendron *Rhododendron ponticum*, and flowers of Polyanthus *Primula* sp., Daisy *Bellis perennis*, Lavender *Lavendula spica*, Hawthorn *Crataegus monogyna* and Daffodil *Narcissus* sp., have been found decorating nests. These are changed regularly, possibly because the female removes them as she does other nest material and the male subsequently replaces the lost decoration. Nesting activity is most intense on warm sunny mornings and evenings. Marples (1936) found that a male continued to decorate the nest when the female was incubating, but in my experience, once the pair bond is formed the female takes the initiative and completes the nest and its lining: it becomes a case of 'you don't bring me flowers anymore'! In fact, the female becomes the dominant member of the pair near the nest hole and it is also she who solicits copulation.

A Starling's nest is a bulky structure of dry vegetation within the nest cavity. The main part of the nest usually consists of dry grasses although fine twigs and pine needles may also be used. Male Starlings will even break small twigs off branches and trees to incorporate into the nest. Within this mass of material is a nest cup which is always situated in the part of the nest cavity most remote from the entrance. This may help to keep the eggs and chicks out of reach of some large predators, such as Magpies *Pica pica* or Crows *Corvus corone*, that might otherwise be able to push their heads far enough through the entrance hole to take the nest contents. The nest cup is usually, though not always, lined with softer material. Finer dry grasses and feathers are the usual constituents of the lining but a wide variety of 'artificial' materials can be used. These include pieces of cloth, string, paper, cellophane, cotton wool, and even cigarette ends. A nest in my Worplesdon nest boxes even had some pieces of computer print-out of an analysis of Starling food intake—the print-out should have been incinerated but one bird obviously found some unburned pieces! In Shetland and Fair Isle, however, where summer temperatures are lower than in southern England, P.G.H. Evans (personal communication) found nests to be much more thickly lined with soft feathers.

Nest building by the male and sexual activity in general take place mainly in the early morning but there is also a subsidiary peak of activity in the late afternoon. Copulation usually occurs close to the nest. As I mentioned in chapter 5, it can occur without any obvious preamble but there is usually some form of pre-copulatory activity. This often takes the form of what Morley (1941) described as 'branch-running', which involves the female approaching the male, who is usually singing, by sidling up to him. At this the male may move away, only to be followed by the female, a process that may be repeated several times before the male either mounts or flies away. I do not know what determines whether the male will copulate or not: in southern England Starlings usually seem to mate in fairly secluded places in trees although they occasionally copulate on the ground. The Spotless Starling, on the other hand, copulates in much more exposed situations and here the male appears to 'invite' copulation by giving soft whistles. On hearing these the female flies to him and solicits by sitting by his side. She may shake her tail from side to side but the decision to mount or not seems to rest with the male—at the female's approach he either mounts or flies away and I was unable to deduce the basis of his reaction.

MATE GUARDING

The apparent dominance of the female in pre-copulatory behaviour can potentially promote a dangerous situation for a male, especially of a communally breeding species. Starlings have an unbalanced sex ratio and many studies suggest that there are about two males to every female. In a breeding colony, therefore, there is likely to be a surplus of unmated males who will be trying to secure mates. In this situation, a female with a determination to solicit copulation might approach the wrong male and be inseminated by him. The true mate must ensure that his genes, and his alone, are those that are incorporated into the eggs of his female for he does not want to 'waste' his energies by helping to promote the continuance into the next generation of the genes of a competing male. This waste would result from the male's protection of eggs that had been fertilized by sperm from the marauding male and from his feeding of chicks that hatched from these eggs.

In order to prevent matings by other males, which may also include rape, the male of the pair remains very close to his mate from a few days before the first egg is laid until incubation begins. Power, Litovich and Lombardo (1981) found that incubation was initiated by females and that males did not sit on the eggs until the clutch had been completed. These authors interpreted this delay in the male's contribution to care of the eggs as being due to his requirement to defend his mate from other males: he could not do this if he was inside the nest. When incubation has begun, the male's interest in mate guarding dwindles and he allows the female to go off to feed on her own. But during the period of mate guarding he stays close to his mate at the nest, in the air, and on the feeding grounds (Plate 8). At the nest the female spends more and more time in the hole as laying progresses, although incubation does not begin until the last, or sometimes the penultimate, egg has been laid. The male remains in attendance close to the nest. Flights from the nest or a nearby branch to the feeding ground are initiated by the female, but as soon as the male sees her depart he follows. Such flights are conspicuous in April; the pairs of birds fly fast, the leading bird, the female, appearing to attempt to take avoiding action and continuously giving a 'chackerchackerchacker--------' call. The male follows his mate's manoeuvres, usually keeping within 1 metre or so of her. This proximity is maintained on the feeding ground, but while the female feeds for most of the time the male periodically stops feeding and sings for a few minutes, watching his mate all the time. Thus the egg-laying phase of the breeding cycle, which is generally assumed to place a strain on the female's resources, is also energetically expensive for the male, for he spends relatively little time feeding but a lot of time singing and chasing his mate whenever she flies between the nest and her feeding area. At this time of year the commonest flock size is two birds, and intruding birds are kept away by a range of antagonistic behaviour by the male of the pair, the extent of his aggression depending on the apparent threat to the female that is posed by the intruder. This mate-guarding by the male is common in essentially monogamous birds (this will be qualified for Starlings below) and it seems to represent the attempt by the male of a pair to ensure that his reproductive efforts are not wasted on the genes of competing males. More intensive observations are needed to assess the relative energy expenditure by male and female at this time of year, but it may well be that the male's investment of energy in his future brood is as great as that of the female who is manufacturing the eggs.

EGGS AND LAYING

Starling eggs are usually a clear, pale greenish-blue, but the colour is slightly variable and ranges from white to pale blue. The shell has a slight gloss. The eggs laid by any particular female are more-or-less identical, and the inclusion of an odd coloured egg in a clutch is indicative that it has been laid by another female, as will be described later in this chapter. The eggs are ovate to elliptical-ovate in shape. Within a clutch they may vary slightly in size and shape but the variation between the eggs of different females is greater. Measurements of a series of British eggs average 30.2 mm long × 21.2 mm at the widest point (Bannerman 1953b) while eggs of birds derived from British stock in North America average 29.2 × 21.1 mm (Kessel 1957). The size of eggs of birds breeding on continental Europe is very similar to this, and Dement'ev and Gladkov (1960) quote an average of 29.4 × 21.3 mm while in the east, at Alma-Ata, Sema (1978) found an average of 29.3 × 21.2 mm. We shall see later that egg size is related to female size and this is reflected in variations observed in the eggs of the extreme subspecies. For example, the eggs of *Sturnus vulgaris zetlandicus* average 31.1 × 22.0 mm (Bannerman 1953b), while those of the small *S.v. minor* average only 26.1 × 19.6 mm (Ali and Ripley 1972).

All Starling eggs are unmarked when laid and the few reports of eggs with fine black or brown spots refer to markings that develop after the eggs have been in the nest for a few days. At Worplesdon we found a higher incidence of spotted eggs in late than in early broods (Feare and Constantine 1980). Using techniques developed for forensic medicine we have subsequently identified the spots as being dried blood, originating from bites by parasites on the brood patch of the incubating bird.

The factors that lead to the onset of laying are not understood, and the date of laying of the first eggs in a colony can vary by up to 20 days or so in different years. On a geographical scale, Evans

(1980) found a strong positive correlation between date of laying and mean April temperature and a negative correlation with latitude, although the latter relationship was complicated by earlier breeding near the mild Atlantic coasts. Dunnet (1955) considered that the rate of growth of leatherjackets (larvae of craneflies or daddy-long-legs), which constitute an important food item of Starlings in winter and spring, had an important effect on the initiation of laying, with early breeding occurring in years when the spring growth of leatherjackets was early. Verheyen (1980) placed more emphasis on the effects of weather on the birds themselves and thought that high temperatures and low rainfall between 05.00 h and 10.00 h, the period of greatest sexual activity, in early April could promote early laying. Jones and Ward (1976), working with an African weaver bird, the Quelea *Quelea quelea*, concluded that both the date of initiation of laying and the number of eggs laid by a female were dependent upon the reserves of protein in her body, especially in her pectoral muscles. Peter Ward (1977) has subsequently suggested that the same relationship may hold for Starlings. The amount of reserve protein that can be accumulated in the muscles is presumably related to the food that the female can find, and since temperature influences the growth rate of leatherjackets, and presumably other soil invertebrates, in the spring it seems certain that both food and social activity are important in determining when laying will commence.

Once laying does begin, those birds that are going to lay an early clutch all do so within a few days. In my Surrey study area all early clutches are usually started within ten days (Fig. 6.1) and in Belgium Verheyen (1980) found, over eight years of study, that the number of days in which all early clutches were started varied from four to ten, with a mean of 6.7.

Between colonies, however, there is much more variation and at three colonies in Surrey the difference between them seems to be reasonably consistent from year to year. Starlings at Tolworth begin laying 10–15 days before those in my own population at Worplesdon, about 30 km to the south-west. In Ewhurst, about 16 km to the south-east of Worplesdon laying occurs about a week later still. The factors responsible for this kind of geographical variation are unknown, but Verheyen did suggest that larger colonies might breed earlier than small ones. I do not know the relative sizes of these three colonies.

When laying begins it is highly synchronous and it seems that

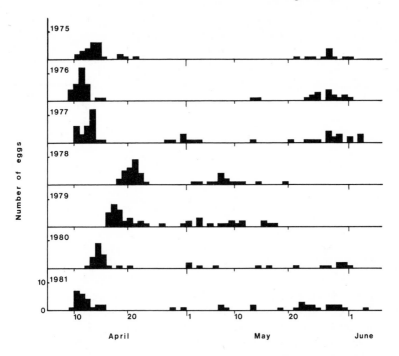

Fig. 6.1. The seasonal pattern of initiation of clutches at Worplesdon from 1975 to 1981.

this synchronization is brought about by social stimulation. In other words, each member of a colony is stimulated by the activities of other members of that colony. In Chapter 5 we saw that singing male Starlings tend to match their songs; this will lead to a synchronizing of singing by males. We also saw that in some birds (though it has yet to be shown in Starlings) male song can influence egg-laying by the female. These two behavioural traits could be instrumental in the achievement of the egg-laying synchrony that is observed but other factors that also play a part will doubtless be discovered.

So far, I have discussed synchrony of laying in terms of the days on which eggs are laid, but recently my colleagues and I (Feare, Spencer and Constantine 1982) have shown that laying is also synchronous during the day. Many song birds lay their eggs soon after dawn but we found that most Starling eggs are laid between 8 a.m. and 10 a.m. (Fig. 6.2). When we looked at the times of laying of each egg in the clutch, however, we found some unexpected

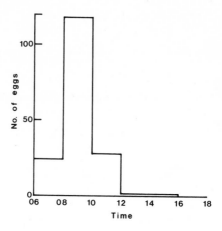

Fig. 6.2. Time of laying of first clutches in the Worplesdon colony in 1979 and 1980. Most eggs were laid between 08.00 h and 10.00 h.

trends. Starlings lay eggs at approximately 24-h intervals, but the first three eggs are laid at slightly less than 24-h intervals, while for the fourth and fifth eggs the interval between laying is slightly more than 24 h (Fig. 6.3). We do not know what underlies these trends. The progressive earlier laying of the first three eggs may result from the increasing number of birds entering the laying phase of their breeding cycle during the first few days of synchronous (in the seasonal sense) laying, and the consequent increased social activity within the colony. The longer interval between the laying of the fourth and fifth eggs is harder to explain on this reasoning, but reduced social stimulation following the peak of clutch initiation in the colony, and a drain on the female's reserves are possible explanations. In addition, there may be a physiological basis for these laying intervals greater than 24 hours, for Follett and Davies (1979) found that in chickens, ovulation occurred later each day; however, this raises problems with the interpretation of earlier laying of the first three eggs! Further work is clearly required on this aspect of laying in Starlings.

I have discussed synchrony of laying, and the factors that might assist synchronous breeding, at some length. But why should Starlings breed synchronously? For Starlings we do not know the answer because this problem has not been studied. In other colonial species, especially seabirds such as the Black-headed Gull *Larus ridibundus* (Patterson 1965), the Gannet *Sula bassana* (Nel-

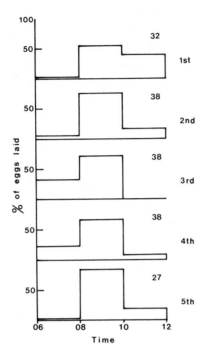

Fig. 6.3. Time intervals during which each egg was laid in the sequence of early clutches in 1979 and 1980 (data for the two years combined). Figures at the top right of each histogram are sample sizes. See text for explanation.

son 1980), and the tropical Sooty Tern *Sterna fuscata* (Feare 1976*b*, among many others), some of the advantages that accrue from nesting at the same time as most other members of your colony have been discovered. In short, those that nest at peak nesting time tend to have a better chance of rearing their young than those that nest at other times. In the seabirds this has been shown to result from, among other things, reduced rates of predation when the ratio of prey (number of birds in the colony) to predator is highest—a phenomenon called predator swamping. Yom-Tov (1975) has suggested, from his work on Crows *Corvus corone*, that synchronous breeding might help to reduce intraspecific interference; in Crows this took the form of cannibalism while we shall see later that the main kind of interference in Starlings is through intraspecific nest parasitism. In addition, there is circumstantial evidence that large numbers of seabirds exploiting the same localized food supplies can learn from each others' experience of where food is or when it will appear, thus enabling more birds to exploit these resources (Feare 1981*a*).

I shall return to and enlarge upon this theme of birds learning from each other when they aggregate together, currently called the 'information-centre' hypothesis (Ward and Zahavi 1973), when roosting behaviour is discussed in Chapter 10. Tinbergen and Drent (1980) have suggested that breeding Starlings do learn from each other the whereabouts and abundance of food, and this may be an advantage of colonial and synchronous breeding. This also, of course, enables the birds to feed together in flocks and we shall see (Chapter 9) that feeding in flocks leads to more efficient feeding by the birds involved. It is difficult to demonstrate advantages with respect to predation since most studies of breeding Starlings have been made using nestboxes. The combination of regular disturbance by human observers, and a uniform shape of box which a predator can readily recognize from a distance, may lead to artificially high levels of predation in colonies under investigation and this may mask any advantages derived from predator swamping.

There is no doubt that the synchronous breeding early in the season is more successful, in terms of output of fledglings, than clutches laid later, but we shall see below that, apart from being less synchronous than early cluthes, late broods differ in a number of other respects that effect their outcome.

INCUBATION

Early clutches are incubated for, on average, 12 days after the laying of the last egg of the clutch. The female takes the greater share in incubation: she incubates throughout the night and for most of the day while the male spends a small portion of the day sitting. At Worplesdon, we have estimated the times devoted to incubation by the sexes during our efforts to catch the incubating birds in order to ring, identify, and weigh them. Table 6.1 summarizes these captures and shows that in early clutches females spend about 70 per cent of the daytime incubating while males cover the eggs for most of the remaining period. Incubation by each member of the pair is not done in one continuous spell, but is broken up into shorter incubation shifts, between which the birds will leave the nest for brief intervals to preen, defaecate, or wipe their bills, or for longer periods to feed (the male also spends long periods singing and defending his territory against intruders).

Table 6.1. The proportion of occasions on which females were caught when incubating Starlings were captured at Worplesdon, 1977–1979 and in 1982

Clutch	Total number of catches	No. of catches on which female caught	% of times female caught
First	321	228	71.0
Intermediate	104	85	81.7
Second	113	99	87.6

In 1979 we watched the activities at two nestboxes throughout the day, recording the arrival and departure times of the birds in order to discover how long incubation shifts are and for how long the nests were left unattended. One of the nestboxes was 'normal' in that it was tended by both male and female, while the second box was cared for solely by the female, the male having deserted or died. At the normal box the male undertook far fewer incubation shifts than the female, but his shifts were slightly longer (Table 6.2). The nest was left unattended for 19.5 per cent of the day, with absences averaging slightly less than five minutes each. At the nest where only the female was present, she undertook

Table 6.2. All-day observations of the activities of incubating Starlings at two nestboxes at Worplesdon in 1979. At nest A both male and female shared incubation while at nest B the male had deserted or died and the female alone incubated the eggs

	Nest A		Nest B
	♀	♂	♀
Total time spent incubating (minutes)	443	211	396
Number of shifts	41	15	27
Average duration of shift (minutes)	10.8	14.1	14.7
Total time nest left unattended (minutes)	158		395
% of time nest left unattended	19.5		50.0
Average duration of absences (minutes)	4.6		14.2

considerably fewer incubation shifts than the female at the first box, but the shifts of the lone female were slightly longer. Despite this, she spent less time during the day on the nest but perhaps compensated for this because she left the nest later in the morning and returned to it earlier at night than did the female with a mate. The lone female's absences were also longer, with the result that her nest was unattended for 50 per cent of the day.

When an incubating Starling is disturbed it flies off as quickly as possible. When it leaves the nest of its own accord, however, it partially covers the eggs with a leaf or other convenient piece of material. (I have seen eggs covered with a piece of clear polythene sheet, leaving them plainly visible). Egg-covering behaviour occurs in some groups of birds, for example, the grebes, that nest in exposed situations and here the function of the behaviour is presumably to hide the eggs from potential predators. It seems strange that a bird that nests in a hole, which itself confers considerable protection from egg predators, should go to the trouble of attempting to cover its eggs when it leaves them. An alternative explanation might be that the covering is an attempt to reduce heat loss in the absence of the parent but the inefficiency with which the eggs are covered renders this doubtful. In Starlings, egg-covering seems to be ritualistic, rather than functional since part of the eggs can invariably be seen. The derivation of this behaviour, however, remains to be discovered.

Associated with the difference in time sharing by the sexes is a difference in their brood patches—areas of skin on the belly that become devoid of feathers during the breeding season (Plate 9). The incubation patch of the female is totally bare and pink, this colour being due to the dilation of blood vessels so that heat can be transferred to the eggs by the sitting bird. The incubation patch of the male, on the other hand, still has a cover of downy feathers and the skin that is visible is much greyer, this being due to a less pronounced vascularization of the abdominal skin. K. Westerterp (personal communication) considers that males do not in fact incubate because he has found that they do not add heat to the eggs; rather, their sitting reduces the rate at which the eggs would cool in the absence of the female.

If males devote so little time to care of the eggs in the nest, how are they to spend their time?

Some time has to be devoted to feeding and to territorial defence, but some males renew courtship activities and obtain a second mate. This second female is often a bird that has entered the colony late in the season, for example a female that is one year old and is breeding for the first time. This female will lay her eggs, fertilized by the polygamous male, two to three weeks after the laying of the early clutches of the remainder of the colony. These clutches of females of polygamous males form a part of what is frequently called the 'intermediate' clutch during a laying season (Fig. 6.1).

Although polygyny has now been demonstrated by many students of Starling biology, its frequency has not been established. Under exceptional circumstances, however, it seems that a male may mate with more than two females and Merkel (1978) recorded an instance (in a new nestbox colony to which young birds tend to be attracted) of one male with five females in a breeding season! Having taken a second mate, a male does not abandon his first. In fact, he devotes most of his time to assisting with the early brood and does not feed the chicks of his second mate; as a result, these polygynous matings result in a much lower breeding success than have the primary clutches (Merkel 1980). The low contribution of the male to the care of these intermediate clutches may, in part, explain the relatively greater amount of time devoted to their incubation by females (Table 6.1). However, many intermediate clutches are not the result of polygyny, but are replacements of early clutches that had been lost or deserted.

Replacement laying usually begin nine to twelve days after the loss of the first clutch, which partly accounts for the great spread in the occurrence of intermediate clutches. Where our own activities led to an unusually high rate of desertion in 1977, 1978, and 1979, the number of intermediate clutches, mainly replacements, was high (Fig. 6.1).

When we caught the birds that had laid replacement clutches we were surprised to find that most of the birds, identified by individually numbered leg rings, were not paired with the mates with whom they had mated for their failed early clutches. Nor did they all attempt to rear their replacements in the same nest boxes where they first laid. Thus the mating system within a Starling colony appeared to take on an unexpected flexibility. This could, of course have been due to our disturbance while undertaking our measurements of breeding birds, but the discovery of similar mate and nest site changes when birds paired in order to lay a true second clutch, after successfully rearing an early brood of fledglings, suggested that mate infidelity and nest site changes were a normal facet of Starling breeding biology (Feare and Burnham 1978). That flexibility is an integral part of Starlings breeding systems is further suggested by our discovery, at Worplesdon in 1981, of two males, during the late (normally true second brood) period, each assisting with the incubation of two clutches simultaneously.

The diversity of matings that results from these events must lead to a pronounced genetic mix in the succeeding generations, but why should Starlings change mates between broods? In 1978, Feare and Burnham showed that the more successful (in terms of output of fledged young) pairs tended to keep their mates for the second broods while less successful pairs swapped mates. We interpreted this as indicating that less successful pairs opted for divorce in the hope that re-pairing might increase their chances of subsequent success. Rudolph Verheyen (1980) proposed a simpler, and more plausible, explanation, suggesting that females whose chicks were undernourished needed more post-fledging parental feeding than well-fed chicks. This would entail a few extra days devotion by the mother of the weaker chicks, rendering her unavailable for re-mating when her male, who often takes a smaller share in feeding young, was ready to pair for a second time in the year. Mate change might, therefore, be regarded as an 'accidental' consequence of the reduced capabilities of under-nourished first brood chicks to fend for themselves and their resulting prolonged dependence on the mother for food. This explanation implies, of course, that the young of females with smaller broods tend to be less well nourished than the young in larger broods, which need not be the case. But the genetic heterogeneity within the progeny of a colony with such a flexible mating system must permit a greater adaptability than if pairs maintained their allegiance to one another. This assumes, of course, that the progeny of the 'new' pairs survive to breed, and also that the abilities of a pair of Starlings to successfully breed do not improve the longer the pair remains together. This certainly does happen in long-lived seabirds (Coulson 1972; Nelson 1980) but is less likely in birds whose chances of surviving to breed for a second or third time are small; this requires further investigation in Starlings, as in many other species, but Perrins (1979) found that older tits breed earlier and were more successful than younger ones.

CLUTCH SIZE

We must now consider the relative success of early, intermediate, and late clutches and the factors that affect this success. The most obvious variable that determines the number of young that can be produced is, of course, the number of eggs laid, and this varies both in time and space.

Most studies of Starlings have shown a seasonal decrease in clutch size, with intermediate clutches being smaller than early ones and second clutches being smaller even than intermediates. This pattern is clearly shown by my own studies at Worplesdon (Table 6.3) and it is typical of many species. The findings by Dehaven and Guarino (1970) and Royall (1966) that second clutches in their Starlings in the United States were larger than the first seem to be exceptional, even in America.

In addition to this drop in clutch size in successive bouts of laying, the number of eggs per clutch declines even during the laying of the early clutches, with those being initiated early being larger than those started towards the end of the first layings (Fig. 6.4). The effect of time of season on clutch size thus operates on a fine scale, but clutch sizes also vary in different years, as Table 6.3 shows. Since a seasonal decline in the number of eggs laid by each female seems typical of most Starling populations, we might expect clutches to be smaller in years when laying begins late than when it commences early. This does indeed happen in Great Tits *Parus major*, while the clutch size of Mistle Thrushes, Blackbirds, and Song Thrushes increases early in the season but declines later (Snow 1969). Our observations at Worplesdon indicate that for Starlings clutch size increases when the laying season is later in

Table 6.3. Mean clutch sizes at Worplesdon, Surrey, from 1975 to 1981

Year	First	Intermediate	Late
1975	4.48		4.17
1976	4.58	3.50	4.50
1977	4.77	4.71	4.50
1978	4.96	4.33	—
1979	4.96	4.07	—
1980	4.86	4.00	3.87
1981	4.61	4.25	4.39

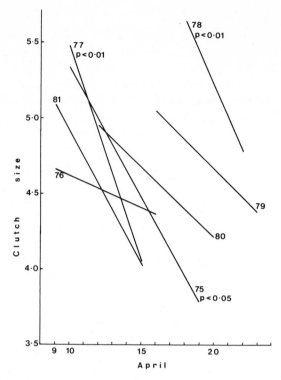

Fig. 6.4. Declines in clutch size during the course of the laying of first clutches at Worplesdon from 1975 to 1981. Significance levels are given where the regression lines are significantly different from horizontal.

starting (Fig.6.5). Here, the clutches laid in the latest years, 1978 and 1979, when laying in the colony did not begin until 16–18 April, averaged about 0.3 eggs larger than those clutches laid by females who started to lay in the earliest years, 1976 and 1981. In 1978 and 1979 laying began so late that successful breeders did not attempt to lay a second clutch. These two years therefore seemed to be 'bad' years for Starlings and it is surprising that in such years the early clutches should be larger than in apparently good years. This phenomenon cannot be explained in terms of the weights of the females since there was no difference in female weights between the early and late years, and we found no statistically significant relationship between female weight and her clutch size. We obviously need a deeper understanding of female physiology prior to egg-laying before this apparent anomaly can be explained

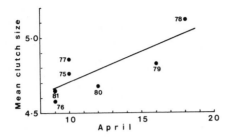

Fig. 6.5. Mean clutch size of first broods in relation to the date on which laying began at Worplesdon in 1975–1981: $r_{179} = 0.20$, $p < 0.01$.

and the levels of pectoral-muscle protein in early and late years will merit investigation (Ward 1977).

Within a breeding season clutch sizes do, however, bear a relation to female weight. When females are feeding young, they are considerably lighter than when they are incubating the early clutch (Fig. 6.6) but by the time they are incubating the second clutch they have almost regained their early clutch weight, but not quite: a comparison of the weights of the same individuals on early and second clutches showed that those incubating the latter averaged 3.6g lighter than when sitting on the first eggs. Although a smaller number of eggs is laid in the second clutch, corresponding with the lower weight of the females, we have found that those eggs that are laid are the same size (using weight as the measure) as those of the first clutch. This again is somewhat surprising since in the early clutches there is a direct relationship between female weight and the weights of the eggs she lays—larger females lay larger eggs (Fig. 6.7). But a comparison of egg weight with female weight in

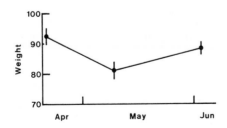

Fig. 6.6. Mean weight (g ± 1 s.e.) of three female Starlings caught in 1977 at different stages of breeding: while incubating early clutches (April), feeding first broods (May), and incubating second clutches (June).

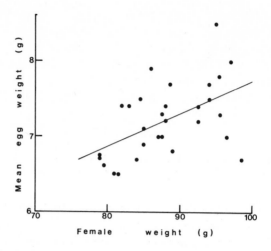

Fig. 6.7. The relation between the weight of a female Starling when caught during incubation of the first clutch and the weight of her eggs, showing that heavier females lay heavier eggs. The data are from 1977; $r_{29} = 0.44$, $p<0.05$.

the second clutches shows no such relationship. There is some variation in the weights of eggs within a clutch but it seems that each female lays eggs of roughly the same size in each clutch, independent of her weight when incubating the second. Egg size may therefore be more strictly related to the female's body size, rather than to her weight but the relation between egg size and the parameters used to assess body size, such as wing length, sternum length, and head length have not been investigated. This constancy of egg size nevertheless emphasizes that the female Starling's main method of adjusting to her different physiological states is through varying the number of eggs that she produces. Birds with a less flexible clutch size, on the other hand, tend to lay smaller, rather than fewer, eggs later in the season (e.g. Sooty Terns, Feare 1976b) or even late in the clutch (Parsons 1972). How this relates to prevailing environmental conditions is not known, but it is generally assumed that the female's egg production is somehow geared to food availability (Lack 1968), possibly through the amount of food that is available to females at, or immediately before, egg-laying (Perrins 1970).

The initiation of egg-laying is doubtless influenced by a complex of factors involving photoperiod, climate, and social stimulation of the breeding birds, as well as their ability to accumulate sufficient nutrients; this ability may also be influenced by climatic effects on the invertebrate prey just prior to breeding for, as mentioned above Dunnet (1955) found that the rapid growth of leatherjackets in the spring was related to soil temperatures. It is therefore to be expected that laying dates will vary over the Starlings' vast breeding range. Figure 6.8 shows that this is so, with the first clutches being laid in early April in the south and west of the range but not until mid-May or later in the north-east of their breeding areas.

It should be noted that Starlings have readily adapted to breeding in the Southern Hemisphere, for birds in South Africa (Liversidge 1962) and New Zealand (Coleman 1974) breed between October and December.

It will be noticed from Fig. 6.1 that it was in years when egg-laying began late in Worplesdon that no second clutches were laid. Anderson (1961) found the same in Aberdeenshire and furthermore showed a significant corelation between the date of laying of the early clutches and the proportion of second ones in that year. Verheyen (1980) did not find this linear relationship, but it nevertheless appears that early laying of the first clutches is a prerequisite for the subsequent appearance of second broods. This has implications on a geographical scale, since second broods seem to occur regularly only in the south and west of the Starlings

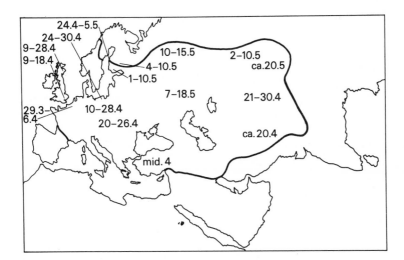

Fig. 6.8. Ranges of laying dates of Starlings in different parts of the breeding area. Laying is earlier in the south and west and later in the north and east.

breeding range (Fig. 6.9) which is where, as we have already seen, Starlings breed earliest. Similarly, Kessel (1953*b*) found that second clutches did not occur in North America when first layings were late.

If the date of initiation of laying is important geographically with respect to the laying of second clutches, does it also produce geographical variations in clutch size? The main source of information on Starlings in the Soviet Union, Dement'ev and Gladkov (1960) does not unfortunately give clutch sizes in sufficiently precise detail to allow a comparison of those in, for example, Krasnoyarskiy and Altai, where extreme late laying occurs, with the earlier breeding populations of Europe. Figure 6.10 shows the ranges of clutch size that have been found in various parts of Europe, and it is evident that there is comparatively little geographical variation. Even in the east of the species' range, at Alma-Ata, Sema (1978) found an average clutch size of 5.3 eggs. In other words, the number of eggs laid in early clutches does not show the increase with later laying in northern Europe that we might have predicted from the Worplesdon observations shown in Fig. 6.5. Although this increase in clutch size with lateness of season at Worplesdon was unexpected, it is equally surprising that there is no apparent increase in clutch size at higher latitudes,

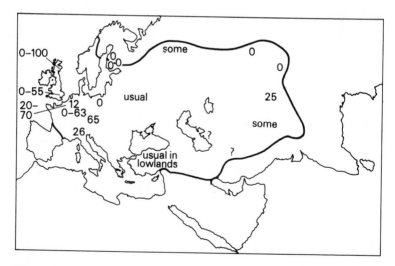

Fig. 6.9. The proportion of second clutches in different parts of the breeding area. Second clutches are more frequent in the south and west than in the north and east.

Fig. 6.10. Mean sizes of first clutches (extremes are given where data are from several years) in colonies that have been studied in Europe.

since this is a common phenomenon in many birds (Lack 1968). For example, Snow (1956) recorded average clutches of six to seven eggs in Blue Tits in southern Europe while British Blue Tits usually lay around 11 eggs.

Geographical variations in clutch size in Starlings may be complicated by a variety of other factors, however, which have not yet received adequate study in this species. For example, Dunnet (1955) and Verheyen (1969) discovered that females breeding for the first time, that is one year-olds, commence laying slightly later than older birds but still within the same synchronous laying period. Kluyver (1933) found that young birds lay smaller clutches than older ones, and this may contribute to the decline in clutch size during the early laying period (Fig. 6.4). Geographical variations in the proportion of first-time breeders could therefore influence overall clutch size.

Earlier, I remarked that laying dates in Surrey showed considerable variation on a local scale and Gromadzki (1980) in Poland and Tenovuo and Lemmetyinen (1970) in Finland have also demonstrated local variations in clutch size. Gromadzki found that the average clutch sizes of early broods in 12 colonies in Northern Poland in 1972 ranged from 4.5 to 5.5 eggs: this range of sizes embraces most of those recorded elsewhere in Europe! Thus clutch size variation on a local scale is probably so great as to mask wider geographical trends. Some of this variation might be attributed to differences in colony size or in breeding density within colonies since Verheyen (1980) reported that larger colonies tended to breed earlier than smaller ones.

Although there has been no field demonstration of a relation between breeding density and clutch size, Luniak (1977) described variations in nesting density from six to 360 pairs per square kilometre and Risser (1975) found that captive Starlings nesting at artificially high densities laid smaller clutches than those nesting at low densities. Variations in colony size and breeding density will obviously result from differences in the habitats in which the birds breed and habitat variety throughout Europe may further help to mask geographical trends in clutch size.

Incipient cuckoos

A fascinating and yet poorly understood aspect of Starling breeding behaviour is what Yom-Tov, Dunnet, and Anderson (1974) called 'intraspecific nest parastism'. This occurs when females, whose identity is unknown, lay their eggs in the nests of other females rather than in nests of their own. This becomes most readily apparent when two eggs appear in a nest within 24h, or when an egg of a different shade from the remainder of the clutch is laid in a nest. Peter Evans (1980) has shown that these criteria grossly underestimate the amount of parasitism in a colony, for he found an even higher incidence of chicks from a parasitic mother; by examining certain of their blood proteins he found that many chicks were not genetically related to the owners of the nest in which the chicks were found. Thus some females behave as incipient cuckoos by laying their eggs in other Starlings' nests, to be incubated and reared by the true nest owners. (There is even a record of a Starling chick being found in the nest of another species, an Indian Mynah, in New Zealand (Wilson 1979) and Kessel (1957) quotes records of Starling's eggs or chicks being found in nests of Bluebirds *Sialis sialis*, Pileated Woodpecker *Dryocopus pileatus*, Magpie *Pica pica*, and Stock Dove *Columba oenas*. This is exceptional.)

Another phenomenon that may be associated with this nest parasitism is the appearance of Starling eggs on the ground during the laying period. These are generally attributed to accidental laying by females who are 'taken short' before they can get back to their nests. In the Worplesdon study, every egg is marked with a spot of coloured nail varnish on the day that it is discovered in a nest so that each egg of a clutch is individually recognizable. All of 58 eggs, 56 of them intact, that have been found on the ground between 1975 and 1981 in our Laboratory grounds have had spots of nail varnish on them! In other words, all of these eggs had been laid in a nestbox but had been subsequently removed. A predator would most likely have eaten them, and since Starlings have been occasionally seen carrying eggs in their bills it is most probable that all of these eggs had been removed from the nests by Starlings. Why these eggs should be carefully desposited on the ground, rather than be dropped by the flying bird, is a mystery. (For an alternative to the 'accidental laying' explanation that used to be in vogue, I strongly recommend a highly amusing article by the late David Lack (1963) commemorating the retirement of Professor Alister Hardy from Oxford University. The paper concerns the unique egg-laying behaviour of 'Hardy's Swift.') These aspects of Starling behaviour pose many questions, the foremost being: who are the females that lay in other Starlings' nests? Do they lay one egg in each of several nests or do they have a nest of their own and lay only one or two elsewhere? How successful are the parasites in ensuring that their progeny survive and do they assist in feeding them? Who is the mate of the parasitic female? Is egg removal in fact related to nest parasitism and, if so, how? These questions suggest an exciting study of Starling social behaviour but I have to admit that I suspect that both nest parasitism and egg removal are increased by the activities of the scientists who investigate Starling behaviour! Nest parasitism has nevertheless been reported from many colonies (e.g. Numerov (1978) in Russia) and P. G. H. Evans (personal communication) has recorded it in relatively undisturbed colonies.

When considering geographical, or even local variations in clutch size, the occasional addition to a clutch by these parasites or the removal of an egg poses obvious complications.

Determinants of clutch size

Despite all these variations in, and the problems in assessing clutch size, a remarkable feature recurs when one reads the relevant European, Asian, and North American literature on Starlings: in all areas the commonest early clutch size appears to be five, or occasionally six, eggs. Why should this be?

David Lack devoted much of his writing to the evolution of clutch size in birds, and included a special study of Starlings (Lack 1948). His main thesis was that the clutch size evolved by a species represented the maximum number of chicks that the parents could rear successfully. This hypothesis held two major assumptions. First, that clutch size was genetically inherited and therefore that natural selection could act on it, and second that the maximum number of young surviving from a brood represented the maximum contribution to future generations that the parents could achieve. Research on Starlings is unfortunately behind that on other species, and we do not yet have long-term studies from which data are available to support or refute these assumptions. From studies on other species, notably tits, it appears that clutch size does have a genetic component but that genetic variation is sufficient to allow environmental factors to influence the number of eggs laid at any time (Perrins and Jones 1974; van Noordwijk, van Balen and Scharloo 1980). With respect to the maximum genetic contribution to future generations, different factors oppose each other and parents have to reach a compromise. In order to ensure that as many as possible of their progeny survive to breed, parents must raise as many chicks as they can to the age of independence. The effort involved in achieving this could, however, put so much of a strain on them that it jeopardizes their own survival and, therefore, their chances of laying another clutch in the same or a subsequent year.

This could be particularly important if the birds' reproductive success increases as they gain experience, as Kluyver (1933) and Gromadzki (1980) showed when comparing the breeding success of females breeding for the first time with that of older females. But ensuring that a large number of young attain independence is not enough, since there is increasing evidence that chicks (of several species) that are heavy when they fledge stand a better chance of surviving the difficult period of learning to fend for themselves than chicks which fledge at a low weight. Thus, the important factor for parents is to produce as many *heavy* young as they can. Crossner (1977) found that chicks in artificially enlarged broods left the nest at lower weights than those from more normal brood sizes, but that if the large broods were presented with an additional supply of food they could achieve the weights of chicks from normal broods that were not given the supplement. In other words, under natural conditions of food availability, birds that lay the usual four to six eggs stand a good chance of rearing the resulting chicks so that they fledge at a high weight, while Starlings with larger broods may be able to raise more chicks but they are lighter at fledging. This strongly suggests, as Lack (1948) predicted, that the food available to the parents is important in determining the number of offspring that they can raise. Crossner did find, however, that chicks in broods of three fledged at a greater weight than those in broods of four to six, but presumably the slightly better chance of survival of these heavier chicks is insufficient to outweigh the advantage of producing five or six chicks at a slightly lower fledging weight.

Lack (1948) also considered second clutches in his analysis of the evolution of clutch size in Starlings. We have already seen that the number of eggs in the late laying is smaller than in first clutches (Table 6.1) and in fact the most common size for second clutches is four eggs. Lack found that this size was the most productive, just as five or six eggs were the most productive in the early broods.

It is worth remembering here that unusually small clutches, besides being unable to produce sufficient chicks with a potential of contributing to the next generation, are uneconomical in energetic terms (Westerterp *et al.* 1982). In Chapter 3 I showed that nestlings benefited from the heat production of their siblings, but if there were too few chicks they had to expend more energy in heat production to maintain their body temperatures. To achieve this, each had to receive proportionately more food from its parents, leading to a lower parental efficiency in terms of the amount of food brought per nestling in relation to the future contribution that the nestling might make to passing on its parents genes.

These energetic relationships within nests built inside holes seem to be an important factor in allowing Starlings, and other hole nesting birds, to lay larger clutches than their cup-nesting counterparts (Lack 1968), and we must now examine the survival of eggs during incubation up to hatching.

HATCHING SUCCESS

I have already commented on the adverse effects of scientists' studying Starling breeding biology. If the visit of a human to a nest-box, especially to catch the incubating bird, has any effect it is usually to lead to desertion of the nest. If the female deserts, the male cleans out the nest, including the eggs, and recommences his courtship rituals in an attempt to mate again: he has usually cleaned the nest within 24 h of his female's desertion (Verheyen 1980). If the male deserts, the female may or may not continue to incubate the eggs and care for the young but the factors that influence her decision are unknown. During studies of breeding success, the loss of an entire clutch is generally attributed to observer disturbance, and such losses are therefore omitted from calculations of the proportion of eggs that hatch. That this is justified is suggested by our work at Worplesdon. Of 184 first, 53 intermediate and 54 second clutches layed during the breeding seasons from 1975 to 1981, we have been able to attribute only five total clutch losses to predation: in one case a Grey Squirrel *Sciurus carolinensis* ate all the eggs before taking over the nest-box for itself, and in the others a predator, probably a weasel *Mustela nivalis*, ate all of the eggs inside the nests (three of these cases in 1978).

Table 6.4 shows that hatching success in colonies in various parts of Europe and North America is usually around 80–90 per cent in early clutches but that there is a suggestion of a slight decline in succeeding clutches. Korpimäki (1978) found that the highest hatching success occurred in clutches of five and six eggs, which

Table 6.4. Hatching success (%) in various Eurasian and North American Starling populations. The percentages of eggs laid that hatch in first, intermediate, and late clutches excludes clutches where all eggs disappeared, probably following desertion after disturbance by observers

	First	Intermediate	Late
England (Worplesdon study)	78–94	63–100	67–88
Scotland (Dunnet 1955, Anderson 1961)	83–91	—	78–89
Finland (Tenovuo and Lemmetyinen 1970)	90–92	—	—
(Korpimäki 1978)	87	—	—
Poland (Gromadski 1980)	75–100	—	—
(Luniak 1977)	89	—	—
Kazakhstan (Sema 1978)	76–93	—	42–79
North America (Kessel 1957)	90	83	80
(Collins and De Vos 1966)	86–99	84–91	80–87
(Dehaven and Guarino 1970)	84	—	82

were by far the commonest clutch sizes in his study (Fig 6.11). Low hatching success in small clutches may be a reflection of the lower efficiency of young birds that tend to lay smaller clutches, while low success in large clutches could result from the inability of the incubating bird to adequately cover all of the eggs.

Unfortunately, few authors have recorded the causes of egg losses during incubation, but our results, together with those of Dunnet (1955), Tenovuo and Lemmetyinen (1970), and Korpimäki (1978) suggest that most of the losses are due to eggs that fail to hatch. This is due both to infertility and to embryos dying in the egg. Tenovuo and Lemmetyinen (1978) found that some eggs simply disappeared, as we did in the Worplesdon study and these are most probably the result of Starlings removing eggs. The eggs found on the ground in our study area all proved to be fertile when they were dissected, and when we 'killed' some eggs, when fresh, by injecting them with formalin, we found that the nest owners did not eject them. Egg ejection was thus not an attempt by nest owners to remove infertile eggs, thereby avoiding a possible waste of heat energy during incubation, but was more likely to be related to intra-specific nest parasitism. A few eggs are occasionally found broken in nests; these may result from fights between the true occupant of a nest and an intruding bird.

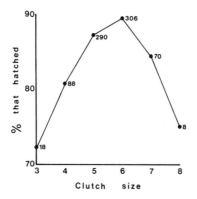

Fig. 6.11. Hatching success of clutches of different sizes. Figures by the side of each point are the number of eggs in the clutches sampled. (From data in Korpimäki 1978.)

7 THE HUNGRY HORDES

HATCHING

Within each nest, the eggs do not all hatch at the same instant but over a period, usually of around 24 h. The process of hatching is itself prolonged since the chick has to cut the top off the broad end of the egg using its egg tooth. This is a hard protuberance, on the tip of the upper mandible, which disappears gradually as the chick grows. The first evidence that an egg is about to hatch is the appearance of tiny cracks radiating out from a central point just above the widest part of the egg—at this stage the egg is said to be 'starred'. From starring to actual emergence of the chick can take up to 24 h but it is usually accomplished in less than 12 h. Once the chick is out of the egg the shell is removed by the parents and dropped out of the hole. Surprisingly, the shell is usually not carried very far and may even be dropped directly below a nest box. This seems to be a dangerous practice since the appearance of shells on the ground must give a potential predator an indication of where it may find a meal; Starlings presumably rely on the protection afforded by the nest hole as their main line of defence against predation.

The spread of hatching over 24 h is usually due to one egg hatching about a day later than the rest. Where we have been able to relate the order of hatching of the eggs with their order of laying, we have found that in 68 cases the last egg to hatch was the last to be laid and in only five instances was another egg the last to hatch. This suggests that incubation usually begins on the day that the penultimate egg is laid.

GROWTH

During incubation eggs lose weight as the embryos within develop and while freshly laid eggs average about 7.5 g, a newly hatched and unfed chick weighs about 6 g. Within 12–15 days, first-brood chicks have increased by 1250 per cent to around 75 g! Weight is the most usual criterion used for measuring growth and weight curves for first and second brood Starlings at Worplesdon in 1977 are shown in Fig. 7.1. This shows that weight increase is most rapid

(a)

(b)

(c)

Plate 1. Roost sites.
(**a**) Starlings arriving to roost on Nelson's Column, Trafalgar Square, London and (**b**) at Marischal College, Aberdeen, a centre that has undertaken much research on Starlings. (**c**) Part of an urban roost in Newcastle, with some of the birds singing. Note the large quantity of droppings that can necessitate expensive cleaning of the masonry. (Photograph: Jacqui Hogan.) (**d**) A rural roost. The guano on the floor is about 20 cm deep and the lower branches of the trees are covered. Some trees have died and others have broken branches.

(d)

(a)

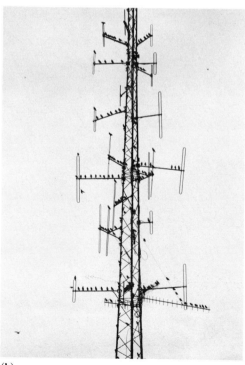

(b)

Plate 2. (**a**) A day roost in the top of a tall tree. The birds are conspicuous but have good all-round visibility. (**b**) A pre-roost assembly on a radio aerial: such flocks can obliterate the radio signals.

Plate 3. (*opposite*) Adaptability in selection of nest sites. (**a**) A natural cavity in the fork of a tree. (**b**) A nest under the eaves of a house. (**c**) A nest behind a hole in the wooden cladding of a barn. In (**a**), (**b**), and (**c**) note the tell-tale droppings beneath the nest entrance. (**d**) An unusual nest site in an oil drum on the Orkneys, where a shortage of trees leads Starlings to select unusual sites. (Photograph: Marianne Wilding.) (**e**) This selection of unusual nest sites in Orkney can present problems: a letter box protected from Starlings by a mesh screen, but the benevolent Orcadians have provided an alternative site beneath, also painted red! (Photograph: Marianne Wilding.) (**f**) Starlings readily adapt to nest boxes. While these are used primarily to investigate breeding biology, in New Zealand they are erected to encourage dense Starling colonies in the hope that the birds will control insect pests. (Photograph: Peter Purchas.)

(a)

(b)

(c)

(d)

(e)

(f)

(a)

Plate 4. Habitats. (**a**) Mixed dense forest in Surrey, presenting many potential nest cavities for Starlings but no open feeding areas. This poor Starling habitat may resemble the appearance of much of Britain before man began creating clearings. (**b**) Completely open country in Lincolnshire, presenting extensive feeding areas but few nest cavities. Such an area supports few breeding pairs and has few day roost sites for winter flocks. (**c**) Park land in Surrey, with mature trees providing many cavities and areas of short grassland nearby. This represents an ideal breeding area for Starlings. (**d**) Open farmland in Hampshire, with tall trees and farm structures providing day roost sites, grazed and liberally manured grassland providing invertebrate food, and cattle feeding areas providing alternative foods. This represents ideal winter habitat.

(b)

(c)

(d)

(a)

Plate 5. Adaptability in feeding methods. (**a**) The Starling is primarily a grassland feeder. (**b**) 'Cattle Egret feeding': feeding in association with ungulates that keep the vegetation short so that soil invertebrates can be located, that disturb mobile insects making them more visible to Starlings, and that deposit dung which constitutes a microhabitat for a wide variety of invertebrates. (**c**) 'Oxpecker feeding': Starlings eat ectoparasites from tolerant domestic animals. (**d**) 'Flycatcher feeding': hawking of aerial insects, especially flying ants, is common in spring and summer.

(b)

(c)

(d)

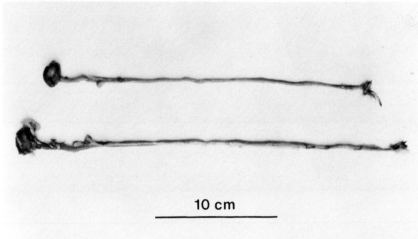

(a)

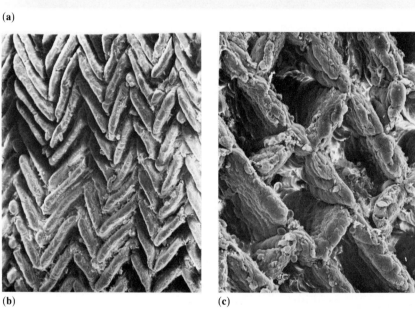

(b)   (c)

Plate 6: Adaptability of the gut. (**a**) The long gut of a Starling adapted to a plant food diet compared with the shorter gut of a bird that is adapted to a diet of invertebrates. (**b**) Zig-zag and (**c**) reticulate villi in the upper and lower parts of the intestine of a Starling. (Scanning electron micrographs by Brian Cresswell.)

(a)

(b)

(c)

Plate 7. Postures of the male.
(a) Low intensity song with throat feathers erected, belly feathers ruffled and wings held slightly away from body. (b) Higher intensity song in which the wings are periodically flicked away from the body. Note also the bending of the tail downwards and the ruffling of the rump feathers, giving a 'hunchback' appearance.
(c) High intensity song with 'wing flailing' or 'wing waving'.
(d) Copulation. The male rotates his wings in order to maintain balance while mounting; this may be the derivation of 'wing flailing'.

(d)

(a)

(b)

Plate 8. Mate guarding.
(a) The male (right) of a mated pair feeds close to his female and (b) stops feeding to indulge in a bout of song, still close to his mate. (c) and (d). The male also remains close to his mate in flight. The female appears to take evasive action and calls almost continuously but the male follows closely.

(c)   (d)

(a)

Plate 9. Some differences between the sexes. (**a**) A male, with an eye that is entirely dark brown. (In this male, in late breeding season, the facial feathers have become abraded so that the facial skin is naked, a common occurrence at this time of year.) (**b**) A female, showing a pale ring in the iris. (**c**) The ill-defined incubation patch of a male. (**d**) The extensive and highly vascularized incubation patch of a female.

(b)

(c)

(d)

(a)

Plate 10. Mortality. (**a**) Ring recoveries propose the domestic cat as a major predator of Starlings but the biases inherent in ring returns may overestimate its importance; however, this nest box was not occupied by birds. (**b**) Starlings commonly feed at sewage farms but there is no evidence that they contract disease there. (**c**) A juvenile Starling with lesions caused by avian pox virus beneath the lower mandible. (**d**) Electron micrograph of the causative agent of avian pox in Starlings. (Photograph: Denis Alexander.)

(b)

(c)

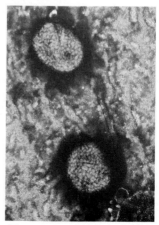

(d)

(a)

(b)

Plate 11. Spacing within Starling flocks in flight. (**a**) Wide spacing between individuals that are undisturbed while flying between feeding areas. (**b**) Close spacing in a flock that has just taken off after being disturbed by a Sparrowhawk, a potential predator.

(a)

(b)

(c)

(d)

(e)

Plate 12. Pre-roost assemblies. Dense flocks rising from (**a**) a stubble field and (**b**) a winter barley field. (**c**) Part of a pre-roost assembly feeding at a pig farm in Norfolk and (**d**) a huge flock descending on a cattle farm in Lincolnshire. (**e**) A meandering stream of Starlings arriving from a pre-roost assembly into the roost in the reed beds at Slapton Ley, Devon. (Photograph: Robin Prytherch.)

Plate 13 (*opposite*). Departure from a roost. (**a**) A flock rises from a roost site before dispersing in all directions to produce a 'wave'. (**b**) 'Ring angels' on the plan position indicator of a radar. A dense ring is visible close to the roost and two rings that have dispersed further from the roost can also be seen. (**c**) Departing Starlings can pose hazards when they compete for air space with jet aircraft.

(a)

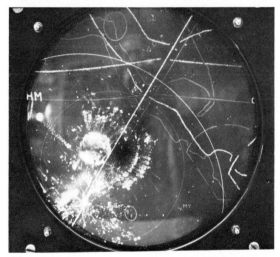

(b)

(c)

(a)

(b)

(c)

(d)

Plate 14. Feeding sites in which agricultural damage can occur. (**a**) Ripening cherries. (**b**) Cattle food, mainly crushed barley, at an indoor feeding unit. (**c**) Pig food at an open air piggery: here, Starlings are also sometimes blamed for the dissemination of some pig diseases, (Photograph: Marianne Wilding.) (**d**) Digging up winter wheat in a pre-roost assembly.

Plate 15. Some examples of crop damage by Starlings. (a) Extensive damage to cherries, with most fruit eaten leaving only the stones. (b) An early ripening cultivar of apple, Discovery, severely pecked by a Starling. (c) Probe holes made by Starlings along the drills in a winter wheat field, with some plant remains lying on the surface.

(a)

(b)

(c)

(a)

Plate 16. Damage prevention. (a) A loudspeaker in a cherry orchard. Starling distress calls are broadcast periodically in order to scare away the birds. (b) A plastic mesh netting excluding birds from mature cherry trees. The netting covers approximately 2.5 ha. (c) PVC strips suspended over the open front of a calf-yard. Ventilation gaps are left between the strips but the curtain prevents Starlings from entering and also provides a slightly warmer environment within the yards.

(b)

(c)

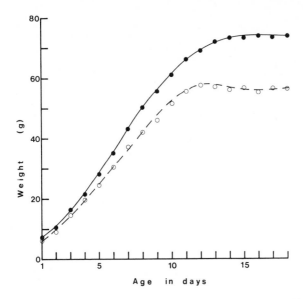

Fig. 7.1. The growth, in weight, of first- (●) and second- (○) brood chicks that survived to fledging at Worplesdon, 1977.

over the first 10 days of life but then the rate begins to slow down. There are, however, other criteria for measuring growth and some of the simplest are wing length, tarsus (knee joint to ankle joint), and culmen (bill from feathering on crown to tip of upper mandible) lengths. These show somewhat different patterns. The tarsus grows very rapidly over the first five days but then its rate of increase slows, and the culmen shows a slightly faster growth rate over the first five days than later, but really its rate of growth is reasonably constant up to fledging (Fig. 7.2). Increase in wing length with age shows a more complicated pattern (Fig. 7.3) for two stages are involved. First, the long bone of the arm, the humerus, and its associated flesh, increase in length but after the fifteenth day the growth of this part of the birds' fore-limb becomes overshadowed by the rapid growth of the flight feathers, especially the primaries. The parameters mentioned above are easy to measure, but if we could as easily measure the size of the digestive system, we would find that it was relatively large, in comparison with our other criteria of size, at hatching and its rate of increase thereafter would not match that of total body weight, tarsus, and wing length. The gut is, of course, important to the

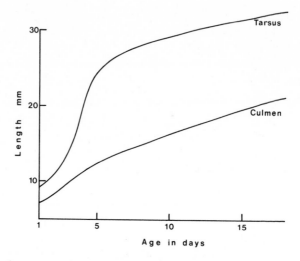

Fig. 7.2. Rate of growth of tarsus and culmen in first-brood Starling chicks that survived to fledging at Worplesdon in 1975.

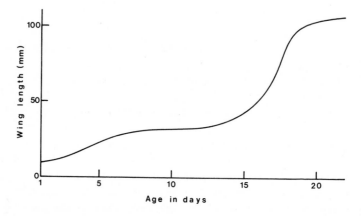

Fig. 7.3. Rate of growth of the wing of first-brood Starlings that survived to fledging at Worplesdon in 1975.

chick from its moment of hatching, because even though it has a yolk reserve that carries over from its life within the egg, it will accept food as soon as its parents provide it. This food must be processed which, of course, requires a highly developed digestive system. At this stage of the chicks' life considerations of energy and protein intake take precedence over walking or flight, so that an advanced state of digestive development is far more important than a long leg or a long wing. Ricklefs (1979*a,b*) has interpreted this as indicating that the various facets of a birds' growth are geared to two requirements, one being the immediate needs of the individual for its current existence and the other a preparation for the kind of life it will have to lead in a few days or weeks hence. If we look at the plumage development of a Starling chick we see an extension of this idea, for the first parts of the plumage to develop are the body or contour feathers, which provide the bird with insulation against heat loss, while the feathers required for flight, the primaries and secondaries on the wings, grow later (Fig 7.3).

Body insulation is, however, only a part of a growing bird's mechanism for reducing heat loss for another component of heat conservation depends on the bird's size. Heat is lost through the bird's surface and the rate of heat loss is thus dependent on the surface area of the chick's skin. Heat is generated by the tissues within the body and so the amount of heat gain is related to the chick's volume. A small chick has a high surface area in relation to its volume but as it grows the ratio of surface to volume decreases—a simple mathematical relationship. Thus a chick's ability to reduce its loss of heat to the environment increases automatically as it grows, irrespective of any form of insulation; the more insulation there is, for example in the form of nest material, the lower will be the heat loss and therefore the energy intake, as food provided by the parents, required to allow for this heat loss. When the contour feathers break out of their sheaths they give the bird its own insulation and its ability to completely regulate its own temperature, as shown in Fig. 7 4. Let us look further at this development.

At hatching the 6-g chick is devoid of feathers, save for a little down on the back, and its eyelids are closed. It is capable of relatively little movement, except that when the nest is disturbed it is able to raise its head and open its bill wide, revealing a bright orange interior. This bright colour is presumably a stimulus to the adults to feed the chick, as has been shown in other species. The chick is able to maintain this begging posture for only a few seconds, after which it collapses back into the nest cup.

On the second day the main change that has occurred is an approximate doubling in size and an increase in strength, so that the upright begging posture, accompanied by faint calls, can be held for longer. The chicks are also more mobile: they can move

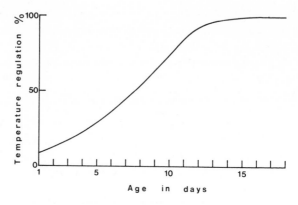

Fig. 7.4. Development of the ability of Starling chicks to regulate their own body temperatures (Redrawn from Ricklefs 1979*b*).

around the nest cup using their legs and wings. The two parts of the bird that are concerned with feeding, the bill and the belly, are disproportionately large. There are two large tufts of down on the sides of the crown, and short hair-like feathers project from the places where the flight and tail feathers will eventually emerge: the function of these is unknown. Increase in size continues rapidly over the next few days, and on the third and fourth days rows of black spots, representing the developing feather sheaths, become visible in well defined tracts, particularly on the back but also where the primaries, secondaries and tail feathers will grow.

The appearance of black spotting continues as tracts of feather follicles develop and extend on other regions of the body but it is not until the sixth day that feather sheaths begin to emerge through the skin, mainly on the sides of the breast and on the rump. Also at this time a few body feathers appear between the main tracts.

The main event on the seventh day is the opening of the eyes (this occasionally happens on the sixth day but may be delayed until the eighth). According to Kessel (1957) the opening of the eyes is marked by a change in the behaviour of the chicks: before the eyes opened chicks responded to a disturbance of the nest by stretching up and begging, while when the eyes had opened, nest disturbance led to the chicks crouching silently in the nest cup. This change in behaviour certainly does occur around the seventh day (except that very hungry chicks will continue to beg when the nest is disturbed) but whether there is a direct relationship with the opening of the eyes is not known. At this stage the chicks may be able to rely on sight for distinguishing their parents from predators or human intruders but the parent's voice may also play a part in their recognition. When the eyes open, however, there is no doubt that the now very mobile chicks can rapidly find their way back into the nest cup if they are lifted out and placed on the edge; previously their movements did not seem to be orientated towards the cup.

From the seventh day onwards feather tips begin to emerge from the shafts or, in some cases, directly from the skin. By the tenth day the chick begins to take on a grey-brown rather than pink appearance as the growing feathers cover the skin and in addition, the flight and tail feathers (remiges and rectrices respectively) break out of their sheaths. Plumage development is now rapid with new feathers emerging and those that have emerged growing quickly. The head is the last region of the chick to become feathered but by the time it is 14 days old the young bird is well covered. Although the flight feathers and tail are still comparitively short the bird becomes much more active and it begins exercising its wings within the nest hole. If it can reach the entrance the chick will look out of the hole: this may be important in enabling the young bird to recognize some features of the surroundings of the nest site. I have also seen 15-day-old chicks catching and eating flies that settle on the side of the nest box, showing that they have already attained a high level of co-ordination. At this age the chicks have stopped increasing in weight (Fig. 7.1) and their body insulation is sufficient to enable them to regulate their own body temperatures (Fig. 7.4), so that the main uses of food at this stage are for activity and feather development in addition, of course, to basal metabolism. These requirements continue until the chicks fledge, which is usually on the twenty-first day. Chicks can, in fact, fly before they are 21-days old and some will fly out of a nest box, when disturbed, from the seventeenth or eighteenth days onward; those that leave the nest prematurely stand little chance of surviving and to avoid this source of mortality it is wise to stop visiting nests when the chicks are 18 days old.

Variations in growth rates

The pattern of increase in weight, shown by the solid line in Fig. 7.1. for Starlings at Worplesdon in 1977, was similar to the growth curves for first-brood chicks found in 1975 and 1976, the only other two years that growth was measured daily in our studies. The dashed line in Fig. 7.1, representing the growth curve for second-brood chicks, shows that growth in weight of Starlings is variable rather than constant, and that in 1977 both the rate of growth and the maximum weight attained were lower in second than in first broods. This poorer attainment of late brood chicks, in terms of their rate of growth and fledging weight, is typical of most years at Worplesdon (Table 7.1) and was also found by Kessel (1957) in New York, and by Ricklefs and Peters (1979) in Pennsylvania. In Dunnet's (1955) study in Aberdeenshire, however, no significant difference was apparent in these parameters of first- and second-brood chicks. In general, though, second-brood chicks do tend to grow slower and fledge at a lower weight than chicks which hatch from eggs laid earlier in the year, indicating that the date on which chicks hatch during the season imposes constraints on their growth.

Table 7.1. The mean weight ($\pm$ 1 s.e.) of 18-day-old nestlings at Worplesdon in different years in first and second broods

Year	First	Second
1975	77.4 $\pm$ 1.1 (81) [1]	69.8 $\pm$ 1.6 (7)
1976	74.8 $\pm$ 0.7 (88)	64.7 $\pm$ 1.5 (28)
1977	79.2 $\pm$ 7.7 (85)	59.4 $\pm$ 2.4 (12)
1978	69.6 $\pm$ 1.0 (34)	—
1979	78.7 $\pm$ 1.2 (30)	—
1980	68.7 $\pm$ 1.0 (48)	74.7 $\pm$ 1.7 (2)
1981	76.3 $\pm$ 0.6 (64)	66.7 $\pm$ 2.6 (15)

[1] Figures in parentheses represent the number of chicks weighed.

Time during the season is only one of several factors that can affect growth, and although I have said that at Worplesdon the growth curves for 1975, 1976, and 1977 were similar, the weights attained differed significantly between some years (Table 7.1), and Ricklefs and Peters (1979) also found annual differences in the growth of Starling nestlings in Pennsylvania. These authors compared the weights of chicks after their growth curves had levelled off (see Fig. 7.1) and also measured growth rate while the growth curves were still ascending, and found statistically significant differences in these parameters in some, but not all, years. These differences applied to both first and second broods, confirming that annual differences in growth do occur.

Variations in growth between years and between first and second broods within a year presumably reflect alterations in various environmental conditions that will be discussed shortly, but there are even variations in growth rate and fledging weight within each brood. For example, these growth variables may differ according to the order in which the chicks hatch, as our Worplesdon data show, with the last chick to hatch in a clutch tending to grow more slowly and with greater weight fluctuations than those that hatch earlier. Although these differences are not statistically significant we shall see later that the last chick to hatch tends to stand a much lower chance of surviving to fledging than earlier ones, and the lower growth rate of the last to hatch may represent a real difference.

Differences are also found when we examine growth in relation to the number of chicks in a brood. Lack (1948), Dunnet (1955), and Kessel (1957) found that chicks from larger broods tended to attain lower weights than those from smaller broods, though the differences were not statistically significant. With the exception of 1979, our data from Surrey do not follow this pattern and in most years it is difficult to detect any trends (Table 7.2). Delvingt (1962*a*) and Westerterp (1973) suggested that the effect of brood size on growth rate would only be apparent under unfavourable conditions. In Surrey, both 1978 and 1979 were characterized by a late start to egg-laying and an absence of second broods (Fig. 6.1), features that we might expect to be characteristics of 'poor' years. In 1978 there was no trend in fledging weight with respect to brood size but weights were generally low, while in 1979 an inverse relationship between brood size and fledging weight was apparent but weights were unusually high. Even the second broods, which from their smaller clutch sizes and low success (see below) appear to be laid when conditions are much poorer, showed no relation between brood size and fledging weight (Table 7.2). However, other factors may intervene to complicate the relationships between brood size and chick growth in the later (intermediate and second) broods, for the parents of these may be younger and less experienced and we have seen (Chapter 6) that males may reduce their contribution to later clutches, especially in polygynous relationships. Clearly, this relationship between the number of chicks and their growth requires further investigation.

Table 7.2. The mean weights (± 1 s.e.) of 18-day-old chicks at Worplesdon in different brood sizes

	Brood size					
	1	2	3	4	5	6
First broods						
1975	76.7 ± 6.1 (3)[1]	71.8 ± 5.0 (8)	81.0 ± 2.0 (21)	75.5 ± 1.5 (32)	70.0 ± 2.1 (5)	83.2 ± 2.0 (12)
1976	80.0 ± 3.2 (3)	72.2 ± 2.6 (4)	75.6 ± 1.0 (36)	73.6 ± 1.1 (40)	75.0 ± 1.6 (5)	
1977	63.0 (1)	73.8 ± 2.8 (6)	75.1 ± 1.4 (12)	71.1 ± 0.9 (32)	70.4 ± 1.0 (35)	
1978			70.3 ± 1.6 (12)	66.5 ± 1.8 (12)	73.0 ± 1.4 (10)	
1979		81.4 ± 1.3 (4)		80.1 ± 1.8 (15)	74.9 ± 1.5 (10)	
1980		67.5 ± 2.6 (6)	70.4 ± 1.9 (14)	68.3 ± 1.3 (28)		
1981		79.7 ± 1.0 (12)	77.4 ± 1.2 (18)	72.2 ± 1.3 (8)	75.9 ± 1.2 (20)	72.7 ± 0.6 (6)
Second broods						
1975	70.0 (1)	69.7 ± 1.9 (6)				
1976	59.2 ± 3.2 (2)	58.9 ± 2.5 (8)	68.4 ± 1.5 (18)			
1977	57.0 ± 2.5 (7)	71.5 ± 5.5 (2)	60.3 ± 1.8 (3)			
1981		60.1 ± 5.2 (6)	71.2 ± 1.4 (9)			

[1] Figures in parentheses represent the number of chicks weighed.

A further possible source of variation in growth of the nestlings is geographical, although comparisons between studies in different parts of the Starling's range are rendered difficult by variations in sample sizes and brood sizes and the number of years over which growth was studied: the relevance of this is clearly seen from the Surrey study (Table 7.2) where significant annual differences in growth were presumably related ultimately to weather. Westerterp (1973) found that the growth curves of his Starlings in Holland were flatter than those of Kluyver (1933) in Holland and of Hudec and Folk (1961) in Czechoslovakia, and Westerterp interpreted his birds' poorer growth as being due to food shortage. Ricklefs and Peters (1979) found that Starlings in Czechoslovakia, Pennsylvania, and British Columbia achieved lower weights than those in Scotland and New York, while the rate of chick growth was higher in North America than in Europe. The factors that lead to these geographical variations in growth, and what they mean in terms of the subsequent survival of the fledglings, are unknown.

CHICK MORTALITY

It is important to realize that the growth rates that we have so far considered have been those of chicks that survived to fledging, but many chicks die in the nest. Most deaths occur during the first few days after hatching (e.g. Korpimäki 1978) and many of these early deaths are of 'runt' chicks, i.e. those that hatch some time after the main batch of hatchings in the clutch. These chicks are rarely able to compete with the earlier hatched nestlings which have already been fed and begun growing, so that the runts grow little, if at all, and die after a few days. Lack (1968 and in other papers) considered that the delayed hatching of one egg, and the consequent smaller size of the last chick, was an adaptation to unpredictable food sources. In good years there would be sufficient food to satisfy the appetites of the larger, stronger chicks and also enough for the runt, so that it too would survive and possibly even catch up with its siblings. In less good years, however, the runt would die after a few days, permitting all of the remaining chicks to grow at a 'normal' rate; the alternative would be for the parents to attempt to feed the entire larger brood in which each chick would have to make a sacrifice in terms of growth rate and final weight attainment.

This lower growth rate of chicks that die is apparent in Fig. 7.5, which also shows that after these early deaths the growth rate of

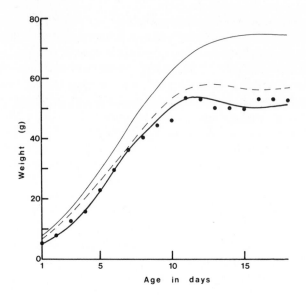

Fig. 7.5. The weights of first-brood chicks that died before fledging at Worplesdon, 1977. Growth rates of first- (———) and second- (- - - -) brood chicks that survived are shown for comparison.

chicks that subsequently died before fledging increased to almost the same rate at which successful second brood chicks grew. After 10 days, however, the growth of chicks that did not fledge again fell below that of second-brood chicks. These poorer growth rates of chicks that fail to fledge are largely the result of a loss in weight for a few days before death; Ricklefs and Peters (1979) showed that these birds also achieved lower rates of wing growth than did those that fledged successfully. This strongly suggests that starvation is the principal cause of death of nestlings and further evidence of this is given below. However, little is known about disease in nestling Starlings and this, and perhaps other factors, may also contribute to the slower growth of some second-brood chicks.

PARENTAL CARE

The maintenance of the growth rates that have been described and the successful fledging of the chicks is dependant upon adequate parental care. This takes several forms involving brooding, feeding, nest repair, and nest sanitation.

During incubation the female plays the major role and she continues to do so when the young are brooded. During the first few days of life the nestlings lose heat rapidly if left unattended and they are therefore brooded for varying periods during the day and for all of the night. Brooding is done mainly (Kessel 1957 and our own observations) or only (Kluyver 1933) by the female. Even when not brooding at night, the female sleeps in the nest cavity, usually on the edge of the nest, until the chicks are seven to nine days old; at this age brooding during the day also usually stops.

The male, on account of his poorly developed brood patch, is presumably less efficient at keeping the chicks warm than the female. He has no recognizable morphological restrictions on his ability to feed the young, but his role in this nevertheless varies from nest to nest. A female can, in fact, rear her nestlings alone and females occasionally do this if their mates die or desert, but Verheyen (1980) found that in cases like this nestling mortality was higher than when the male assisted with parental care. The second females of polygamous males are also committed to feeding their chicks alone and when these females are, in addition, young and inexperienced, their breeding success is low (Merkel 1980).

Our studies at Worplesdon have shown that, on average, 70 per cent of visits to the nest with food are by the female, while Tinbergen (1981), in Holland, found that the provision of food for the nestlings was shared approximately equally by the sexes. Even where the female makes the greater number of feeding visits, this need not indicate that she brings more food for the chicks since the harder-working female may have to be less selective in her choice of food than the male. This possibility requires investigation.

Where the rate of bringing food to the nest has been measured by automatic recording, using a camera and flash to photograph the entering bird's bill and food items, the sexes of the provisioning birds have not been distinguished. These studies have nevertheless shown that rates of feeding the chicks are subject to variation due to a number of factors.

Dunnet (1955) found that the rate of bringing food to the nest varied considerably during the day, with the highest rates of about 20 visits per hour tending to occur between 04.00 and 10.00 in his Scottish study area. On some days there was also a smaller peak in the frequency of nest visits in the late afternoon, a feature also noted by Kessel (1957) in New York. The causes of these daily variations are not understood and several factors may be involved.

For example, Tinbergen and Drent (1980) found that the bringing of some prey items back to the nest was related to daily variations in the availability of these food items. Daily patterns of food provisioning could also be influenced by the requirements of the young or even of the adults. During incubation, parents spend less time on the nest on warm than on cold days and they tend to spend less time incubating in the middle of the day than in the morning and evening. This is presumably related to daily variations in temperature which will determine the rate at which uncovered eggs will lose heat. Loss of heat from chicks can be compensated for by increasing energy supply and the higher rates of feeding in the morning and evening may partly reflect the chicks' elevated energy demands at lower ambient temperatures. In the early morning the chicks could also simply be more hungry, after a night's fast, than at other times of day and by their more insistent begging they may stimulate their parents to bring more food. The adults themselves are subject to certain constraints, for in addition to feeding their offspring they must also feed themselves and undertake other essential activities such as preening. When Starlings are searching for food they tend to select large food items for the nestlings, but if they encounter small items the adults eat them themselves (Tinbergen 1981), as has also been found in certain tits (Royama 1966). It may not be possible for the parents, whose energy expenditure while feeding young is great, to subsist on these small items and parents may therefore have to devote an extended period of foraging to satisfy their own food requirements, preferably when the chicks' own demands are minimal. All of the above factors could contribute to the daily variations in the rate of feeding, but there is further variation on a longer-term scale, related to the age of the chicks.

We have already seen that chicks undergo several changes during growth. It is axiomatic that they become bigger, both in body proportions and in weight, though the main phase of development of different parts of the body occurs at different times in the growth period. This suggests that the chicks' food requirements will vary during growth and in Chapter 9 we shall see that this can involve age-related dietary changes. This requires associated changes in the parents' selection of food items, about which little is known in this context, but the rate of food delivery has been studied in relation to the age of the nestlings. Dunnet (1955) found that the amount of food required daily by a chick increased up to the tenth day and then levelled off. Similar results have been obtained by Westerterp (1973) and Tinbergen (1981), both of whom recorded a rapid increase in the number of parental visits to the nest during the first 10 days, followed by a levelling off at around 300 visits per day until about the fifteenth day, after which the rate fell. The weight of food brought at each visit also rose over the first 10 days, after which it too levelled off but did not decline towards fledging time. The result of these changes in rate of parental visiting and in quantity of food brought at each visit was that the total amount of food delivered each day increased from about 40 g on the first day to around 200 g on the tenth, declining after the fifteenth day to about 150 g at fledging time (Tinbergen 1981). Clearly, parent Starlings adjust their foraging efforts according to the demand of their young but there must be a limit on the abilities of parents to satisfy the demands should they become excessive.

That this is true is demonstrated when the amount of food brought daily is compared in broods of different sizes. Tinbergen (1981) computed an index of the energy delivered to each chick per day for chicks between 10 and 15 days old, when the amount of food brought by the parents reached its maximum. This energy index decreased linearly from 300 units per chick in broods of two, to 200 units per chick in broods of nine. This reduction in the amount of food brought to chicks in larger broods parallels the reduced weights attained by chicks in larger broods (Lack 1948; Dunnet 1955; Kessel 1957; Tinbergen 1981).

Parents are capable of increasing their efforts, however, for each chick in a brood of six receives considerably more than half of the food given to a chick in a brood of three. In experimental modifications of brood size, by adding or removing chicks, Tinbergen (1981) found that when brood size was increased from two to nine chicks the amount of time spent foraging by the female parent increased from 9.57 h to 10.81 h each day; the amount of time she spent flying more than doubled, rising from 1.56 to 3.48 hours. These increases were made possible by sacrificing time that would otherwise have been devoted to preening and other non-feeding activities but other changes in the female's behaviour were also apparent, for when feeding a large brood she fed closer to the nest and was less selective in the kinds of food that she brought back. Tinbergen and Drent (1980) further showed, by presenting the female Starling with satiated young and then replacing them with undernourished chicks, that the changes in female foraging behaviour were mediated by the state of hunger of the chicks. Presumably the more insistent begging of hungry chicks stimulated the mother to increase her rate of delivery of food, even though this could mean a fall in the quality of the food.

Even within a brood of a particular size parental behaviour is influenced by the hunger of the chicks. Visits to the nest by the parents are not always made at regular intervals and at Worplesdon we have found that after a long gap between feeds, the next parent to visit the nest makes a rapid sequence of visits with food; again, this is presumably in response to the begging of the hungry chicks.

The final factor to be mentioned in this discussion of the rate of feeding the chicks is weather. The depressant effect of rain on this feeding rate was demonstrated by Westerterp (1973) and had previously been suggested by Svensson (1964) and Bogucki (1972). Westerterp thought that persistent rain would make it difficult for the adults to find food but the reason for this is not clear. Some food items, e.g. earthworms, might be rendered more readily available during rain while the effect on flying insects, which are less often taken, could be the reverse. Perhaps the effect of persistent rain is directly on the parents: the frequent entrances into the nest hole must lead to considerable feather abrasion which in turn will reduce the waterproofing and insulating properties of these feathers. This might lead the parents to be reluctant to feed in the open in heavy or prolonged rain.

Further aspects of the feeding of the young, particularly with respect to species composition of the prey, will be considered in Chapter 8 but the estimates of rate of parental feeding and weight of food brought given above can be used to provide a rough idea of the amount of food required for the successful rearing of an early brood of Starlings, and this amounts to around 2.5 kg. The most recent estimate of the Starling population of the British Isles is between four and seven million pairs (Sharrock 1976). By extrapolation, we can calculate that the annual food requirement for the rearing of the chicks of these British Starlings is something over 10 000 tonnes, most of this consisting of invertebrates! This very rough figure allows for a failure of about 20 per cent of clutches but it does not take into account the food requirement of the parents, which must itself be considerable. At Worplesdon parents travel up to 500 m from the nest for food but journeys usually average about 100 m, i.e. a round trip of 200 m. With around 7 000 feeding trips per fledging period (Kluyver 1933) the parents must fly about 1 400 km while feeding a brood, indicating a high energy demand of their own. Nor does the above estimate of 10 000 tonnes include the food consumed by second broods, the parental feeding of which has been poorly studied: such studies would be valuable since they could show how parent Starlings respond, in terms of their rate of provisioning of the chicks and their selection of food items for the young, to presumed poorer feeding conditions.

Nest repair and sanitation

The remaining aspects of parental care of the young, nest repair and sanitation, will be considered together since they probably serve the same function. Nest repair has not, in fact, been studied in any detail but incidental observations reveal that nest material, soiled by faeces, is removed and replaced by clean material. Whether the clean nest lining is periodically renewed does not appear to be known.

Nest sanitation involves the removal of faeces by the parents with the apparent aim of maintaining the nest free from fouling. This has often been implicitly assumed to prevent the build-up of disease or parasitic organisms but in his study of Starlings, Kluyver (1933) attributed to nest sanitation a function associated with temperature regulation of the chicks. This explanation was also held by Tinbergen (1981), both authors considering that in a badly fouled nest the chicks would become wet and so be susceptible to chilling due to the loss of their own body insulation.

The evolution of nest sanitation behaviour by the parents has been paralleled by developments in the behaviour and physiology of the chick, for rapid removal of faeces from the nest is facilitated by the occurrence of defaecation immediately after a feed and, at least in the early days, by the enclosure of the faecal material within a gelatinous capsule. These two features ensure that the chick defaecates while the parent is present and that the faeces (or faecal sac) are of such a consistency that they can readily be removed by the parent. Both parental and chick behaviour varies however, with respect to nest sanitation, during the growth of the young.

At first, the young extrude their droppings immediately after feeding but even when there is some delay the parent waits in order that the faecal sac can be removed. This is normally carried out of the nest by the parent and dropped a few metres away from the nest hole, but sometimes the parent bird may swallow the sac, as happens in some thrushes when two sacs are deposited at the same time (Thomson 1964). At this stage the nest material remains clean and dry, and our studies at Worplesdon indicate that this usually remains true up to the tenth or twelfth day. After this time, the parents appear to become less assiduous at removing the faeces which, therefore, begin to accumulate, initially around the rim of the nest but later sometimes in the nest cup as well. This build-up of faeces in the nest seems to result from a decline in the parental determination to remove the droppings, an increasing tendency for the chicks to defaecate in the absence of a parent, and the production of faeces that are less cohesive than when enclosed in a gelatinous capsule. The onset of these changes, occurring generally after the tenth day, coincides with the increasing ability of the chicks to regulate their body temperatures through the development of body feathers and their increasing body size (Fig. 7.4). The coincidence of these events supports the suggestion by Tinbergen (1981) that nest sanitation is related to temperature regulation rather than to the prevention of disease or parastic infestation. While Tinbergen thought that the main effect of poor sanitation lay in the wetting of the chicks' feathers, thereby facilitating greater heat loss, less extreme fouling of the nest could have greater significance for smaller, unfeathered young through the removal of the insulation properties of the nest material itself. In some preliminary experiments, I have found that nest material contaminated with faeces conducts heat away from the nest cup more readily than does dry material; the significance of nest sanitation could therefore be of greater importance to unfeathered young than to larger chicks that are developing plumage.

The failure of parents to remove droppings is not due entirely to the lessening of their response to increasing contamination of the nest. Kluyver (1933) demonstrated that the adults' ability to maintain their sanitary activities was related to the consistency of their chicks' droppings, with wet droppings being harder to remove adequately than dry faeces. To a limited extent, parents may be able to compensate for the occurrence of wet droppings by removing and replacing contaminated nest material rather than taking away the excreta alone, but the significant discovery by Kluyver was that the wetness of the faeces was related to the diet of the chicks, those chicks receiving a high proportion of leatherjackets producing more watery droppings than nestlings fed on a wider variety of invertebrates. This was confirmed by Tinbergen (1981) but the reason for it is not understood.

In our studies at Worplesdon, where second broods are more frequent than in Holland, it is readily apparent that these later broods suffer much more severely from fouled, wet nests (even as early as seven days after hatching) than do first broods. This is due partly to some of the second nests being built on the top of already damp early nests but an inadequacy of the diets of second broods may also be a contributory factor.

FLEDGING SUCCESS

The growth of chicks and the factors that enable them to fledge successfully have been discussed, and it is now time to consider the extent to which chicks are successful in leaving the nest. In Chapter 6 I pointed out that estimates of hatching success must be interpreted with caution because disturbance by observers undoubtedly increased egg losses. Similar reservations must be held concerning fledging success, i.e. the proportion of chicks that hatch that ultimately produce flying young. I have compared the success of chicks that were weighed daily with that of chicks that were weighed on only their twelfth and eighteenth days and found no significant differences in their weights at fledging or in their fledging success. Peter Evans (1980) and I have, independently, also compared the growth and success of chicks whose parents were both ringed and wing-tagged with those of parents only bearing rings and again we found no significant differences, suggesting that the effect of observer disturbance on fledging success is far less critical than it is on hatching success. (Wing-tagging of adults does, however, cause an increase in the incidence of nest desertion.) When examining data on breeding success we must, nevertheless, recognize that different workers employ different kinds of nest box, different schedules of visiting nests, and different handling techniques which may have subtle effects on the success of the nests.

Two ways of assessing breeding success are used. One measures the number of eggs that are laid in a study colony each year, the number of chicks that hatch, and the number that subsequently fledge. This requires almost continuous monitoring of the nests throughout the breeding season and is likely, therefore, to introduce some adverse effects of human disturbance. The second measure of nesting success is more simple and only requires knowledge of the number of nests in which eggs are laid and the number of these that produce at least one fledgling. Using this form of assessment, human disturbance is kept to a minimum, but the two techniques do measure different parameters of breeding success.

Tables 7.3 and 7.4 show the results of studies in various parts of Europe and North America. Let us first consider the simpler of the two measurements. At Worplesdon (Table 7.3) the proportion of nests that produced at least one hatchling varied considerably from year to year. It must be noted, however, that from 1977 to 1980 inclusive we were catching adults on their nests and, in addition to ringing them, we put identification tags on their wings: this procedure caused some birds to desert their nests. Desertion was most pronounced in 1978 and 1979, years which we have already seen appeared to be 'bad' for Starlings, since they bred late and did not lay second broods. If we omit these years of wing-tagging, we see that in the absence of this excessive disturbance the proportion of first-brood nests that survived to hatching was 83 per cent in 1975 and 1981, and 100 per cent in 1976. These values are similar to those obtained by others workers: Collins and de Vos (1966), Dehaven and Guarino (1970), and Kessel (1957) all found the

Table 7.3 Success of early and late nests at Worplesdon, Surrey. A nest was considered to have hatched successfully if at least one egg hatched, and to have fledged successfully if at least one chick fledged

Nests		No. of hatched young	No. (and %) that produced fledged young	No. (and %) that produced young	% of those which hatched young that produced fledged young
1975	Early	29	24 (83)	22 (76)	92
	Late	12	9 (75)	6 (50)	67
1976	Early	30	30 (100)	28 (93)	93
	Late	18	16 (89)	13 (72)	81
1977	Early	32	25 (78)	20 (62)	80
	Late	19	17 (89)	8 (42)	47
1978	Early	27	11 (41)	9 (33)	82
1979	Early	25	10 (40)	9 (36)	90
1980	Early	27	17 (63)	15 (56)	88
	Late	6	4 (67)	1 (17)	25
1981	Early	23	19 (83)	19 (83)	100
	Late	19	10 (59)	7 (37)	70

Table 7.4 Breeding success of Starlings in terms of the proportions of chicks and of eggs that survive to produce fledglings

Location	Clutch	% of chicks that fledge	Overall success: % of eggs that produce fledglings	Source
Europe				
Finland	Early	29–55	24–44	Tenovuo and Lemmetyinen 1970
	Early	74–98	57–95	Korpimäki 1978
Poland	Early	80–89	—	Gromadzki 1980
Scotland	Early	93–96	79–85	Dunnet 1955
	Late	83–89	64–78	
	Early	90–92	74–84	Anderson 1961
	Late	95–96	74–85	
England	Early	82–86	67–81	Feare (unpublished)
	Late	38–67	21–45	
Holland	Early	—	77	Lack 1948
	Late	—	70	
North America				
Ontario	Early	89–99	78–91	Collins and De Vos 1966
	Late	88–94	67–76	
New York	Early	68–94	75–84	Kessel 1957
	Late	62–96	63–75	
Pennsylvania	Early	64–79	—	Ricklefs and Peters 1979
	Late	18–59	—	
Colorado	Early	—	80	DeHaven and Guarino 1970
	Late	—	62	
Arizona	Early	—	57	Royall 1966
	Late	—	45	

success of first-brood nests to range from 73 to 91 per cent. In the Worplesdon studies we have found that birds incubating second clutches are much more prone to desert after disturbance than those with first clutches, and from 1977 onwards the low successes recorded in Table 7.3 reflect our attempts to catch birds with second broods in order to record mate changes (Feare and Burnham 1978). The figures for 1975 and 1976, which were not subject to this disturbance, are again within the ranges recorded by the three studies mentioned above, namely 41 to 80 per cent.

These figures demonstrate two important aspects of Starling breeding biology. First, the second brood, which we have already seen tends to be smaller and to fledge at a lower weight than the first brood, is generally less successful than early nesting attempts. Second, Starlings' nests are typically highly successful. Newton (1972) analysed the British Trust for Ornithology's nest record cards for the Chaffinch *Fringilla coelebs* and found that, over the whole breeding season, nest success ranged from 18 to 60 per cent in different years. In Blackbirds *Turdus merula*, Snow (1958) found that in garden habitats around 50% of nests produced fledged young but in woodland, which presumably has a more natural array of predators, success was as low as 14 per cent. Newton (1972) also recorded high nest losses to predators in several other finches, especially early in the season. The main difference between the nests of Starlings and those of the thrushes and finches is, of course, that while Starlings nest in holes which confer some protection, the open, cup-shaped nests of the other species are exposed to a variety of predators and also to the weather. If we compare the success of Starling nests with those of other hole-nesting species, such as the tits (Perrins 1979) we find closely similar values. We saw earlier that the hole-nesting birds also lay larger clutches than birds that build open cup nests. Thus the rearing of young in cavities is an important feature that enables Starlings to successfully rear more chicks than many of the other familiar birds (though some of them may compensate by attempting to nest more than twice in a season).

The general conclusions drawn above from the success or otherwise of nests are supported by the analysis of the number of eggs that survive to produce fledglings (Table 7.4). First broods are highly successful and much more so than second broods; in most years and in most places over 70 per cent of the eggs laid produce a chick that leaves the nest successfully. Again, this figure is high in comparison with other species that lay eggs in exposed cup-shaped nests. Murton (1965) recorded 44 per cent of Woodpigeon *Columba palumbus* eggs producing fledglings in August, but lower proportions in other months, and in Song Thrushes in Britain 55 per cent of eggs were successful (Silva 1949).

In Chapter 6 I described the Starlings' hatching success (Table 6.3) as high, but it seems, nevertheless, that the egg phase of the breeding attempt is more susceptible to loss since the first column in Table 7.4 shows that, in most places, over 90 per cent of first-brood chicks that hatch eventually leave the nest as fledglings. Predation and the direct influence of weather (e.g. rain and cold) play little part in this low nestling mortality, most of which is attributed to starvation, especially of the last chick to hatch in a clutch. Similarly, starvation is the major cause of the higher mortality of second-brood nestlings, but here the chicks in entire clutches may die progressively as the parents fail to provide sufficient food.

Even though starvation is the main mortality factor, there are records of Starling chicks dying from the effects of inclement weather, predation, and other causes. The effects of extremes of temperature and high rainfall may well be exaggerated where the studies have been conducted in nest boxes, since these nest sites tend to be more exposed than nest cavities in trees, cliffs, or buildings; nest boxes have three sides, a top and a bottom through which heat can be gained or lost. The list of predators that are known to have taken Starling broods is small. In my own studies a Weasel *Mustela nivalis* has been responsible for the loss of one brood and a Grey Squirrel *Sciurus carolinensis* may have taken another. Dunnet (1955) recorded a domestic cat taking nestlings as they looked out of the entrance of a nest box. Records of broods being taken by birds are scarce but the woodpeckers appear to constitute the group of predators most frequently involved. In Europe, Great Spotted Woodpeckers *Dendrocopus major* and in North America Gila *Centurus uropygialis* and Red-headed Woodpeckers *Melanerpes erythrocephalus* have been reported killing Starling nestlings. It also seems likely that snakes, which occasionally predate hole-nesting birds, will take Starlings but I have found no specific references. In South Africa and Australasia a different complex of potential nestling predators is doubtless available but their activities, with respect to Starlings, do not appear to have been reported in the literature.

A further potential source of mortality, or at least loss of condition, for nestlings is the presence of parasites in the nests. In Britain, two species of parasites can be extremely numerous in nests, especially in second broods, and the spotted eggs that appeared in some nests (Feare and Constantine 1979) were found to be due to spots of blood emanating from bites on the incubation patches of parents. The insects involved are the Hen Flea *Ceratophyllus gallinae* and a fly *Carnus haemapterus*. The former lives in nests and requires a blood meal before laying eggs in spring and early summer. Adults can emerge from the nests, in the absence of birds, over a long period and they sometimes leave in swarms (Rothschild and Clay 1952) in search of future hosts. Only the adult *Carnus haemapterus* feeds on the birds' blood, for the larvae are saprophagous, feeding on decaying matter in the Starling's nest material. When the adult fly emerges it is winged and disperses, but on finding a host's nest it sheds its wings and then feeds. The effects of these parasites on Starlings are not known but the heavy infestations in some second-brood nests may affect the growth of already undernourished chicks. Rothschild and Clay (1952) stated that the continuous scratching of domestic poultry heavily infested with *Ceratophyllus gallinae* led to poor health and reduced egg yields. In New Zealand Starling nestlings are infested with a blood-sucking mite *Ornithonyssus bursa*. Powlesland (1977) found that, although a heavy infestation of 50 000 mites in a nest box containing four chicks could take 3.5 per cent by weight of the blood of each nestling daily, this had no obvious effects on the growth or well-being of the birds.

At fledging, Starlings lose the safety of their nest holes and are suddenly thrust into an environment where their parents can offer only limited protection. The youngsters have only a few days in which they must learn how to feed themselves and begin to recognize what constitutes potential danger. This brief period when they gain independence from their parents is perhaps the most hazardous time of a Starling's life and it is here that the young sustain a heavy mortality through starvation, predation, and even accident, such as falling into ponds, hitting windows, or becoming road casualties. The gaining of parental independence in Starlings is the more remarkable in that it occurs so rapidly, in first brood chicks usually within 10–12 days. For comparison, young Spotted Flycatchers *Muscicapa striata* do not gain independence until around 18 days old (Davies 1976), young Rooks remain with their parents for about two months (Coombs 1978), some terns take at least six months (Ashmole and Tovar 1968, Feare 1975), while some larger birds take even longer to attain independence.

The rapidity with which Starlings learn to fend for themselves and the high mortality incurred render this period one of the most important for students of the species' population dynamics. It is, unfortunately, one of the most difficult periods of the bird's life to observe since the juveniles spend so much of their time out of sight in trees. In fact the attainment of independence has been studied in very few species but presumably the tendencies for chicks to feed themselves and for the parents to stop feeding them are gradual processes, as Davies (1976) found in Spotted Flycatchers. Recently-fledged Starlings certainly spend most of their time sitting in trees while the parents collect food, usually within 200 m of the fledglings. The chicks recognize their parents and begin begging noisily while the adult is still some distance away, but they remain on their selected perches and the adult repeatedly feeds them there. After a few days, however, the juveniles spend more time following their parents round the feeding grounds and fly or run to the adult whenever they see it obtain a food item. They approach with begging calls and wings fluttering and the parent either feeds the chick or eats the food item itself: the basis for this decision is not known although the size and quality of the food will doubtless be important factors. Even during the chicks' early days, when they sit and wait for food, they explore the branches around them and peck at various objects. At first, most seem to be rejected but the proportion that is swallowed increases as the birds develop and, when following parents in grass fields, juveniles make frequent exploratory pecks at the ground and increasingly these are followed by swallowing movements. This has not, however, been studied quantitatively in Starlings. Interestingly, P. G. H. Evans (personal communication) has found while catching adult and juvenile Starlings in feeding parties, that 90 per cent of the adults accompanying juveniles were females.

In juvenile birds the top of the skull has two soft translucent areas on each side of the mid-line. In Starlings, the hardening of these areas, by a process called ossification or pneumatization, occurs gradually over the first six to seven months of life, so that young Starlings become difficult to separate from birds older than one year, on their skull characteristics, by the late autumn or early winter. During the intervening period the skull is weaker than when fully ossified and, since the physical structure of a bird's skull is closely adapted to the feeding methods employed, young Starlings may be less proficient than adults at the open-bill probing that is characteristic of the family (Beecher 1978 and also see Chapter 1). Recently-fledged juveniles also have shorter bills than do adults, restricting the depth to which they can probe and the rapidity with which the mandible tips can be moved to catch agile prey, and juveniles are also presumably less proficient than adults at locating prey items. In other words, even after juveniles have become independent of their parents and are fully able to sustain themselves by their own feeding efforts, they may still be incapable of feeding in a fully adult way and therefore be restricted in their selection of feeding methods and consequently the habitats which they can exploit.

So far, breeding success has been considered in terms of the number of fledglings produced but breeding can only be regarded as totally successful if some of these fledglings survive to breed themselves. There have been no detailed or long-term studies of the rate of return to the colony of Starling fledglings: at Worplesdon we have, to date, found only 19 birds that were ringed as nestlings being subsequently recorded in the colony as breeding adults. The pattern of these returns does, however, raise an interesting question. As shown in Table 7.5, all but one of those returns were of birds produced in early clutches and the one exception originated in an intermediate clutch: although the sample is admittedly small, there have been no returns of second-brood chicks. Second-brood chicks have a low fledging success and are usually low in weight at fledging. If the post-fledging survival of second-brood juveniles is as poor as the data in Table 7.5 suggest, why do Worplesdon Starlings bother to lay second clutches? In some years they do not, and in years when second

Table 7.5. The number of birds fledged in the Worplesdon colony in 1975–80 and the number of these that have been found breeding in the colony in 1976–81

	First	Intermediate	Second
No. of fledglings (18-day-old) ringed	366	63	49
No. found breeding	18	1	0
% found breeding	5.3	1.6	0.0

clutches are laid it seems that the parental effort involved in rearing a small number of chicks to fledging is barely worth-while. For the present we must simply assume that this effort is not wasted and that the small proportion of second brood juveniles that does eventually breed is sufficient to provide those parents that do rear them with a genetic advantage in future generations. More long-term studies of breeding in different parts of the species' range will be needed to confirm this assumption. In particular, it will be important to examine the post-fledging dispersal of the sexes and of different weight classes, for differences in their subsequent return will have critical implications with respect to the interpretation of the preliminary Worplesdon results presented in Table 7.5.

8 A TIME TO DIE

' . . . . . . for the purpose of illustrating the rate of increase we will presume that in 1921 there were 100 000 pairs of Starlings breeding in Great Britain (which is considerably under the actual figure), and that each pair reared three pairs of young, half of each sex, and that all lived together with their offspring. The progeny and parents in a single year would total 800 000. At the end of 1922 this number would have increased to 3 200 000, the addition in 1923 would make the total 12 800 000, while at the end of 1924 there would be over 51 000 000 birds.' So wrote W. E. Collinge (1924–7) in his assessment of the impact of British birds on agriculture. He concluded his remarks on the Starling with the emotive sentence 'In short, the Starling has become a plague in the land and a source of great natural loss.'

The most recent estimate of the number of breeding Starlings in Britain is between four and seven million pairs (Sharrock 1976) and Collinge's predicted rate of increase has clearly not occurred. When introduced into a new and yet adequate environment, however, Starlings can increase their numbers dramatically as Davis (1950) showed for the USA. Collinge's calculations omitted to take account of mortality, which we have already seen leads to a nestling production considerably below the 'three pairs' of young per nest cited above. Since we are not overrun by Starlings (some farmers might disagree!), Collinge's figures indicate that the mortality incurred by our Starling population each year must be very high. But we are not, thankfully, knee-deep in Starling corpses either and so in this chapter we must discuss how many Starlings die and from what do they die.

Although vast numbers of birds (and other animals) do die each year, the finding of a corpse is a rather unusual event. The scientist who wishes to measure mortality cannot, therefore, simply go around collecting bodies and say 'this number of birds has died this year.' We cannot even use the disappearance of ringed birds from our nestbox colony to indicate how many have died between breeding seasons because we are by no means certain that birds reared in a colony are going to return to that colony to breed, or that adults that cease to nest in a nestbox might not have found a 'natural' cavity in which to breed in preference to a box. Thus the study of mortality necessitates a vastly different approach from the study of breeding biology where direct observation is usually the most satisfactory technique.

The indirect approach used most frequently in mortality investigations involves the marking of birds with individually numbered leg rings. A proportion of the marked birds that die will be recovered and the relative numbers recovered at different ages can be used to calculate mortality and longevity. When recovered, the cause of death of at least some of the birds will be recorded and these data can be used to estimate the relative importance of different mortality factors. There are several obvious and widely appreciated limitations in using this 'mark–recapture' technique. The birds that are ringed must represent a random sample of the population and those that are recovered must constitute a random sample of those that die. These two conditions are probably rarely fully met. The proportion of birds ringed that are subsequently found dead is usually small and therefore sample sizes tend to be small—this leads to problems of statistical analysis. Many other problems could also be listed, but as long as the limitations are appreciated, the mark–recapture technique remains the best available for the estimation of mortality in most bird species.

The Starling is, in fact, a better subject for study in this respect than many other birds, since it is common and can be easily caught. As a result large numbers have been ringed since bird-ringing began early in this century. Under the British Trust for Ornithology's ringing scheme alone, by the end of 1979, 776 120 Starlings had been ringed (Spencer and Hudson 1980). Of these, 27 841 had been recovered, representing a recovery rate of about 3.6 per cent. British data were analysed up to 1957 by Coulson (1960), and similar analyses have been undertaken in other countries; the considerable volume of British recoveries that have accrued since 1957 still awaits complete analyses, although some preliminary results are presented below.

ESTIMATES OF MORTALITY

In studies of Coulson (1960) and Delvingt (1962b) the youngsters ringed in the nest and those ringed as fledged young are treated together. This unfortunately precludes the estimation of the supposedly high mortality that accompanies the attainment of independence. By comparing the proportions of juveniles in the recoveries each month, Coulson found, however, that juvenile mortality was higher during summer than later in the year. But the fall in the proportion of juveniles from 76 per cent in July, August, and September to 56 per cent subsequently may still underestimate the mortality associated with early life. Firstly, the critical period for fledglings is likely to occur in late May and June, when the majority fledge, which is a period not covered by Coulson's analysis. Secondly, while adults tend to remain close to their breeding areas in summer the juveniles range more widely and tend to inhabit areas more remote from human habitation, such as moorlands and coastal salt marshes. Birds that die here are much less likely to be recovered than those dying near towns, and thus the number of juveniles recovered along with adults may substantially underestimate the relative juvenile mortality.

No actual mortality *rate*, in terms of proportion of birds dying each month, can therefore be given for the immediate post-fledging stage, but mortality rates for the first year of life have been calculated (although the different behaviour and ranges of juveniles and adults mentioned above may again lead to an underestimation of first-year mortality).

The values obtained in various studies are given in Table 8.1, together with the annual mortality rate of birds after their first year for comparison. In all cases where first-year mortality has been differentiated from mortality later in life, the value for the former rate is the higher. In none of the studies, however, was the

Table 8.1. Annual mortality rates estimated from ring recoveries

Country	First year	Adult	Source
Britain	66	52	Lack and Schifferli 1948
Britain	56	53	Coulson 1960
France	60	50	Lebreton and Landry 1977
Belgium	66	54	Delvingt 1962*a*
Holland		50	Kluyver 1933
Switzerland	73	63	Lack and Schifferli 1948
Germany	73	64	Schneider 1972
Czechoslovakia	68	68	Beklova 1972
USA	60	50	Kessel 1957
USA		57	Fankhauser 1971
New Zealand		33	Flux and Flux 1981

difference statistically significant. Nevertheless, in view of the suspected underestimation of first-year mortality rates indicated above, I suspect that the differences are real, but more critical studies, especially on post-fledging survival, are needed to verify this.

The picture presented by Table 8.1 may well be an over-simplification, however, since Perdeck (1967a) has shown that different groups of birds passing through Holland have different mortality rates, as shown in Table 8.2. Furthermore, Perdeck found that in some of the groups first-year mortality was significantly higher than annual mortality later in life. The mortality rates of first-year birds increased the later they were caught and Perdeck related this to the ultimate wintering area of the birds that migrated through Holland. A high proportion of recoveries of those birds ringed in early autumn were from the British Isles, whereas later caught birds tended to winter on the Continent. Perdeck attributed the lower mortality of birds that wintered in Britain to the milder winter climate of this country, implying that high first-year mortalities of birds wintering on the Continent were due to food shortage resulting from colder winter weather.

The figures available suggest that, on average, 55 per cent of Starlings that are at least one year old will die each year, but Table 8.1 shows a range from 50 to 64 per cent for Europe and north America. Delvingt (1962b) pointed out that the values obtained for Germany and Switzerland were higher than those for Belgium and Britain, and suggested that annual mortality might increase towards the north and east of the geographical range. The northern and eastern populations are certainly more strongly migratory

Table 8.2 First year and subsequent annual mortalities (%) of Starlings caught and ringed as juveniles during different periods in winter in Holland (from Perdeck 1967a)

Date ringed	First year mortality	Adult mortality
1 Sept–23 Oct.	45.3	48.8
24 Oct–8 Nov.	59.9	47.7
9–30 Nov. [1]	66.2	53.7

The difference between first-year and adult mortality of birds ringed in the period 9–30 November is statistically significant than those in the south and west, which doubtless subjects the former to added mortality factors, but Delvingt's interpretation seems, nevertheless, premature. The estimates of mortality that we have are based on a variety of ringing schemes, on different sample sizes, and in different years and in view of all of the other biases that enter calculations of mortality from these mark–recapture data, this suggestion of geographical variation in annual mortality rates must be regarded as tenuous. Indeed, Coulson (1960), who specifically examined the mortality rates of British resident Starlings and immigrants from continental Europe that wintered in the British Isles, found no significant difference between them. Contrary to Delvingt, Coulson found that the group of countries with the lowest mortality rate, Poland, Finland, and the USSR, were the most northerly and easterly, but again the regional differences were not stastically significant. Nor did Coulson find any significant differences between the mortality rates of Starlings in different parts of the British Isles, suggesting that climatic, agricultural, and human population differences between regions within Britain have little influence on Starling mortality. This contrasts with Perdeck's (1967a) comparison between Britain and the Continent as a wintering area.

Coulson also examined the British data for annual variations in mortality. In the 12 years in which he regarded sample sizes as adequate (more than 100 ringed birds available at the beginning of the year), annual mortality ranged from 40 to 66 per cent. The factors responsible for this variation are not known: the only feature examined, the severity of winter in terms of snow and frost, showed no clear correlation with the mortality recorded over the year as a whole.

Preliminary results of an analysis of British Trust for Ornithology ringing returns indicate longer term changes in annual mortality rates of British Starlings (R. J. O'Connor, personal communication). Figures available so far show mortality rates of 41–66 per cent in different regions of Britain between 1920 and 1938, the average being around 50 per cent. Between 1940 and 1958, annual mortality was somewhat higher, ranging from 45 to 68 per cent and averaging around 55 per cent. Between 1960 and 1978, however, mortality has been much lower, from 33 to 49 per cent, in different areas and averaging about 36 per cent. These figures, especially the national averages (estimated by me from regional data supplied by the BTO), *are* preliminary but they do suggest long-term changes in mortality rate and, furthermore, that British Starlings may currently be experiencing particularly favourable conditions.

In New Zealand, Flux and Flux (1981) have also found a low mortality of about 33 per cent. This was based on less than 100 recoveries but in their nestbox study, in an admittedly unusual situation, they found an average of 72 per cent of marked birds returning to breed in successive years. This represents a maximum annual mortality in this study area of 28 per cent and Flux and Flux thought that this unusually low mortality might be due to the absence of severe winters; this is in accord with Perdeck's (1967a) conclusions for European birds but contrasts with Coulson's (1960) findings.

In America, Davis (1959) obtained samples of Starlings from roosts and noted that in these samples there were more males than females and that the relative proportions of both the sexes and ages changed during the year. These changes were attributed to a differential mortality of the sexes but the actual values obtained by Davis were exaggerated owing to the false assumption that both sexes bred in their first year. This criticism was raised by Coulson (1960) who was nevertheless able to infer a differential mortality of males and females from the ring recovery data and from the sex ratios of juvenile and adult Starlings in Britain.

It is well established that most Starling populations are biased in favour of males and Coulson quoted an average of 66 per cent males for European populations. This must be regarded as a very rough figure, however, since the methods of obtaining samples varied widely. In my own studies I have found that sex ratios differ at different feeding sites and recently my colleague, Ron Summers (personal communication), has found that the sex ratio differs in different parts of winter roosts. This renders an estimation of 'the' sex ratio of Starling population extremely difficult, but there is no doubt that in most places and at most times males outnumber females by almost two to one. In the first year, however, the admittedly scant data indicate a sex ratio that is closer to unity, and this 1:1 ratio persists until at least the first winter of life. To produce the almost 2:1, male:female ratio of the second year, therefore, more females than males must die between the first winter and the onset of year two which, in Coulson's study, began on 1 August of the year following birth. Using a change in sex ratio from 46 to 62.5 per cent males, and an average first-year mortality of 56 per cent, Coulson concluded that during their first year males must experience a mortality of only 39 per cent while that of females is 70 per cent. Coulson attributed this differential mortality to the fact that males generally do not breed in their first year whereas females do, and he considered that a greater vulnerability to predation led to the high female mortality, when these birds were breeding for the first time. This high mortality thus came towards the end of the females' first year of life and was quite independent of post-fledging mortality. Charman (1965) who based his observations on the change in sex ratio of roosting birds, concluded that the differential mortality occurred before the end of the winter and therefore the females died long before breeding. This finding relies on the assumption that the sampling of birds in roosts, by shooting, is random; recent work by R. W. Summers (personal communication) suggests that this may not be the case.

After the first year the mortality rates of male and female are similar. In Britain, Coulson (1960) found female mortality (49.9 per cent) to be slightly higher than that of males (46.3 per cent) but the difference was not statistically significant. Fankhauser (1971) found female mortality to be higher than the annual mortality of males in the United States but the difference was again small, while Suthers (1978) using smaller samples, found a greater difference in the mortality of the sexes.

Unfortunately, most Starlings are ringed as adults and therefore their exact age is unknown. This means that the sample of known age birds which is available for estimating annual mortality rates after the second year of life is small, and the mortality rates calculated from these small samples are consequently less reliable than those calculated for the first and second years of life. Kessel (1957) appreciated this shortcoming but claimed, nevertheless, that the annual mortality rate increased somewhat after the third year: the mortality rates for the first three years were based on 1179 ringed birds while the rates thereafter were determined from a sample of only 97 birds.

Beklova (1972), who again worked with small samples, claimed that in Czecholslovakia the annual mortality rate decreased from 68 per cent in the first year to only 14 per cent in the eleventh year, but increased thereafter. Beklova's initial sample consisted of 997 Starlings ringed as 'young', but the data on which the mortality rates after the third year were calculated were based on a sample of only 63 birds! Much larger samples are required before this suspected influence of senility on the mortality rate can be proven.

LONGEVITY

If about half of the Starlings die each year, how long can an individual be expected to live? With a reasonably constant annual mortality rate, the 'expectation of further life', as it is known in demographic terms, is also constant. The expectation of further life is the time that an individual at a particular age might be expected, on average, to survive and in those studies of Starlings where over 100 ringed birds have been at risk at the beginning of a year, this value falls between 1.0 and 1.5 years. In other words, the average life of a Starling can be expected to be between 12 and 18 months. Similarly a bird which has attained an age of one year can be expected to live a further 12–18 months. Thereafter, sample sizes in the studies that have so far been undertaken are too small to yield reliable results, and Beklova's (1972) calculation of an expectation of further life of 3.7 years for an eight-year-old Starling, based on a sample of nine birds, must be regarded as suspect. If we accept that 1.0–1.5 years is a reasonable expectation of life for a juvenile, this means that many individuals will die before attaining this age but, conversely, many will live much longer. In Britain, the maximum recorded longevity for a Starling is 16 years 10 months; in the United States it is 17 years 8 months, while the oldest Starling ever recorded is a bird ringed in Germany in 1934; it was recovered in 1955, 21 years 4 months after being ringed. (Delvingt (1962*b*) reported a Starling that was ringed in Switzerland and recovered in Belgium over 23 years later, but the bird had, in fact, died long before its discovery was reported.)

CAUSES OF DEATH

We now know that something over half of the Starlings die each year but it would be interesting to know at what time of year most of them die since this may provide clues to the cause of death. The only quantitative assessment we have of seasonal changes in the number of birds that die stems from the distribution during the year of ring recoveries (Fig. 8.1). Coulson (1960) showed that most of these occurred between January and May and there tended to be a dearth during the summer and autumn. In North America, Kessel (1957) found a broadly similar pattern of recoveries but with an even higher proportion found between January and March. At first sight, this suggests that the heaviest mortality occurs during the winter and breeding season. This view may well be strongly biased, however, since it is precisely at these times that Starlings are in their closest contact with human habitations and

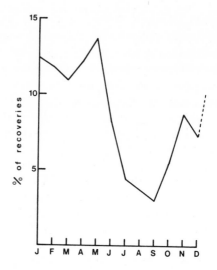

Fig. 8.1. The seasonal pattern of recoveries of ringed adult Starlings in Britain. (Redrawn from Coulson 1960).

birds that die are most likely to be discovered. Similarly, the frequency of recoveries fell during the summer when Starlings, especially juveniles, tend to frequent areas more remote from human dwellings.

Some of the other data presented by Coulson (1960) support the suggestion that the picture presented by the seasonal distribution of recoveries is erroneous. I have already mentioned that he found no clear relationship between annual mortality and the severity of the winter. This casts doubt on the idea that winter is a critical time for Starlings and indeed Dunnet (1956) found that they had little difficulty in maintaining fat reserves in winter, even when the ground was covered by snow; he thought that in north-east Scotland autumn may prove more difficult. During exceptionally severe winters Starlings undoubtedly do suffer a high mortality. In the winter of 1962–63 in Britain, Dobinson and Richards (1964) reported that many had been killed during the prolonged hard weather but conditions like this are unusual and this scale of winter mortality is certainly not the norm. In any case, this 'heavy' mortality (1333 corpses were reported) may well be an artefact since in severe weather Starlings move closer to habitation, rendering any birds that do succumb more likely to be found than other species that are less attracted to conurbations. It is notable that Dobinson and Richards (1964) detected no marked change in the number of breeding Starlings in the spring following the severe winter, suggesting that winter mortality is not a determinant of density in the following breeding season.

The evidence for heavy mortality in winter is not, therefore convincing but the high mortality in the breeding season, indicated by the recovery rate in Fig. 8.1 may be similarly spurious. The several studies of Starling breeding referred to in Chapters 6 and 7 did not mention parental loss as a notable contribution to nest failure, although the death of a parent could result in apparent desertion, a phenomenon recorded by most workers. At Worplesdon, however, most desertions of first brood nests, attributable to our activities, were followed by a re-nesting attempt, indicating that the parents had not died. During the breeding season reserves of fat and protein are depleted (Ward 1977) and if depletion is too severe this might prove fatal. In our Worplesdon studies, however, we have found only two adults, both females, dead in their nest-boxes out of 362 nest box occupations between 1975 and 1981. We have also found the remains of an adult in a Little Owl's *Athene noctua* nest, but this adult was wing-tagged and therefore may have been more prone to predation. The adults could, of course, die away from the nest and indeed Coulson (1960) proposed that the heavy mortality of females breeding for the first time was related to their vulnerability to predation when devoting so much of their time to foraging on the ground. Thus the supposition that mortality is high during the breeding season is based only on circumstantial evidence and is not supported by observation or by measurement of adult disappearance.

After the breeding season the adults are low in weight (Al-Joborae 1979) and their protein and fat reserves reach their maximum depletion (Ward 1977). When in such apparently poor condition they commence moult, with its concomitant demands for energy and nutrients. The summer is a time, however, when many of the more frequent items of the Starlings' diet are in short supply. Cereal grains and many seeds are not yet ripe and available; earthworms descend out of reach or aestivate and leatherjackets pupate before emerging as adult craneflies in late July, August, and September (Dunnet and Patterson 1968). Thus Starlings may well be faced with problems similar to those encountered by Rooks *Corvus frugilegus*, which experience a period of food shortage in the summer (Feare, Dunnet and Patterson 1974). In

Rooks, this results in a heavy mortality of juveniles by starvation, but most deaths of adults seem to occur during the breeding season (Holyoak 1971). Adult and juvenile Starlings appear to segregate into different feeding sites in summer: the adults continue to feed in grassland while juveniles tend to be more arboreal, eating defoliating caterpillars, and, later, soft fruit. This segregation may free juveniles from competition with more experienced adults for scarce invertebrate food sources in grassland (Feare 1980), but as segregation only occurs at this time of year, this suggests that summer may represent a time of food shortage, and therefore high mortality, for Starlings. P. G. H. Evans (personal communication), who has devoted considerable time to catching Starlings throughout the year, found that the birds that he caught during the summer tended to be weaker than at other times of year; this again suggests that summer may be a time of hardship.

This argument that mortality is highest in the summer and lower at other times of year is contrary to the patterns indicated by the seasonal occurrence of ring recoveries (Fig. 8.1) and it is readily apparent that a study of Starling mortality and its causes is desperately needed.

Since most theories of population regulation in animals ultimately hold food shortage as the principle determinant of population levels (e.g. Lack 1966; Wynne-Edwards 1962) it is surprising that starvation has not been more frequently identified as a cause of death in Starlings. Keymer (1980) attributed a high proportion of deaths within winter roosts to starvation and hypothermia, but the rate of mortality in the roosts was extremely low (personal observations). Other sources of mortality have been identified but their relative contributions are unknown. These included predation and disease, and while the latter may not prove fatal by itself, debilitation might increase susceptibility to predation or to other causes of death. In October I have watched migrating Starlings arriving on the east coast at the end of their sea crossing. Some were so weak that they failed to make the landfall and dropped into the sea and there is no doubt that weaker birds that did reach the coast would there be more susceptible to predation than fitter members of the flocks. Whether these weak birds are diseased or simply had insufficient reserves of 'migratory' fat is unknown; nor is it known how significant mortality during migration is in Starling population dynamics, and therefore to what extent migrants might be disadvantaged in comparison with residents where both occur together in the same part of the geographical range.

The impact of predators on adult and juvenile Starlings (as opposed to eggs and nestlings) has not been ascertained, but in Britain Starlings have been recorded in the diets of most birds of prey and of several mammals (Table 8.3). Avian predators take Starlings throughout the year but large winter roosts can present a special attraction. On a world scale the list of predators could presumably be substantially extended. For example, Starlings are recorded in the diet of the Black Kite *Milvus migrans* in Europe, and in North America Red-tailed Hawks *Buteo jamaicensis*, and other American 'hawks' are regular attenders at roosts, most of which also house large numbers of blackbirds (Icteridae). In New Zealand the Swamp Harrier *Circus approximans* is often mobbed by flocks of Starlings and some are doubtless taken occasionally (Falla, Sibson, and Turbott 1979).

Data on the incidence of Starlings in the diet of predators are available for few species, but for none of the avian predators do Starlings constitute a major item of prey and the influence of these predators on Starling populations must be negligible (Newton and

Table 8.3 British predators in whose diets Starlings have been recorded

Birds:	
Red Kite	*Milvus milvus*
Goshawk	*Accipiter gentilis*
Sparrow Hawk	*Accipiter nisus*
Buzzard	*Buteo buteo*
Rough-legged Buzzard	*Buteo lagopus*
Merlin	*Falco columbarius*
Peregrine	*Falco peregrinus*
Hobby	*Falco subbuteo*
Kestrel	*Falco tinnunculus*
Little Owl	*Athene noctua*
Tawny Owl	*Strix aluco*
Short-eared Owl	*Asio flammeus*
Long-eared Owl	*Asio otus*
Barn Owl	*Tyto alba*
Eurasian Crow	*Corvus corone*
Mammals:	
Brown Rat	*Rattus norvegious*
Domestic Dog	*Canis familiaris*
Stoat	*Mustela erminea*
Weasel	*Mustela nivalis*
Domestic Cat	*Felis catus*

Marquiss 1982). Collinge (1924–7), however, claimed that Little Owls destroyed 2.25 per cent of Starlings even though this prey item constituted only 2 per cent of the diet of the Owls. How he came by this proportion destroyed is not clear but in view of the relative densities of the two species and the low percentage of Starlings in the diet, Little Owls cannot possibly have such an impact.

Mammalian predators are similarly unlikely to influence the number of Starlings. Brown Rats take only moribund birds in roosts; Stoats take eggs and chicks and only rarely an incubating adult, and domestic dogs on farms seem only occasionally to display an interest in a sick or dying bird. Cats may be more significant and indeed ring recoveries indicate that cats are one of the main causes of death in cases where this cause has been identified (Plate 10). Coulson (1960) found this to be particularly true in London, and, in view of the number of cats in the County of London he concluded that cats must be an important predator of Starlings. Coulson showed, further, that most cat predation occurred during the breeding season; he attributed this to the amount of time that adults had to spend foraging on the ground while feeding their young, rendering them more vulnerable to ground predators at this time of year. Cat predation was also moderately high in winter but was low in summer and autumn, following the overall pattern of recoveries which, as argued above, was probably biased towards the times when Starlings live close to man and to cats. At such times any bird caught by a cat has, as Coulson noted, a good chance of being found by man and reported. Thus far more deaths due to cats are likely to be discovered, identified as cat kills, and reported than are deaths due to other predators or other causes, leading to an excessive emphasis on cats as predators. In Coulson's analysis, 11 per cent of ring recoveries were identified as killed by cats, while 67 per cent were simply 'found dead'. The majority of Starling deaths are likely to occur where they are unlikely to be found, i.e. away from human habitation and also from cats, so that to consider that 11 per cent of deaths are due to this particular predator must greatly exaggerate the importance of the lap-loving tabby!

Table 8.3 omits a mammalian predator that is potentially much more significant than the cat—man! Man's effects on Starlings are both deliberate and accidental. In Britain, killing for food is comparatively rare even though birds are shot in winter roosts for export to certain European countries to make pâté. Starlings are killed for food in some European countries and in Spain some corn fields are planted specially to attract roosting birds so that they can be trapped for sale in local markets (Parsons 1960). Killing in an attempt to prevent damage of various kinds is more widespread and will be discussed in more detail in the last chapter. In his analysis of ring recoveries, Coulson (1960) found that Starlings reported as shot were the most numerous of all records where the cause of death was identified, accounting for 15 per cent of all recoveries. Many of the biases discussed above must apply to this 'shot' category and although Coulson attributed the higher annual mortality rate of shot Starlings to control efforts in fruit-growing areas, where the damage occurs in the summer, the main mortality indicated by ring recoveries occurred in winter. Shooting in the summer is unlikely to have a marked effect on the population since Tahon (1980) has shown that the annual killing of an average 20 per cent of the Starlings inhabiting the Saint-Trond cherry growing area of Belgium has no effect on the population in the following year. The amount of shooting in Britain in winter is similarly unlikely to be sufficient to affect population levels but the scale of mortality reported to be inflicted on roosting Starlings in North Africa, using sprayed poisons (Steinbacher 1960), could potentially have more serious implications for those migrants: more data are required on the extent of the operations and on the number of birds killed in order that this potential can be assessed. Poisons are also used in Britain, albeit illegally, to kill Starlings and Cadbury (1980) recorded the use of mevinphos, alpha-chloralose, and endrin; only small numbers of Starlings were actually reported as having been killed but more were suspected to have been involved.

In the United States, where a number of poisons and other killing techniques are registered for use against Starlings and other bird pests, large numbers have been killed in recent years. The mortality inflicted has been insufficient to stem the increase of the introduced Starling population (Dolbeer and Stehn 1979) and the use of these techniques has come under criticism from scientists (and conservationists) who feel that alternative approaches to bird-damage problems should be sought (Dyer and Ward 1977).

It seems highly unlikely that the damage-prevention measures taken in western Europe, many of which do not involve killing, have been responsible for the decline in the number of Starlings in parts of the north of their range, as has been claimed (Orrell and Ojanen 1980, Feare 1981*b*).

Nor does accidental death, resulting from human activity, seem to be an important factor in Starling population dynamics although there is little quantification of this mortality. Recently there have been reports of Starlings dying in oil flares during the birds' migration across the North Sea, but the extent of the losses incurred is unknown. Some quantification of the number of birds killed by vehicles on roads has been attempted in a survey in 1960–61. The amount of road covered by the survey was small and the sample was certainly not representative of Britain's roads as a whole, but Hodson and Snow (1965) appreciated these problems and estimated that around 2 500 000 birds died annually on the roads. Of the 5269 birds recorded dying on the sample stretches of road, 77 or 1.46 per cent were Starlings. Using this figure (but accepting that further biases may be involved) to extrapolate to the national road system, about 36 000 would have been killed annually on roads in the early 1960s. There are now more roads, more traffic, and faster vehicles than 20 years ago and the pattern of road deaths may well have changed but no more recent survey has been undertaken.

Birds are also killed by aircraft and Starlings are involved in bird strikes in Britain, Europe, and America. Being comparatively small birds, individual Starlings tend to cause minor damage and the number of Starling strikes that is reported probably underestimates the number that actually occurs. Rochard and Horton (1980) found that between 1966 and 1976, 86 Starlings were involved in 57 reported collisions with aircraft in Britain and there appeared to be no seasonal variation in the incidence of strikes, though samples were admittedly small. Aircraft do not, therefore, represent an important mortality factor for Starlings but flocks of these birds near airports can pose a serious threat to aeroplanes: In 1960, Starlings were responsible for the crash of a Lockheed Electra at Boston, Massachusetts, killing 62 of the passengers; this is the worst bird strike, in terms of loss of human life, that has so far occurred.

Another accidental cause of death identified by Coulson (1960) involved ringed birds having fallen down chimneys; these accounted for 2.96 per cent of the recoveries of ringed birds. The birds involved probably enter the chimneys in search of roosting or nesting places but, owing to the biases associated with recoveries near human habitation, the proportion of Starlings over the country as a whole that die from this cause must be much less than three per cent.

A more insidious form of mortality stems from man's use of chemicals in his surroundings, especially as aids to agriculture. The effects of accumulated pesticides on animals at the tops of food chains, especially the birds of prey, have been well documented (e.g. Ratcliffe 1981 for the Peregrine *Falco peregrinus*, one of the most severely affected birds on the global scale) but birds lower down food chains have also occasionally experienced locally heavy mortality as a result of eating dressed cereal seed (Hamilton, Hunter, Ritchie, Ruthven, Brown, and Stanley 1976). Somewhat surprisingly, Starlings seem to have suffered little from this use of toxic chemicals, even though they eat both insects that are sprayed against and sown cereals whose seeds are dressed with insecticides and fungicides. However, although heavy mortality from these chemicals has not been recorded in Starlings, Grue, Powell, and McChesney (1982) have demonstrated that parental behaviour can be modified following the ingestion of organophosphorus pesticides. Sublethal effects, such as this, are difficult to detect but may nevertheless exert significant effects on wild populations that are exposed to pesticides.

Internal parasites

It is readily apparent from the foregoing that our knowledge of the contributions of most mortality factors towards the Starling's overall mortality is very limited. We know even less about the effects of the many parasites and diseases to which Starlings are susceptible; some of them do kill, at least sometimes, and others may contribute towards a general debilitation that could make the afflicted individuals more prone to other mortality factors. Most studies of parasites and disease have been orientated towards potentially economic aspects and our knowledge of infestations and infections that are of no agricultural or human health significance are likely to prove extremely fragmentary. Starlings are, however, prime candidates for the transmission of some parasitic infections to aviary birds, for example in zoological gardens, and this has led to a closer study of these infections in Starlings than in many other species (Keymer 1982a).

The internal parasites that infest the digestive and respiratory tracts have received considerable attention from workers in both

Eurasia and North America, and this has resulted in an extensive list of species for which the Starling can act as host. The majority of these species occur very infrequently and only a few parasites occur regularly and in large numbers, and the rates of infestation of these vary seasonally and with the age of the host. Most of the parasites also occur in several other bird species and none is absolutely specific to Starlings.

Few protozoan parasites have been recorded but both the alimentary and circulatory systems are infected. Coccidiosis is an important disease in poultry, and in Starlings is caused by *Eimeria balozeti*, among other organisms. Coccidia may be present in a host without any apparent ill-effects but clinical signs can range from lethargy to death. Starling blood cells are infected by two protozoan parasites in Britain but the incidence of both *Leucocytozoon* and *Haemoproteus* seems to be low although the number of birds that has been examined is small (Cheke, Hassall, and Peirce 1976). In America, Haslett and Schneider (1978) found antibodies to *Toxoplasma gondii* in Starlings : toxoplasmosis is an infection to which human children, and to a less extent adults, are susceptible but its effects on Starlings are unknown.

The internal parasites, generally termed helminths, comprise the nematodes (roundworms), trematodes (flukes), cestodes (tape worms), and acanthocephalans (spiny-headed worms). Starlings have been recorded as hosts for over 80 species of helminth parasite (Hair and Forrester 1970; Cooper and Crites 1976) and many other species will doubtless be recorded in future. Although fewer New World helminths have been found in Starlings than have Old World species, the presence of any New World forms is interesting in demonstrating the lack of host specificity of many species, and the readiness with which Starlings can become infested, when introduced into a new geographical area, without adverse effects on their population.

The helminth parasites of British Starlings have been the subject of a detailed study by Owen and Pemberton (1962). They examined 135 juvenile and 223 adult birds, all but seven of which were shot near Leeds, and recovered 15 species of parasite from the juveniles and 11 of them from adults. Most species were recovered from only a few of the birds: in juveniles only four species and in adults only two species occurred in over 40 per cent of the birds. Most parasites had a higher incidence of infestation in juveniles than adults, although with the tape worm *Aploparatsis dujardinii* the reverse was true and the incidence of the most frequently occurring tape worm *Hymenolepis farciminosa* was the same in both age groups.

The incidence of infestation also showed a seasonal cycle, both in the number of parasites per bird and in the number of species per bird as shown in Fig. 8.2; this again emphasizes the higher infestation rates of juveniles. This higher incidence of parasitism during the spring and summer was also found by Boyd (1951) in North America and by Markov (1940) in Russia and probably results from two factors. First, the intermediate hosts of the parasites, which include snails, slugs, earthworms, and other invertebrates, are more active during the warmer months of the year and the reproductive cycles of the parasites are geared to this activity. Second, invertebrates constitute a greater portion of the Starling's diet in the spring than at other times of year (Al-Joborae 1979) and nestlings are fed almost entirely on them (Dunnet 1955; Kessel

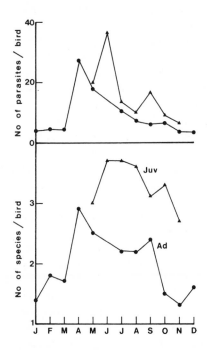

Fig. 8.2. Seasonal variation in the parasitic infestations of adult and juvenile Starlings in northern England. Infestations are expressed in terms of mean number of parasites per bird (top) and mean number of species per bird (bottom). Data from Owen and Pemberton (1962).

1957; Tinbergen 1981 and many other authors). This dependence of nestlings on invertebrates for food may also partially explain their high incidence of infestation but, for some parasites at least, other factors are involved. The nematode *Capillaria exilis* and the tape worm *Hymenolepis farciminosa* have annual cycles of infestation and elimination and their incidence may thus be related to the food of the birds but the nematodes *Porrocaecum ensicaudatum* and *Syngamus trachea* occur commonly only in young juveniles. This indicates that an early infestation of these two parasites confers some immunity on the infested birds. *Syngamus trachea*, the gape worm, used to be an important disease of poultry before intensive rearing became common (Keymer 1982*a*) and it can still cause problems in outdoor turkey and game flocks. The adult gape worm lives in the trachea and if the beak of an infested bird is opened wide the red rematodes can be seen. They can cause bleeding in the throat and the blood, together with an abundance of worms, can cause coughing and choking which sometimes kills the host. In Britain almost all nestling Rooks *Corvus frugilegus* and Jackdaws *C. monedula* are infested (Mettrick 1960) while the infestation rates in Starlings were found to be 55 per cent for nestlings and 32 per cent for adults. In Aberdeenshire rookeries the infestation was readily evident from the coughing of the juvenile Rooks (personal observation) but I have never encountered this coughing in Starling nestlings at Worpledon. Owen and Pemberton (1962) found, however, that the number of gape worms averaged 2.2 per infested juvenile and 1.1 per infested adult Starling, whereas coughing juvenile Rooks had many more. Few adult Rooks are infested and thus they too are capable of developing an immunity to this parasite.

Records of adverse effects of helminth parasites on Starlings are scarce but heavy infestations of some, if not all, species must place an extra drain on the birds' reserves. There is some indirect evidence for this, for during an investigation into the effects of change of diet on the structure of the alimentary canal my student B. Cresswell (personal communication) noted that a Starling with a heavy tapeworm infestation had unusually long intestinal villi: this may be an adaptation to enable the gut to improve its absorptive capacity when in competition with a heavy parasite fauna. Freeland (1981) has recently shown that a heavy parasitic burden can disadvantage male mice by resulting in a loss of seniority in a dominance hierarchy. More direct manifestations have occasionally been recorded, for example Keymer (1982*a*) noted that in Starlings a mild enteritis was associated with infestations of the spiny-headed worm *Plagiorhynchus formosus*; he also reported adverse effects of many of the helminth parasites recorded from Starlings but these adverse effects were usually described from clinical signs or lesions observed in aviary birds.

Ectoparasites

Starlings are also prone to infestations of external parasites. Unlike the internal parasites, however, the ectoparasites tend to drop off their host when the host dies and many undoubtedly go unrecorded except when birds are collected specifically for ecto-parasitic examination. Some parasites spend very little time on their host, for example various biting insects, and the only evidence that we have to indicate that Starlings are parasitized by them is the presence within the bird of organisms transmitted by the biting insects. The protozoan blood parasites *Leucocytozoon* and *Haemoproteus* have Simuliid flies (black flies) and Hippoboscids (louse flies) as vectors respectively. The presence of antibodies to certain viruses (see below) indicates that Starlings are bitten by mosquitoes and their blood is also doubtless taken by various midges. Other arthropods have a closer association with their host, however, and more is known about their infestations.

Starlings can be infested with several biting or chewing lice of the insect Order Mallophaga, commonly called feather lice by bird ringers. They are dorso-ventrally flattened, allowing them to rest beneath the feathers on the skin surface where they are least likely to be dislodged by preening. They eat feathers and their waxy sheaths but some species also ingest blood. Four species, *Menacanthus eurysternus*, *Myrsidea cucullaris*, *Brueelia nebulosa*, and *Sturnidoecus sturni*, have been recorded from Starlings, the different species being structurally adapted to infest different parts of the host's body. Kettle (1977) found that most of the Starlings he examined in southern England had louse populations of less than 10 individuals, but that juveniles tended to be more heavily parasitised. Their heavy infestations ended during their moult in July–August. Heavy infestations of lice are usually associated with other forms of malaise in the host, possibly as a result of reduced preening activity that might otherwise keep louse numbers down, and Starlings do not appear to experience adverse effects of louse infestations alone.

Louse-flies, Hippoboscidae, also live in the plumage where they can move rapidly. They may or may not have wings but their important characteristic is that they suck blood and are involved in the transmission of blood protozoa such as *Haemoproteus* and *Plasmodium*. The latter is the organism of avian malaria and *P. relictum* has been reported from Starlings (Garnham 1966).

Other blood-sucking insects that infest Starlings, especially in their nests, are fleas and in our Worplesdon nest-boxes *Ceratophyllus gallinae* can be numerous, especially in intermediate and second brood nests. The fleas bite the chicks and also the incubation patches of the incubating or brooding adults: the resulting pin-pricks of adult's blood can become black, brown, or reddish spots on the eggs (Feare and Constantine 1980). Similar blood spots can also result from the bites of a Dipteran fly, albeit a fly with unusual habits. *Carnus hemapterus* parasitizes a wide range of birds but it is particularly common in the nests of hole-nesting birds such as tits, woodpeckers and, of course, Starlings (Rothschild and Clay 1952). The fly lives in the feathers of the host but eggs are laid in the nest; on hatching, the larva also lives in the nest where it is saprophagous, eating decaying matter in the nest. When the adult flies emerge from the pupae they are winged, presumably to permit these adults to locate a host should flight be necessary, which it is often not since the complete life cycle can be passed within the nest of a cavity-nesting bird. On settling on a host, however, the wings are shed and the adult spends the rest of its life on that host.

The remaining ectoparasites that have been recorded from Starlings belong to the arthropod class Arachnida, and are the ticks and mites. Ticks are blood-feeding arthropods and are well-known as vectors of diseases. In Britain, Starlings are parasitized by three species of tick: *Ixodes ricinus*, the sheep tick, *Ixodes arboricola*, and *Haemaphysalis punctata*. The sheep tick is probably the commonest tick of Starlings in Britain. On moorlands this tick is the vector of the virus of a disease known as louping ill, a serious infection of sheep and grouse which can also infect man (Duncan, Reid, Moss, Phillips, and Watson 1978), but we do not know whether the disease occurs in Starlings. In North America the introduced Starlings have been recorded as hosts to *Ixodes brunneus*, a tick that parasitizes many bird species, and *Haemaphysalis leporis-palustris*, which is the American Rabbit tick but which has also been found feeding from a wide variety of birds

(Boyd 1951). Migrant birds can be instrumental in the spread of some tick-borne diseases (Hoogstraal 1972) and the discovery of *Hyalomma marginatum*, the vector of a number of human and animal virus diseases, on Starlings in the southern USSR may implicate these birds in the epidemiology of these diseases (Shcherbinina 1971).

The mite infestations of Starlings are poorly known but Powlesland's (1977) study of the effects of *Ornithonyssus bursa* on chicks has already been mentioned. The red mite of poultry *Dermanyssus gallinae* has been recorded; in cage birds it can cause anaemia (Keymer 1982*a*) but this has not been investigated where the mite has been found on Starlings. The mange mite *Microlichus avus* can cause feather loss and also produce skin lesions in Starlings (Keymer 1982*a*), and these mites might be dependent on another ectoparasite for their dispersal, for they have been found being mechanically transported on the wings of hippoboscid flies.

Disease

We now turn to the smaller infective organisms, the fungi, bacteria, and viruses that cause diseases in Starlings. One of the commonest of all avian diseases is caused by a fungus, *Aspergillus*. Aspergillosis produces a wide variety of symptoms ranging from mild debility to sudden death (Keymer 1982*b*), and while birds recently brought into captivity seem to be particularly susceptible, wild Starlings have been found to be infected (Keymer, personal communication).

Samples of Starlings have been subjected to bacteriological examination, usually in attempts to discover whether they act as carriers of organisms of medical or, more commonly, veterinary significance. In some instances, the causative bacteria of diseases of farm stock have been isolated from Starlings on farms during outbreaks. *Mycobacterium avium* was discovered in Starlings on a farm, in the United States, where pigs had contracted avian tuberculosis (Bickford, Ellis and Moses 1966) and in Britain *Leptospira laura* was isolated from Starlings shot on a farm where this organism had been causing abortion in cattle (P. Bloxham, in Feare 1980). In cases like this it is not known whether Starlings have spread the disease to the farm animals or *vica versa*. In general, the shooting of healthy Starlings at farms or other feeding sites, even at sewage farms, has revealed an extremely low incidence of bacterial infection. At roosts, a higher incidence of infection has been found in dead or moribund birds (Faddoul, Fellows, and Baird 1968; Keymer 1980) but even here Ian Keymer found that most deaths resulted from starvation and hypothermia.

The most frequently occurring infection in Starlings may well be the various serotypes of *Salmonella*: I say 'may well be' because Salmonellae are in fact the most frequently sought bacteria in examinations of wild birds. Some of the serotypes are responsible for food poisoning in humans and others produce sickness in domestic animals. Interestingly, the phage type of *Salmonella typhimurium* that Keymer isolated from a Starling found dead in a roost was a phage type that is not normally infective to cattle. Thus the role of Starlings in disease transmission from farm to farm receives no support from this instance. Although at a very low incidence, *Salmonella* infections appear nevertheless to be widespread in Starling populations, for they occur in the United States and *S. hessarek* has recently been discovered in Starlings found dead in a roost in Israel (Singer, Weissman, Yom-Tov, and Marder 1977); these birds must have originated from breeding populations in eastern Europe or western Asia. In America Faddoul *et al.* (1968) and in Britain Keymer (1980) have isolated *Erysipelothrix insidiosa*, suggesting that this organism may also be widespread, and other bacteria that are generally of widespread occurrence, e.g. *Yersinia pseudo-tuberculosis* which has been found in Starlings, may also prove to occur widely in these birds. There must also be a wide range of infections that remain to be isolated from Starlings but it seems that all of them, like those already known, will occur at a very low incidence. This means that none of the bacterial diseases recorded so far can be regarded as significant in terms of the overall mortality of Starlings and this is likely to be true of those that will be isolated in future.

Our knowledge of viral infections of Starlings is even more limited, to some extent because the isolation and identification of viruses is, in comparison with bacteriological examinations, such an expensive process. This has, of course, led to an even greater bias towards those diseases that are potentially of economic importance.

Newcastle Disease and Fowl Plague (an influenza virus) are viruses that, for legislative purposes, are together termed 'foul pest' in Britain. Newcastle Disease originated in Java and began spreading from there in 1926. The main mechanism of spread has been the movement of cage birds, especially the air transport of birds of the parrot family (Lancaster and Alexander 1975), but Starlings have been found to be infected with the virus. Once infected, Starlings can potentially act as agents for the spread of Newcastle Disease though proof that this has actually happened is lacking; such evidence would be very difficult to obtain, however. Similarly, there is no direct evidence that Starlings are involved in the transmission of influenza viruses although both these birds and domestic poultry are infected by the same serotypes. Farmers in Norfolk have noted the coincidence of recent outbreaks of Fowl Plague in turkeys with the autumn arrival of immigrant Starlings. Although the farmers would like to be able to blame these outbreaks on some external agency, their claim that Starlings are involved remains speculative. The serotype of influenza that was found in turkeys in Norfolk has been isolated from Starlings—but only in Israel (Lipkind, Weisman, Shihmanter, and Shohman 1979).

A virus disease that certainly can kill Starlings is avian pox, which produces wart-like lesions (Plate 10) particularly on the bird's head round the eye and the base of the bill (Blackmore and Keymer 1969). The expression of the disease seems to be seasonal: I have caught birds with lesions only in July and August and they (three) have been juveniles. The incidence of birds with visible lesions in wild populations is undoubtedly low but it has not been quantified. Avian pox does raise problems in our captive birds, however, and this may result from our bringing into captivity of a juvenile with lesions (before we knew what they were) in July 1979. In both 1980 and 1981 we have captured apparently healthy Starlings and held them in our aviaries but in July and August many of the juveniles have developed lesions. Some of these juveniles have died and others with visible lesions we have killed in an attempt to control the disease, but by the time we have killed some of these birds we have noticed that lesions have become smaller or disappeared. It is also notable that our captive adults have rarely developed visible lesions, suggesting that juvenile Starlings are susceptible to avain pox but that survivors become immune. Since none of our freshly caught adults exhibited clinical signs in July and August it appears that these birds are already immune; perhaps a high proportion of the wild population is exposed to the virus in early life but survives and develops immunity. Starlings have, nevertheless, been implicated in the spread of pox to captive Rothschild's Mynahs *Leucopsar rothschildi*, resulting in the death of birds showing visible signs of infection, but not of birds in the same aviary that did not develop obvious symptoms (Landolt and Kocan 1976). Williamson (1968) thought that the avian pox infective in Starlings was specific to the Sturnidae. A study of the epidemiology of avian pox in Starling populations would clearly be interesting but, as with other diseases, our current knowledge does not highlight this infection as a significant cause of mortality.

Starlings will undoubtedly prove to be infected with a variety of viruses but the discovery by Aspock, Graefe, Kunz, and Radda (1972) of antibodies to tahyna, yellow fever, and dengue fever viruses in Starling blood introduces more complexity into their parasite–disease relationships. These are classed as arboviruses (an abbreviation for *ar*thropod *bo*rne *viruses*) meaning that they are transmitted by (and replicate within) arthropods which, in this case, are usually mosquitoes. Thus the presence of antibodies to these viruses in Starling blood indicates that mosquitoes must, as previously mentioned, be included in the list of ectoparasites. The effects of these arbovirus infections on Starlings are unknown but yellow and dengue fevers are well known diseases of man in the tropics. The discovery of yellow fever antibodies is particularly surprising since Starlings do not migrate across the Sahara to the areas of Africa where the disease is endemic in man.

Starlings have also been found to be involved in the epidemiology of other arboviruses, although their involvement appears to be peripheral to the main lines of transmission. In the southern Ukraine, Sidenko, Semenov, Stepanovskaya, Karaseva, Sochinsky, Polyakov, Gretov and Solomko (1972) have found antibody reactions to tick-borne encephalitis and Japanese encephalitis and have also isolated viral agents of the group B arbovirus type from the blood of migrant and resident Starlings. These authors considered that Starlings, and other migrants, could be involved in the geographical dissemination of these viruses. Mal'kov, Dargol'ts, and Voronin (1966) found Starlings, among other species, to be infested with the tick *Ixodes persulcatus* in an area where this tick was involved in the circulation of tick-borne encephalitis. Antibodies to Omsk haemorrhagic fever have been found in Starling blood (Casals, Henderson, Hoogstraal, Johnson, and Shelokov 1970); this virus is transmitted to man through tick bites or through close contact with infected Muskrats *Ondatra zibethica* but the precise transmission pathways for this virus are unclear. It seems that Starlings will prove to be involved in the epidemiology of further viruses but their role may again be minimal, as is likely to be the part played by the viruses in the birds' mortality.

From the foregoing it is apparent that no known disease contributes significantly to the Starling's annual mortality. Nor do parasites or predators account for a major share of the 50 per cent or so of Starlings that die each year. Even where man attempts to control their numbers he seems largely unsuccessful and man's environment is obviously not hostile to Starlings. It thus seems that when man attempts to inflict excessive mortality, this is simply absorbed into the overall mortality pattern of the species and man's efforts are not added to the naturally occurring mortality. This has an important theoretical bearing on attempts to prevent damage by killing the birds, for in order for the number killed by man to have any influence on population levels, this number must approach, or preferably exceed, the average annual mortality. If we take Sharrock's (1976) lower estimate of the number of Starlings breeding in Britain, four million pairs, in order for us to reduce this number we must kill over half of them, and over half of their offspring, *each year*. It is obviously unrealistic for us to expect to be capable of such a reduction, which in any case would be undesirable from many points of view, the most persuasive of which would be the economics of such an operation.

If we eliminate predators, parasites, and disease as major causes of mortality, we come to the end of this chapter without establishing what causes the death of most Starlings. I suggested earlier that summer might be a period of food shortage and that many birds, in poor condition after the breeding season and then commencing moult, might die of starvation. If food supplies limit populations, as has been suggested by many authors (e.g. Lack 1966; Wynne-Edwards 1962 and many more), then we might expect most deaths to be due to starvation, but in Starlings competition for nest sites could also contribute to population regulation. Despite all of the studies of many aspects of Starlings biology (the bibliography at the end of this book represents only a portion of the literature on the species) we simply do not know what regulates their populations or at what time of year the regulation occurs. Food shortage must nevertheless be regarded as a prime candidate and we shall now examine the food and feeding behaviour of our subject.

9 A BALANCED DIET

All animals need an adequate supply of food for survival, but 'food' is a very general term and an animal's requirement is for a wide variety of components. There are times when 'food' may seem to be abundant but the nutrient content of what is available may be inadequate to permit the predator to perform some particular activity. For example, most birds need an extra supply of calcium immediately before and during egg-laying in order that they can secrete the eggshells. Some stored calcium in the bones can be mobilized at this time but the quantity available from this source is hopelessly inadequate to meet the demands of egg-shell formation. In order to obtain sufficient calcium, the birds select certain calcium-rich foods at this time: snail shells and grit are items that are commonly eaten, while some arctic birds eat bones of dead animals (Jones 1976; Perrins 1979; Maclean 1974; Seastedt and Maclean 1977).

Our knowledge of avian nutrition is currently very basic and we do not know the precise requirements for a 'balanced' diet for any wild species, though rather more is known about the dietary needs of domestic poultry. The balanced diet will, in any case, vary at different times of year and at different stages in the bird's life. A nestling needs large amounts of protein for growth; a breeding female needs calcium and she also needs added protein for egg formation; in winter the main requirement is probably for a rich energy source to permit birds to survive long, cold nights; in summer, the protein needs of moulting birds may be more specific since feathers contain large amounts of the amino acids that contain sulphur: cystine and methionine. There are doubtless seasonal demands for vitamins and minerals but nothing is known of these requirements in wild birds.

At present, therefore, we are unable to describe what constitutes a balanced diet for Starlings in terms of the nutrient content of the food, but we can ask three questions, answers to which will give us an insight into the birds' needs. These questions are: (i) of what is the Starling's digestive system capable; (ii) what do Starlings eat, and (iii) how do they find their food? The first question necessitates a study of the morphology (and chemistry, though our knowledge here is particularly poor) of the gut; the second involves investigating the food eaten, its quantity, and seasonal variation, while the third question examines those aspects of behaviour that permit the bird to locate and eat food items and, where there is a choice, to select from the various items available.

DIGESTIVE SYSTEM AND ITS ADAPTABILITY

Many books describe Starlings as 'omnivorous' birds but they cannot, of course, eat everything they encounter while foraging. Limits on the size of items that can be eaten are imposed by the size of the bill and mouth, and although a Starling's bill does not allow the bird to chew large items to break them down, it can break off small pieces of soft foods, such as fruits. Bill and body structures also preclude some of the feeding methods of other birds; the term omnivorous simply means that the bird can eat both animal and plant foods but even this tends to over-estimate its capabilities, for the structure of the gut itself poses dietary limitations.

The Starling's gut consists of an oesophogus that leads directly from the mouth into the gizzard; there is no crop, so that these birds cannot gorge themselves on an abundant food and digest it over a long period, as pigeons can. The amount of food that can be eaten in a bout of feeding may be restricted by the size of the gizzard and by the rate at which it can process the food that enters it. The gizzard's function is to physically break down food items (in this it is usually helped by pieces of grit that are eaten to aid the muscular action of the gizzard wall) and to mix with the food those enzymes secreted by the glandular anterior part of the stomach, called the proventriculus. Digestion, the chemical breakdown of food into constituents that can pass through the walls of the cells lining the intestine, is completed in the intestine and it is here that most of the digested food is absorbed. At the lower end of the intestine are two caeca whose function seems to be mainly one of absorption. Below the caeca is a short rectum which leads to the cloaca where both faeces and urine are voided. This gut and its associated structure and enzymes is capable of digesting and absorbing a wide variety of food-stuffs of plant and animal origin but, even though the lumen of the gut possesses a flora of bacteria, Starlings are unable to digest large quantities of cellulose, the basic structure of most plants. Thus Starlings cannot be obligate herbivores in the way that ruminants are, and their consumption of plant material is usually restricted to seeds and fruits which contain readily digested carbohydrates and smaller quantities of protein and lipid.

When eating vegetable food however, the properties of the gut required for efficient digestion are different from those required for the breakdown and absorption of animal foods. Seed-eating birds have proportionately longer intestines than insectivorous birds and Al-Joborae (1979) has shown that the Starling's digestive system is capable of fairly rapid adaptation when the diet is changed (Plate 6). When captive Starlings are switched from an animal to a plant diet the length of the gut increases and the gizzard enlarges. Al-Joborae also found that the rate of passage of food through the gut increased. However, he was unable to detect any improvement in digestive efficiency in the longer gut when compared with a digestive system, adapted to an animal diet, that was given plant food. One of my students, B. H. Cresswell (personal communication) has recently shown that the changes that accompany dietary alteration extend beyond mere lengthening, for he found that, on switching from an animal to a plant diet, the length of the intestinal villi (Plate 6) increased, especially lower down the intestine. Savory and Gentle (1976) recorded a similar change in Japanese Quail *Coturnix coturnix japonicus* and the effect of this must be to increase the absorptive area of the intestinal lining. Digestive-system adaptation can occur quickly: Al-Joborae found that gut length changed within 14 days while Cresswell recorded a significant decrease in intestine length within four days of a switch from plant to animal food. These experiments have demonstrated an interesting capability in captive birds, but do they reflect something that happens in the Starling's real world? Al-Joborae (1979) found that gut lengths changed seasonally, being longer in winter and shorter in the breeding season (Fig. 9.1); this parallels the seasonal change in the proportion of plant food in the diet but other environmental factors such as photoperiod, may also stimulate the gut modifications.

These physical alterations of gut morphology are presumably only the most obvious adaptive changes that occur, and there must also be modifications of the relative concentrations of enzymes secreted into the digestive system (Hofer and Schiemer 1981). This has yet to be ascertained in Starlings, as has the physiological stimulus that promotes the lengthening and shortening of the gut

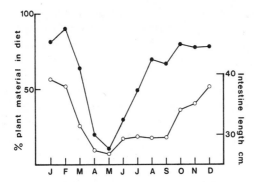

Fig. 9.1. Annual change in the proportion of plant material in the diet (●) of Starlings collected near Oxford and the change in the length of the intestines of these birds (○). (From data in Al-Joborae (1979) and reproduced with his permission.)

and its components when the food varies. These point to exciting areas of research for the future.

DIET

Geographical considerations

The diet of the Starling is diverse, as this adaptability suggests, and a wide variety of organisms have been recorded as prey. Most studies of the diet have been restricted to the breeding season and have concerned the food brought to the young. Kluyver's (1933) results amply demonstrate the broad spectrum of food that is collected. He identified 17 933 items brought to nestlings, including over 230 species of invertebrates, three species of vertebrate (newt, frog, and lizard), and two species of plant. The invertebrates consisted of earthworms, snails, woodlice, centipedes, and millipedes, grasshoppers, earwigs, beatles, bees, and ants and their allies, flies, and spiders. Other workers have recorded a similar diversity of food items brought to the nestlings and have added other families of insects to the list of prey (e.g. Coleman 1977; Gromadzka and Luniak 1978; Gromadzka and Gromadzki 1978; Havlin and Folk 1965, Szijj, 1957). Where studies have run over several breeding seasons the species composition has been found to vary annually and variations have also been found in the food brought to first and second-brood nestlings within the same year (Havlin and Folk 1965). It is apparent, therefore, that Starlings respond to the availability of a tremendous variety of potential food by eating different items at different times and it follows from this that there will be spatial differences in the composition of the diet, both on a local and on a wider geograpical scale (Kalmbach 1922). The local variation of food brought to nestlings was well demonstrated by Gromadzka and Luniak (1978) who compared the diet of nestlings in Warsaw with the diet in the rural areas of Poland. In the latter, invertebrates formed the main constituents of the diet while in urban Warsaw invertebrates accounted for only 66 per cent of the food, the remainder consisting of household waste such as sausages, meat, macaroni, and bread.

On a wider geographical scale the diets of nestling Starlings are characterized by big differences in species composition (e.g. Coleman 1977; Gromadzka and Gromadzki 1978; Kalmbach 1928) reflecting the geographical distribution of invertebrates. For example, one of the main food items in Europe is the leatherjacket, the larva of the cranefly or Daddy-long-legs *Tipula paludosa*. This insect is not present in New Zealand, where its place in the nestlings' diet is taken by different soil-inhabiting larvae, the Greasy Cutworm *Agrotis ypsilon* and the Grass Grub *Costelytra zealandica*. This geographic variability, together with the Starling's flexibility within each geographical and local area, renders a list of the recorded food items unwieldy and relatively uninformative and I have therefore made no attempt to assemble such a list. It is in fact unnecessary and the diversity expressed by this compilation would be somewhat misleading, for in each area and at each time of year the birds' diet is dominated by a few items which contribute most, in terms of energy and nutrients, to the total food intake. For this reason, most authors do not attempt to identify each food item, rather they categorize the invertebrates into families and give specific identity only to those items of major importance (Schneider 1972). Dunnet (1955), for example, found that leatherjackets constituted the main food in his Aberdeenshire study while Tinbergen and Drent (1980) concentrated their attention on two food items, leatherjackets and the caterpillar of the Antler Moth *Cerapteryx graminis*, which were the main prey brought to the young in their study in Holland. If we examine the food categories that are brought to the young in different parts of the world, however, a general pattern emerges (Table 9.1). There are indeed regional differences but the two kinds of food items collected in most areas are larvae of the insect orders Coleoptera

Table 9.1. The major invertebrate food categories in the diets of adults and free-flying young Starlings in different geographical regions

	Poland (Gromadzki 1979)	Hungary (Szijj 1957)	Czechoslovakia (Havlin and Folk 1965)	USA, New York (Lindsay 1939)	USA, Texas (Russell 1971)	New Zealand (Coleman 1977)
Insecta						
Coleoptera	+	+	+	+	+	+
Lepidoptera	+	+			+	+
Diptera	+		+			
Hymenoptera	+		+			+
Homoptera			+			+
Orthoptera		+			+	
Myriopoda						
Diplopoda			+	+		
Arachnida						
Araneida			+			+
Annelida						
Oligochaeta						+

(beetles) and Lepidoptera (butterflies and, particularly, moths). The kinds of larvae that are preyed upon most heavily are those, like the leatherjacket (Diptera) and the Antler Moth caterpillar, that live on or just under the soil surface. It is this kind of organism that the open-bill probing (Fig. 1.1), permitted by the Starling's bill structure and associated musculature (Beecher 1978), has evolved to exploit and therefore this broad similarity of the diets of populations throughout the world is to be expected.

Seasonal variations in diet

The animal groups listed in Table 9.1 are those eaten by free-flying birds. At some times of year these groups may not be available since the invertebrates themselves have annual cycles. Leather-jackets, for example, are available only until June–August when they become inactive pupae from which adult craneflies emerge subsequently. The adult females mate and lay eggs which hatch into leatherjackets, but for their first few months of life they are too small to be worthy of a Starling's hunting effort and it is only from mid-winter that they are eaten in large numbers (Dunnet 1955). The availability of earthworms is also determined by a behavioural cycle, for when the soil is dry in the summer they either descend out of reach of birds or become inactive and aesti-vate, depending on the species (Dunnet and Paterson 1968). The result of these cycles of prey availability is that at different times of year Starlings eat different kinds of food, the precise nature of which again varies geographically. Russell (1971) showed that the monthly consumption of eight families differed widely, for exam-ple carabid beetles were eaten mainly in winter and spring while noctuid moths were preyed upon in spring and summer (Fig. 9.2). Szijj (1957) showed similar seasonal variations in diet in Hungary. In general, winter in temperate climates is a time of relatively low insect abundance and this is probably what stimulates the greatest dietary switch—that from an insectivorous to a plant diet. The switch is never complete for both invertebrates and plant material are eaten in all months of the year but, as Fig. 9.1 shows, vegetable material predominates in the autumn and winter with animal food being the main dietary constituent in spring and, to a lesser extent, in summer. Most omnivorous birds eat invertebrates at most times of year and Berthold (1976) found that plant foods constituted a reserve that could be exploited when invertebrates were less readily available. The nutrient provided by the invertebrates is

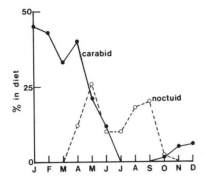

Fig. 9.2. The percentage (by number) of representatives of two species (noctuid moth caterpillars and carabid beetles) in the diet of Starlings in Texas throughout the year, showing the high preponderance of carabids in winter and of noctuids in summer. (Data from Russell (1971)).

animal protein and its absence from the diet leads to weight loss and death (Berthold 1976). Only specialist herbivores such as pigeons and Waxwings *Bombycilla garrulus* are able to survive without this animal protein. The effects of the absence of invertebrate food on male Starlings were clearly shown by Al-Joborae (1979) who found that while the testes of birds fed on insects grew normally in spring, the testes of those Starlings maintained on a plant diet did not develop at all.

Kalmbach (1922) and subsequent authors have shown that the amount of animal and plant material, taken over the year as a whole, varies geographically and in the early studies these estimates were used to assess the relative 'benefit' or 'harmfulness' that Starlings were likely to confer in different agricultural regions. The results of studies of the composition of food of free-flying birds have to be interpreted with caution, however, since there are considerable problems of obtaining quantative information.

Studies of the food of nestlings involve the photographing of each item brought to the chicks (Dunnet 1955; Tinbergen 1981) or the placing of collars around the chicks' necks so tht they cannot swallow the food given to them by their parents (Kluyver 1933; Havlin and Folk 1965); this food can then be collected by the observer. Both of these techniques allow the direct measurement of quantity and size of the food items. Analysis of the food of free-flying birds, on the other hand, relies on the examination of the gizzard contents of birds that have been shot. In many studies, birds were shot in roosts so that the researcher did not even know where his birds had been feeding. The gizzard contents are a mixture of undigested and partially digested food, some of which are easy to identify while others are not: some items are even difficult to detect. These differences are due to the different rates of breakdown of different food items, for while hard objects like cereal grains take a long time to digest, soft bodied animals like earthworms rapidly lose their identity (Coleman 1974). Some insects leave readily identifiable remains, such as a chitinous head capsule, but earthworms can often be detected only by the presence of their setae, visible under a microscope. Once the various items have been identified there are three ways of formulating a picture of the birds' diet: (i) an attempt can be made to count the number of individuals of each species or group in the sample; and (ii) the volume, or (iii) the weight of the components within the gizzard can be measured. Each of these methods gives a somewhat different result and in view of the other problems mentioned above the relationship between the diet as interpreted from the gizzard contents and that actually eaten by the bird is very difficult to determine. In quantifying the seasonal changes of diet it is again, therefore, necessary to use rather broad categories to describe the food items.

Dunnet (1956) recorded adult staphylinid and carabid beetles and their larvae and also spiders, in gizzards throughout the autumn and winter in Aberdeenshire. Earwigs (*Forficula auricularia*) and harvestmen (Arachnida, Phlangida), on the other hand, occurred only during the autumn All of these prey were relatively infrequent compared with the main autumn and winter foods which were weevils (Curculionidae), leatherjackets, and oats. Of the insect foods, weevils predominated in the autumn but from November leatherjackets occurred with increasing frequency. Oats were present in the gizzards from September through to February and were practically the only food eaten when the ground was covered with snow. Their increasing reliance on vegetable foods (or household waste) in severe weather has been noted by other workers (Taitt 1973).

In southern England and in Continental Europe, Starlings make use of resources that Dunnet did not find in Aberdeenshire, namely fruits of various kinds. In the last chapter I shall discuss damage to cherries: these, and other species in the genus *Prunus*, together with a wide variety of other fruiting plants, have evolved in association with birds and the plants rely heavily on birds for the dispersal of their seeds (Herrera & Jordane 1981). In England Al-Joborae (1979) found fruit in the stomachs of birds sampled near Oxford in most months but August to November were the main times of fruit consumption, while in cherry-growing areas the fruit damage occurs from mid-June to August. In Czechoslovakia, Havlin and Folk (1965) recorded the sequence of fruits eaten during the autumn: in June and July, cherries; August, cherries and grapes; September, grapes and elderberries *Sambucus nigra*; October, cultivated fruits (e.g. apples), elderberries, and rowan berries *Sorbus aucuparia*, and in November, sloes *Prunus spinosa* were eaten. This follows the sequence of ripening of the fruits, and Starlings generally wait until fruits are ripe before eating them. When ripe, fruits tend to be softest and their sugar content is high: both factors are probably important in the birds' selection of fruit, though this has not been investigated. The main cue used by the birds to determine 'ripeness' may well be colour, since where cultivated fruits occur in white and coloured forms the latter suffer most damage: red cherries are preferred to white and blue grapes are taken in preference to white ones (Havlin and Folk 1965).

Daily variation in diet

In addition to the seasonal changes in diet outlined above, there are also daily cycles but as yet these are only sketchily known. In winter, at my study site at Bridgets Experimental Husbandry Farm in Hampshire, there appear to be peaks of feeding on grain each day, when the Starlings first arive at the farm from the night roost in the morning and again in the pre-roost assemblies before returning to the roost in the late afternoon. For the remainder of the day there are always many birds feeding in grass fields, presumably on invertebrates. Tinbergen and Drent (1980) found a diurnal cycle in the bringing of bibionid flies to nestlings and this was related to the restricted time of emergence of these flies (this restriction may be an anti-predator response). In this case the collection of flies was related to their availability but the basis of the dietary variation in winter is not known; it may be related to varying states of hunger and satiation, anticipation of a long night of enforced fast and to a requirement for animal protein (see below).

Diet and age of young birds

Tinbergen (1981) found that when parents were foraging they

swallowed small items themselves and only collected the larger ones for the chicks. This suggests that food item size is a critical factor in determining what parents select for their young and Tinbergen showed that very young nestlings were given smaller caterpillars than older chicks. There are further criteria of selection, however, and most authors have found variations in the chicks' diet as they grow older (although Gromadzka and Gromadzki 1978, found no such variation). During the nestling period there are inevitable changes in the availability of different potential food items and some of them will increase in size during this period, as Dunnet (1955) showed with leatherjackets. Thus, this natural variation in availability and in size could be a component of the variations in the food of the young as they grow. It seems more likely, however, that diet changes do result from active selection by the parents. Very young chicks generally receive small, soft bodied invertebrates with which their developing digestive systems can presumably cope (Al-Joborae 1979) but there may be other reasons underlying food selection. Perrins (1979) noted that large caterpillars could inflict serious bites on tit nestlings and very small Starling chicks may be equally susceptible to such bites. More important as a basis of selection may be food quality; the relative merits of leatherjackets and caterpillars (Tinbergen 1981) were mentioned in Chapter 7. The apparently widespread giving of spiders to young tits (Perrins 1979) and Starlings (Kalmbach and Gabrielsen 1921; Kluyver 1933, Al-Joborae 1979, Tinbergen 1981) may indicate that spiders contain some nutrient that is vital to small chicks but the identity of this nutrient is as yet unknown.

Shortly after fledging there is evidence of a further age-related difference in food selection, the contrast here being between the diets of adults and juveniles. Brown (1974), Tahon (1978), and Feare (1980) have found that damage by Starlings to cherries in the summer is due largely to juveniles and Feare (1980) considered that this resulted, at least in part, from a tendency for juveniles to be arboreal in summer while adults continued to feed mainly in grassland at this time. I have already commented on the juveniles' weaker skulls (through lack of pneumatization), shorter bills, and lack of experience in catching agile prey. These characteristics would not be detrimental where birds were eating soft fruit and the separation of the feeding areas of the age groups may well release the juveniles from a competitive situation, with their elders for scarce invertebrates, in which the juveniles would be unlikely to succeed.

Daily food requirement

There have been remarkably few studies of the amount of food that a Starling (other than nestlings) needs to remain alive and perform activities such as breeding, migration, and moult. Kendeigh, Dol'nik, and Gavrilov (1977) derived formulae, involving body weight and ambient temperature, from which the daily energy budget of a passerine bird can be calculated. The daily energy budget is the energy of basal metabolism plus the energy required for all other activities. Gromadzki (1979) used these formulae to calculate the daily energy budgets of adult Starlings for the months that they reside in Poland. Since only a part of the energy in the food eaten is assimilated, the remainder passing out in the faeces, the amount of energy that must be ingested is greater than the daily energy budget, as shown in Fig. 9.3. In addition Gromadzki calculated that further energy, 35 k cal day^{-1} in April and 25 k cal day^{-1} in October, was required for the accumulation of

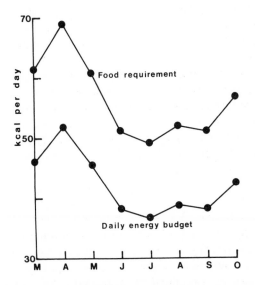

Fig. 9.3. Calculated daily energy budget and food requirement of Polish Starlings from May to October. The difference between the two is due largely to the proportion of the food eaten that is not assimilated but merely passes through the gut. (Data from Gromadski (1969)).

energy reserves for migration. In his calculation of daily food requirements from the daily energy budget, Gromadzki assumed a constant assimilation efficiency of 75 per cent but in fact assimilation efficiency varies with the kind of food being eaten.

Taitt (1973) recorded energetic assimilation efficiencies of 72–74 per cent for Starlings eating mealworms but, when the birds were given poultry pellets, assimilation efficiencies were only 40–45 per cent, thus Starlings eating the latter have to eat a greater weight per day than when feeding on the invertebrate food. Taitt found that her birds ingested daily about 50 k cal of mealworms but about 90 kcal of pellets: in terms of dry weight of food eaten this represented around 9 g and 23 g respectively. Both of these intake rates provided an existence energy of approxmately 40 k cal day^{-1}. The consumption of the additional weight of food required when birds are eating a largely vegetable diet is made possible by increasing the rate of food passage through the alimentary canal (Al-Joborae 1979), rather than by increasing the amount of time spent feeding. But the amount of food eaten is also dependent upon the kind of diet to which the birds are adapted. In Al-Joborae's experiments, Starlings given animal food ate 7–18 g day^{-1} (dry weight) while those eating plant food consumed 30–40 g day^{-1}. In terms of energy, these weights represent intakes of 50–60 k cal and 80–100 kcal day^{-1} respectively; these figures are similar to those found by Taitt (1973). On switching the diets of the two groups, however, the daily consumption of the birds that had been on a plant diet, and therefore, had large gizzards and intestines, dropped rapidly to about 20 g: the birds that had been eating invertebrate food were less able to increase their daily consumption when switched to plant food, presumably because their small guts could not cope with the much large volume of food the birds really required.

When to feed

In winter a Starling could potentially spend most of the day feeding, stopping only to drink, rest, or perform other essential activities such as preening. Their allocation of time to these various activities has not been studied but my impression is that most bouts of feeding are ended by disturbance by a wide variety of external influences or even by other Starlings. If feeding were not interrupted, however, it is still doubtful whether the birds would feed continuously, for feeding still occurs in bouts, the duration of which may depend on the kind of food that is being eaten. At Bridgets Experimental Husbandry Farm, I found that the higher the proportion of the birds that fed on grassland, the higher was the proportion of the birds that was feeding on each of my censuses. This suggested that when they were feeding on grassland invertebrates they had to devote more time to feeding than when they fed on barley (Feare 1981c). I have been unable to measure the feeding rates of birds feeding in grass fields because it is difficult to see their bill movements, but they ate barley at a rate of 0.54 g min^{-1} (Feare and Swannack 1978). At this rate they could satisfy a daily requirement of around 30 g (Taitt 1973; Al-Joborae 1979) in about an hour. Apart from the requirement of animal protein, discussed previously, it is unlikely that a Starling could ingest its daily requirement in one hour because the gut is not big enough to cope with that amount of food in such a short time. Thus the length of a bout of feeding could be governed by the capacity of the gut and the rate of passage of food through it, rather than by any behavioural factors. This has not been studied in Starlings, but during our work on the effects of feeding space on feeding behaviour (Feare and Inglis 1978) it was notable that each individual fed on turkey starter crumbs for only a few minutes at a time, followed by a period of resting, bathing, preening, and singing; we do not know what made the birds stop feeding at a particular moment.

When a Starling returns from its winter feeding site to the roost in the evening, it must decide whether to fill its gizzard at the farm and use additional energy in carrying the extra weight involved to the roost, or whether to travel light in the expectation that the gizzard can be filled close to the roost. Once again, we do not know how birds arrive at this decision, but the principles involved may be similar to those that concern a parent returning to its nest box carrying a load of food for its chicks.

Tinbergen (1981) examined the relationship between time devoted to feeding, number of food items collected, and the distance that the parent had to travel. The collection of food for the young presented the parent with a time-consuming problem for the presence of a leatherjacket in the bill hindered the collection of a second one since the adult could not probe into the soil so efficiently. To overcome this problem the bird had to put the first item down when digging for the second: this necessitated subsequent re-location and picking up of the first leatherjacket. Thus, to collect two food items it took the Starling more than twice as long as it did to collect one and the delay due to 'hindering' increased more as further items were sought. If a bird had to travel a long way to the feeding ground, however, it was more economical for the parent to collect and carry back a few items whereas when feeding close to the nest the bird could afford to make repeated trips in order to collect single leatherjackets. Thus the birds were able to balance the effort to be devoted to collecting food with the distance that they had to fly back to the nest. That the problem was one really of time was shown when Starlings fed on an area where moribund leatherjackets were lying on the surface of the ground. Here, 5.8 leatherjackets were collected per bout of feeding because the 'hindering' effect was eliminated; where parents had to dig for leatherjackets they collected only 1.2 per feeding visit.

Where to feed.

In any feeding area a bird may encounter and sample a variety of prey but major dietary switches usually entail moving to a new feeding area. When Starlings were feeding their young on leatherjackets and caterpillars, Tinbergen (1981) and Tinbergen and Drent (1980) found that these items were obtained from grassland and salt marsh respectively and that the birds had to decide which area to visit to satisfy different needs of their chicks. Here, a relatively minor change of diet from one invertebrate to another nevertheless necessitated the exploitation of two distinct feeding areas.

More fundamental alterations of diet may require vastly different areas in which to forage, as shown by the divergence of feeding areas of adults and juveniles in summer mentioned above. Damage to cherries is due mainly to juveniles, but even in an area where cherries are not grown, Feare (1980) found that in July and August flocks of Starlings feeding in trees consisted predominantly of juveniles, while flocks feeding in grass fields comprised mainly adults. The foods obtained from these two feeding areas may satisfy different nutritional needs of the age groups; alternatively, the separation of their feeding ranges may relieve naive juveniles from competition with experienced adults for the scarce invertebrate resources in grass fields in summer. The feeding relationships within mixed age-group flocks in grassland and the relative nutritional contents of the foods eaten in the two areas need investigation before these problems can be resolved.

Whether similar age-related utilization of feeding sites occurs at other times of year is not known, largely because the ages of feeding birds are much more difficult to determine once the juveniles have moulted into their first winter plumage. Seasonal variations in the proportion of Starlings feeding at sites yielding different foods does present this possibility and there are suggestions of sexual differences in the utilization of some feeding areas (Feare and Inglis 1978).

Throughout the year, Starlings spend a high proportion of time feeding in pasture but their exploitation of other feeding sites varies seasonally (Dunnet 1956; Gromadzki 1969, 1979; Williamson and Gray 1975). Alternative feeding sites are used especially in winter, as shown in my studies at Bridgets Experimental Husbandry Farm near Winchester (Fig. 3.3). Here, the two principal sites available in winter are grass fields surrounding the farm buildings and cattle troughs from which the cows' high energy foods, for example crushed barley, are usually taken by the birds. During prolonged snow, which is rare in southern England, these cereal-based foods constitute one of the only resources available to Starlings (Dunnet 1956; Taitt 1973), but at other times grassland is extensively used for feeding, even when feed-lots are being utilized and damage is occurring (Fig. 3.3).

This suggested that a shortage of invertebrate food might not be the factor that makes Starlings eat vegetable food in winter. This idea was supported by the absence of any density-dependent limitation of the number of birds feeding on grassland or of the proportion of them that was feeding while in grass fields; in other words, the invertebrate food available in grassland around the farm did not appear to impose any limitation on the number of birds that could feed there (Feare 1981c). Why, then should any Starlings feed on barley from the cattle troughs?

The reason seemed to be connected with the birds' time allocation to feeding, for while those feeding on animal food from grassland had to devote a high proportion of the short winter day to feeding, those eating barley could potentially obtain their daily requirement in about an hour. This could leave the remainder of the day for activities like resting and preening, which could be performed in situations, such as dense foliage, where predators would find the birds hard to locate and the Starlings would receive greater protection from adverse climatic factors, notably wind and rain, that might otherwise increase their energy expenditure. But if eating barley carries so many advantages, why should Starlings expend so much time and energy searching grass fields for inverte-brates?

We have already seen that animal protein is essential for weight maintenance and even for the survival of carnivorous birds (Berth-old 1976) and the incorporation of some invertebrate food into the diet is therefore a basic requirement. At present, however, we do not know how much animal protein is required; from the foregoing observations it is apparent that it need constitute only a proportion of the daily food intake. If the necessary animal food can be collected in a relatively short time and the remainder of the day's feeding devoted to eating barley, the birds ought to be able to fulfil their daily feeding activities in a small proportion of the daylight hours, even in winter, and therefore accrue some of the advan-tages of energy conservation and predator protection that a bird on a strictly plant diet would achieve. The majority of the farm population, however, spent over half of the day feeding (Feare 1981c).

When Starlings that were feeding in the food troughs were caught in mist nets, these birds were found to contain an unex-pectedly high proportion of males and in experiments with captive birds, Feare and Inglis (1978) showed that, when feeding space was limited, as at a cattle trough, males were dominant over females and could restrict the access of subordinate birds to the troughs during bouts of feeding. Thus the high proportion of males in the samples caught at the cattle troughs at Bridgets Experimental Husbandry Farm (and at cattle feedlots elsewhere) could result from the competitive exclusion of females; these must spend a high proportion of their day feeding in grassland. This may not, however, be the complete story since females could have different nutrient requirements from males, and especially a need for a higher protein intake.

Jones and Ward (1976) considered that the main determinant of the date of laying and of the clutch size of Quelea was the amount of protein that was stored in the pectoral muscle of the females. Ward (1977) has subsequently suggested a similar importance of pectoral-muscle protein in Starlings and he demonstrated a rapid fall in the level of this protein in females during the breeding season. We do not know the composition of this protein that can be stored for use during breeding, nor do we know for how long it can be stored. If females can derive an advantage, in terms of breeding early and laying a large clutch, from maintaining high protein levels in winter, then females may elect to spend a greater proportion of their time feeding on grassland invertebrates. The increased risks of predation and added energy expenditure, due both to the longer period spent feeding and to the lack of protection from climatic factors, that are consequent upon feeding for long periods in the open, may even contribute to the higher mortality of inexperienced first-year females.

From the foregoing it is apparent that grassland is the main feeding site used by Starlings for most of the year (Fig. 3.3) but grass fields vary in their quality with respect to food availability. This variation is due to different densities of food organisms that are present in different fields (old pastures support a higher earthworm density than recently grown grass—Edwards and Lofty 1972) and to various factors that affect the availability of these organisms to the birds. One of the more important of these factors is the height of the vegetation and grassland feeding birds prefer to feed when the grass is short (Brownsmith 1977), a feature not restricted to Starlings (Eiserer 1980; Feare, Dunnet, and Patterson 1974). Brownsmith (1977) showed that in short grass (< 6 cm high) the rate of movement of foraging Starlings was more rapid and the duration of stationary periods was shorter than when feeding in tall grass, though the reasons for the differences were not clear. Starlings are also attracted to freshly cut grass (e.g. Tinbergen 1981) which seems to offer a temporary prey abundance, but again the precise reasons for this have not been established (Eiserer 1980). Greater prey availability, greater ease of prey detection or capture, and clearer all-round vision might all contribute to the above findings.

HOW TO FIND FOOD

We have already seen one way in which Starlings find their food for at any moment they must decide where to feed in the range of potential feeding sites that is available to them. In some instances the decision is made easy: there is no point in feeding in trees in winter when the trees bear no fruit or harbour no caterpillars, and there is no point in trying to feed in fields when they are covered in snow. When such obvious restrictions are not in force, however, Starlings must learn which are the best areas to suit current nutritional needs. In the breeding season, adults are restricted by the distance that they can economically travel from the nest in order to procure their own and their chicks' food. While breeding, adults become very familiar with their feeding range, such that they can rapidly switch from one kind of food item to another when the need arises (Tinbergen and Drent 1980). But what happens in winter, when no such ties to a restricted area exist?

Spaans (1977) found that Starlings did not usually return to the same geographical area in sucessive winters and our own work in southern England supports this conclusion: few of the birds that we have ringed at Bridgets Experimental Husbandry Farm in winter (they are nearly all migrants) have been subsequently retrapped there. Migrant Starlings do not, therefore, build up a knowledge of a particular winter feeding area that can be used year after year. This seems, at first sight, to put them at a disadvantage compared with our own resident Starlings which spend much of the winter in the vicinity of their nest sites, defending these and at the same time feeding in familiar places. Wintering migrants do, however, consistently use the same feeding site once they have established themselves in an area at the beginning of the winter (Bray, Larsen, and Mott 1975).

By conspicuously marking birds, caught at the calf yard at Bridgets Experimental Husbandry Farm, with plastic wing tags and identifying them subsequently at and around the farm, I was able to demonstrate this fidelity to a feeding area in winter (Feare 1980 and Fig. 9.4). At this time the situation is complicated, however, by the birds' apparent necessity to return to a winter roost each night. In this particular study the roost has ranged from 5 to 14 km from the farm, but each morning the marked birds returned to feed in the same general area. For some birds, we had sufficient sightings to plot their individual feeding distributions around the farm, which showed that these birds maintained an even greater fidelity to the feeding site in which they became established at the beginning of the winter. This fidelity concerned not only a particular cattle yard or a field, for the birds habitually returned to feed in the same corner of a field each day (Fig. 9.5). In addition, much of the time that was not devoted to feeding was spent in a day roost where small groups gathered to rest, preen, or apparently just sit with occasional bouts of singing. Each marked individual tended to have its own preferred roost site, this being a particular branch of a particular tree or bush to which the individual habitually returned. Such fidelity to winter feeding and day roost sites must enable the birds to learn the best feeding areas (and alternatives, should these be necessary) and the whereabouts

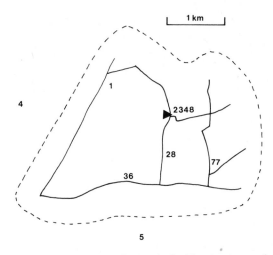

Fig. 9.4. Sightings of Starlings caught, marked with wing-tags and released at Bridgets Experimental Husbandry Farm (arrow) during the 1975–6 and 1976–7 winters. Within the study area (enclosed by dashed line), marked birds were searched for by driving round the roads (continuous lines) and walking. Sightings outside the study area were reported by the public.

and most likely routes of attack of potential predators: in other words, the gaining of an intimate knowledge of a small area of land by daily use must play a part in maximizing the Starlings' chances of surviving the winter.

If familiarity with a winter locality can enhance survival, why should Starlings settle in a new area each winter rather than return to that which permitted their survival the previous winter? Spaans (1977) thought that his discovery of low fidelity to feeding areas between winters might have been due to the fact that Holland (where his analysis was undertaken) represents an inferior winter habitat than Britain: Perdeck (1967*a*) had shown that birds that wintered in Holland had a higher mortality than British winter migrants. The findings that Starlings do not tend to return to Bridgets Experimental Husbandry Farm each winter suggests, however, that other factors must be involved. For example, the invertebrate availability at a particular area may fluctuate widely from year to year, in which case there would be no advantage in returning to a previous winter's feeding area. For the present, this explanation must remain speculative, but there is no doubt that the spatial distribution and availability of certain food items can vary, even on a daily basis.

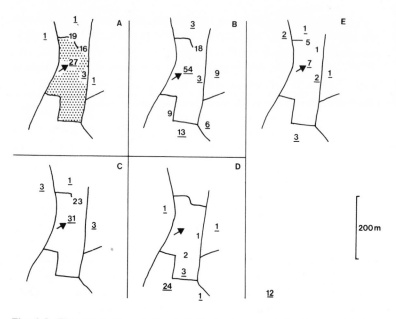

Fig. 9.5. The distribution of five individual wing-tagged Starlings at Bridgets Experimental Husbandry Farm in the winters of 1975–6 and 1976–7. The birds were caught, marked, and released at the calf feedlot (marked by arrow) and the figures denote subsequent sightings during the winter. The stippled area is the farmyard. Underlined figures are birds seen feeding; other figures are birds in daytime roosts. Birds A, B, and C fed mainly in the feedlot while birds B and C fed mainly in grass fields, but all individuals demonstrated a strong fidelity to their particular feeding sites.

Leatherjackets are active mainly at night and in the morning they descend to varying depths in burrows. Any that descend below about 2.5 cm are out of reach of the birds' bills and are therefore unavailable; the proportion of leatherjackets that is available is small, with less than 1 per cent of them being removed by Starlings (Tinbergen and Drent 1980) during a bout of feeding. In addition to a daily redistribution of leatherjackets, a further problem faces a hunting Starling, for leatherjackets, in common with many other potential food organisms, are not uniformly distributed in a grass field but they occur in patches. Tinbergen and Drent (1980) likened their distribution to a contour map with areas of high abundance merging into areas of low abundance or total absence. The problem facing a Starling is how it should locate the areas of high abundance. These authors showed that the mechanism employed involved both trial and error, and a good memory.

A Starling that begins feeding in a new part of a grass field does not know where it is likely to find leatherjackets. The bird walks, repeatedly probing into the turf in search of prey. Most of its first efforts are likely to be unproductive, but when it does locate a leatherjacket it tends to concentrate its hunting effort in that immediate area. If more leatherjackets are found, the bird has located a patch of available prey and its frequency of successful probes tells the bird it should remain in that area. When an adult which is feeding young has collected sufficient food, it must return to its nest to feed the chicks and then needs to begin hunting for a high reward area again. Tinbergen and Drent found that this was where memory played a part since the bird did not begin hunting completely afresh; instead, it returned to the general area where it had found a high prey availability in its last foraging mission (Tinbergen 1976). The bird had, therefore, remembered the location of this patch of available leatherjackets and had memorized some, as yet unidentified, environmental cues that could help it to return to that area. The sensitivity of this memory of environmental information was later shown in greater detail by Tinbergen (1981), who found that in many instances a bird that had had a successful bout of feeding would return to within one metre of its previous feeding site.

Having established the existence of this memory, Tinbergen and Drent wanted to know what enabled the bird to assess the success of a feeding session; that is, what criteria did it use to decide whether to return to that area or to search for another one? During a series of visits to a patch that a bird had discovered, its behaviour followed a characteristic pattern. In particular, its feeding rate rose to a peak and then subsequently declined. Tinbergen and Drent thought that this pattern resulted from two effects: first, the rising feeding rate during the first stages of exploitation stemmed from the bird's increasing familiarity with the distribution of available prey in the patch and second, the decline was due to the bird's depletion of the available leatherjackets in the local area. Eventually, the bird failed to return and searched for another patch of prey, and Tinbergen and Drent suspected that the Starlings could be using their own intake rates during a visit to assess the worth of returning.

These authors found, when observing one of their nesting females, that she returned to a feeding site if her intake rate, expressed as milligrams of food collected per minute of her absence from the nest, was above a certain threshold value. Figure 9.6 shows that this threshold value was about 180 mg min^{-1}, a figure that was also demonstrated experimentally. Thus starlings do indeed appear to use their own intake rates as a measure of the profitability of a feeding site. We have already seen, however, that factors other than food weight can influence the birds' behaviour; in particular, food quality can determine where they feed. An excess of leatherjackets in the chicks' diet promotes the production of excessively wet faeces that soil the nest (Chapter 7) and Tinbergen (1981) demonstrated that, when given a choice, parent Starlings selected caterpillars that did not have this effect.

To obtain the *Cerapteryx* caterpillars the Starlings had to fly to a salt marsh which was further away than the grassland where they could find leatherjackets. The caterpillars also lived at a lower density than leatherjackets and the combination of these two factors meant that the parent had to devote more energy and more time in its search for caterpillars: to use Tinbergen and Drent's (1980) terminology, *Cerapteryx* is an expensive prey. We saw in Chapter 7 that due to their greater time commitment, fewer caterpillars were brought to large than to small broods and Tinbergen (1981) showed that the parent's intake of caterpillars also fell while it was feeding a large brood. In addition, we saw that when

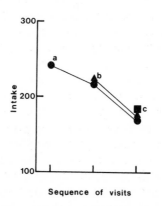

Fig. 9.6. The food intake rate (mg of leatherjackets/min of absence from the nest) of a female Starling on three sequences of visits to the same feeding site. In case (a) she returned twice and in case (b) once before her intake rate fell to about 180 mg min^{-1}, after which she did not return. In case (c) her intake rate was only 180 mg min^{-1} on her first visit and she did not return. This (180 mg min^{-1}) seems to be a threshold that determines whether a bird will or will not return to a particular feeding site. (Redrawn from Tinbergen and Drent 1980.)

Tinbergen replaced well-fed chicks in a nest with chicks that had been starved, the parents stopped bringing caterpillars and instead brought leatherjackets that they collected nearby until the chicks were satisfied. Thus in this situation the parent's selection of a place in which to feed was determined by at least three factors: prey availability, nutrient content of the food, and the state of hunger of the chicks.

These factors that Starlings use in the selection of feeding sites have been discovered through research during the breeding season, but it is likely that similar rules will govern feeding behaviour at other times of year. Food availability and quality will determine what foods they should eat (and hence where they should eat) and this may be influenced by the birds' own state of hunger. For example, when Starlings arrived at Bridgets Experimental Husbandry Farm from their night roost they crowded more densely into the calves' feeding troughs than they did at other times of day. When Starlings leave their winter roost in the morning their gizzards and intestines are empty and their first need may simply be to eat as much food as possible—an inferior diet of cereal grains seems to suffice for this. Thereafter, their satiation can allow them to be more selective in their choice of food and quality may become more important. In the evening, especially when assembling prior to entering the roost, the main requirement may again be to fill the gut as quickly as possible and many of these assemblies are, in Britain, on winter-sown cereal fields where the birds achieve a high intake rate (Wadsworth, in Feare 1980) that enables them to enter the roost with as much food as possible inside the gizzard. Here again, quantity sems to take precedence over quality and the feeding site is determined by a high availability of readily obtainable food.

In this chapter we have seen how remarkably adaptable the Starling is in many aspects of its feeding biology, the adaptability including its morphology (and probably physiology) and behaviour. Joost Tinbergen's work has illustrated the parts that learning and memory play in permitting an individual to locate and exploit the best prey in the most efficient way to provide the bird with the correct intake of essential nutrients, even though we know very little about these.

I have, however, omitted one important clue that can be used by Starlings searching for a good feeding site—the presence and behaviour of other birds. Starlings are, as emphasized in Chapter 1, gregarious and in Chapter 10 I shall examine their flocking and communal roosting behaviour.

10 GATHERINGS

The question most frequently asked of anyone who shows an interest in Starlings is 'How do they gather so quickly when food is put out in a garden, driving other birds away?' This may be an annoying habit as far as the garden bird-watcher is concerned but this is where we can all see in action several aspects of their behaviour that contribute to their success. Their ability to discover the new food source so quickly relies on two aspects of their feeding behaviour that were discussed in the last chapter, memory and feeding in bouts. Starlings do not, as we have seen, search randomly for food; they remember where food is more likely to be found and search preferentially in those places. Thus a bird table where food is regularly placed becomes a focal point for their searching activity. We have also seen that by feeding in bouts Starlings have ample time for other activities and in winter, when bird tables are most extensively used by these and other birds, Starlings are able to spend a considerable amount of time resting, preening, singing, or apparently just sitting. But a 'sitting' bird is aware of what is happening around it, keeping an eye open for predators, for other Starlings, and for new food supplies. Should a sitting bird see food being placed in one of the areas that it has in vision, it may fly down to sample the new food source.

I also mentioned, in Chapter 5, that plastic models of feeding Starlings can be used to attract birds to a catching area and the attractiveness of 'feeding' models has now been demonstrated in various species (Krebs 1974; Drent and Swiestra 1977; Inglis and Isaacson 1978). If the bird that flew down from its vantage point on, say, a television aerial, began feeding intensively on the food source that it sampled, other birds that saw its activity, and are ready to begin a bout of feeding, might well fly down to join it. And then we have a flock!

ADVANTAGES OF FLOCKING

This may give the impression that the formation of a flock is the accidental result of an accumulation of birds at a good feeding site. The toleration of conspecifics nearby is, however, a biological property of Starlings and other flocking species and the formation and maintenance of a flock holds advantages for the participants, though there may also be disadvantages. Let us first consider the rates of feeding of Starlings at a simple but artificial site, a cattle trough where the birds were eating mainly crushed barley, and examine the relationship between the rate of feeding and the number of birds in the feeding flock (Feare and Inglis 1978).

When few birds were feeding at the trough their peck rate was low (Fig. 10.1) and it was readily apparent that a reason for this is that these individuals spent a relatively high proportion of their time looking around, rather than feeding. As the number of birds on the trough increased so their feeding rate increased and this ability to maintain a high feeding rate in a flock is an obvious advantage. Mutual toleration has its limits, however, and when too many birds assembled at the restricted feeding site represented by the trough fighting ensued and, as a consequence, the feeding rate fell. It should be noted, however, that the fighting does not result from a limit imposed by the abundance of the food, for there was enough for Starlings and cattle as well, but restricted access to the trough exerts a limit on the space in which the birds can feed. If

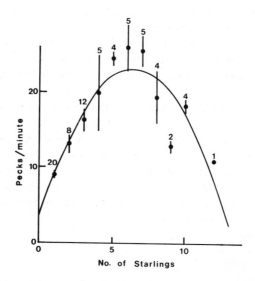

Fig. 10.1. The feeding rate (barley fragments eaten per min) of Starlings feeding at a cattle trough in relation to the number of Starlings on the trough. The maximum feeding rate was attained when between five and seven birds were feeding.

too many birds are present they get too close to each other and then infringe each others' 'individual distance', a distance within which an individual will not tolerate another. In crowded situations like this the dominant birds tend to fare better than subordinates, in terms of being able to remain longer at the feeding site, but the amount of fighting involved leads to a reduction in the intake rate of even the most dominant members of the flock. Thus it is disadvantageous for all birds when the number at a restricted feeding site, such as a cattle trough or a bird table, becomes too large.

Starlings are highly gregarious birds, however, and even when food is not concentrated in a few scattered localities, the birds do not distribute themselves randomly but congregate in certain areas. In such flocks, as seen commonly in fields, fighting occurs infrequently because there is plenty of space, and the flock members are therefore able to derive more benefit from the increased feeding rates permitted by foraging within a flock. Since this appears to be an important advantage of feeding within a flock rather than feeding alone, we must now ask how these higher feeding rates are achieved.

The functions of flocking in birds (and other animals) have been the subject of speculation and investigation for many years and most studies have concentrated on the improvement of feeding rate and on the avoidance of predation as the prime advantages of being in a group. Several means whereby being a member of an assemblage can confer protection from predators have been postulated. The movements of individuals within a flock may have a confusing effect on a predator, making it difficult for the predator to select and attack a particular target. If it does get as far as selecting a target, the predator may then be somewhat reticent in forcing home its attack owing to the danger of damaging collisions with other flock members: the resulting delay may permit the selected prey to avoid its adversary. The confusing effect of numbers can be enhanced when a flock mobs a predator, especially when distracting calls are also given (Chapter 5). Numbers by themselves can confer a degree of protection for the more birds that a flock comprises, the lower is the chance that a particular individual will be predated. A further advantage can be derived from numbers since in a feeding flock each bird apportions its time between probing or pecking, walking to a new area, and looking around. The larger the flock, the greater is the chance that at any particular moment at least one bird will be looking around with the possibility of detecting an approaching predator. These, then, are the various theoretical mechanisms whereby life within a flock could help to reduce the chances of becoming the victim of a predator's attack, but does flocking reduce the rate and success of predation in practice?

Owing to their comparative rarity, rates of predation of Starlings are difficult to observe and measure in the field. Experiments by Powell (1974), using captive birds, do show that birds within a flock have a better awareness of approaching predators than do birds feeding alone. Powell exposed single birds and groups of 10 feeding Starlings to a dead Cooper's Hawk *Accipiter cooperi*, preserved with its wings outstretched in a flying position, that was allowed to 'fly' down a wire over the cage of subject birds. He found that the average time taken for a single Starling to detect the predator and react by taking off was 4.1 s, whereas the flocks reacted in an average of 3.2 s, this difference being statistically significant. Thus a flock does indeed possess more acute powers of perception of predators than an individual. This leads to a prediction about the time that must be spent looking around: the greater observational efficiency of a flock should permit members to devote less time to looking around than is required of lone individuals. This was suggested by my own observations, mentioned above, of Starlings feeding at a cattle trough but Powell (1974) recorded the times spent foraging and being vigilant in his captive birds. Single birds spent 47 per cent of their time looking around; individuals in groups of five devoted only 30 per cent of their time to surveillance, and this decreased to 12 per cent in flocks of ten birds. Conversely, the proportion of time devoted to feeding increased as flock size increased. A similar relationship between the proportion of time spent in surveillance and flock size has been found in Starlings feeding in grassland (Fig. 10.2). Here, Jennings and Evans (1980) discovered further that there were differences in the amount of time spent vigilant according to the position of an individual within a flock, with birds occupying central positions spending less time vigilant and more time feeding than peripheral birds. Jennings and Evans concluded that Starlings could adjust their apportioning of time to feeding and vigilance according to their assessment of their own risk of predation: this interpretation assumes that peripheral birds have a higher predation risk than central ones, which is most likely to be the case with mammalian

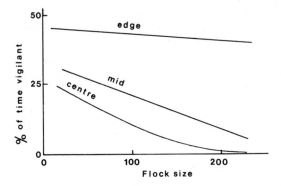

Fig. 10.2. The proportion of time spent vigilant by Starlings in different positions in flocks of different sizes, showing that birds at the centre of flocks devoted the least time to vigilance, and this time diminished as flock size increased. (Drawn from data in Jennings and Evans (1980)).

predators. Barnard (1980) found that House Sparrows adjusted the proportion of their time that they devoted to surveillance according to the risk of predation in different habitats and such a relation may hold for many flock-feeding birds.

An inverse relationship between the proportion of time spent vigilant and flock size has now been found in many flocking species (e.g. Lazarus 1979; Elgar and Catterall 1981) and we can conclude that flocking serves a dual function of defence against predation and permitting more efficient feeding. There are further connotations with respect to feeding, however, which can lead to a greater feeding efficiency of the individual and a more efficient exploitation of a food source.

In my description above of Starlings feeding at a cattle trough, I talked in terms of an increase in feeding rate as the number of birds on the trough rose in Fig. 10.1. These feeding rates were measured by counting the number of food items (fragments of barley) eaten during one minute of observation; no attempt was made to record time spent vigilant and the recorded increase in the rate of food intake in the rising part of Fig. 10.1 probably resulted from the decreasing vigilance of members of a larger flock. When we attempted to simulate the trough-feeding situation using captive Starlings we found, however, feeding rate relationships within the flock (Feare and Inglis 1979). The feeding rates of some individuals were significantly correlated with the feeding rates of their nearest neighbours on the trough: in other words, a bird fed rapidly if its neighbour was feeding rapidly and vice versa. This suggested that, for some birds at least, there was a strong tendency to imitate a neighbour, leading to social stimulation within the flock which, if a high proportion of the birds followed suit, could maximize the food intake of the flock as a whole. Whether this maximization is ever achieved in the field is not known; the finding that birds joining a flock did not selectively land close to a rapidly feeding bird or to a bird of a particular social status might militate against it (Feare and Inglis 1979). In Quelea, Lazarus (1979) found that the onset of feeding could be stimulated by the presence of feeding, rather then non-feeding, neighbours but he failed to record any influence of the neighbours on rates of feeding. There are certainly strong indications that flock members perform more efficiently, in terms of both feeding and predator avoidance, than solitary Starlings but the contribution of flocking to the Starling's success may be more deep-seated than I have so far suggested. Thompson, Grant, Pearson, and Corner (1968) measured the rates of heart-beat of solitary Starlings and flock members when tape-recorded distress calls were played to the birds. Grouped birds showed a greater and more prolonged increase in heart rate than lone individuals, suggesting that birds in flocks might have a heightened physiological responsiveness that could influence behaviour more generally than suspected so far. A rewarding area of research is indicated here.

Although flocking is obviously an integral part of Starling behaviour, carrying with it the advantages mentioned above, flocking also helps birds to discover and exploit localized and transient patches of food. Localization and transience are features of many of the Starling's food sources—the daily re-distribution of available leatherjackets that we saw in Chapter 9; the appearance of some prey items, such as bibionid flies (Tinbergen and Drent 1980) at specific times of day; the ripening of specific fruit trees in the summer and autumn; and the sudden appearance of super-abundances of food items exposed by the cultivation of fields or harvest of crops. In the last two examples the colouring of the fruit and the presence of farm machinery respectively may provide Starlings with adequate cues to the availability of the 'new' food resources. Where such obvious cues are absent, however, the utilization of a patch of food may commence with the chance discovery of the patch by a wandering individual. If this bird then exhibits signs of abundant food, for example by rapid pecking, other birds may be rapidly attracted to the area. This is akin to the bird-table situation discussed above. As more birds accumulate the members of the flock begin to benefit from the relaxed vigilence and more efficient feeding permitted by flock membership and a high food intake is achieved. This kind of exploitation of a transient resource by the aggregation of animals has been termed feeding by 'local enhancement'. Since the food in these local patches is ephemoral, irrespective of the attention of birds, over-exploitation of the resource is not a problem and the birds receive maximum benefit by taking as much as they can while the food is available. Here we see, therefore, that the advantages of predator avoidance and high feeding rate that result from flocking are supplemented by an efficient utilization of transient and localised food supplies.

FLOCK SIZE

In Fig. 10.1 we can see that the most efficient flock size, in terms of maximizing intake rate, was between five and seven birds on the cattle trough. Such extreme localization of food and restriction of feeding space is unusual, however, and we must consider flock sizes in more 'natural' feeding sites, such as grass fields.

I have already remarked (Chapter 6) that in early April the most usual flock size is two, these being mated pairs, and yet casual observation reveals that in winter flocks are much larger. Seasonal variation in the size of flocks feeding in fields was described by Davis (1970) and by Williamson and Gray (1975): they showed that small flocks in spring and summer were replaced by larger flocks in autumn and winter (Fig. 10.3). The latter authors also found that larger flocks tended to occur in their study area, in Maryland, USA, during the times of migration when more birds were present. Flock size must, of course, depend to a certain extent on the number of birds present in the area. For example, at my own study site at Bridget's Experimental Husbandry Farm, winter flocks occasionally exceeded three hundred birds while during the breeding season there were never more than two hundred birds on the farm.

During the period October to March of the 1975–6 and 1976–7 winters I recorded the sizes of 417 flocks feeding in grass fields at Bridgets Experimental Husbandry Farm. Even during this period, when up to 2000 Starlings fed at the farm each day, 58 per cent of the flocks contained less than 50 birds and only 6 per cent con-

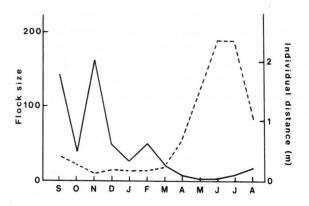

Fig. 10.3. Annual change in the size of flocks of feeding Starlings and in the distance between individuals within these flocks ('individual distance'). The largest flocks and the smallest individual distances occurred in winter. (Redrawn from Williamson and Gray 1975.)

tained more than 250 birds. Even when there were many birds available to form flocks, therefore, the flocks still were mainly small. Expressed in a way that overcame the difficulty of varying numbers of birds on the farm during the winter, 70 per cent of the flocks consisted of less than 10 per cent of the population of the farm at that time, and only 2 per cent of the flocks consisted of more than 40 per cent of the Starlings on the farm. Again, the emphasis was on small flocks, irrespective of how many birds were feeding at the farm. These winter flocks were still, however, larger than in the breeding season when flock size reached a minimum in early April, as mentioned above.

Between November and March there were no seasonal differences in flock size, but in October there were more large flocks (over 200 birds) than in the other months. On the farm, there tended to be larger flocks immediately after arrival from the roost in the morning and prior to departure for the roost in the evening. It is well known, however, that flock sizes increase as the birds prepare to roost in the evening and close to the roost, where flocks from the surrounding feeding areas coalesce, pre-roost assemblies can contain hundreds of thousands of Starlings.

In addition to annual and diurnal changes, flock size may also vary according to the food source being utilized. When available in early winter, maize, barley, and wheat stubble fields at Bridgets

E.H.F. occasionally supported flocks of over 500 Starlings while flocks on grass fields usually contained less than 50 birds. On grass fields, I found no difference between the sizes of flocks on fields containing cattle or sheep and in those without stock, but the precise relationship between the Starlings' utilization of fields grazed by cattle and the food available in the grass and in dung of various ages is obscure.

Large flocks tend to be characteristic of the dense concentrations of food found at cattle feeding areas in winter, although at the large feedlots of the North American plains, where the number of cattle can run to tens of thousands and Starlings occur in hundreds of thousands, the definition of a flock becomes difficult: the birds in different parts of the feedlot should perhaps be regarded as separate flocks.

The number of Starlings comprising a flock is thus subject to variation, but other parameters of flocking behaviour have also been found to change according to season and to the food being eaten. Williamson and Gray (1975) found that the spacing between birds within flocks was greater in the small spring and summer aggregations than in the large flocks encountered in winter. Patterson, Dunnet, and Fordham (1971) found a similar inverse relationship between flock size and individual spacing in Rooks. The distances between individuals in Starling flocks on stubble and germinating cereal fields, and in cattle feeding areas, have not been measured but it is readily apparent that in these situations, and especially the last, birds feed much closer together than when feeding in grassland (cf Plates 7 and 14). This suggests that flock size and spacing are both features that can be modified to confer different advantages to Starlings feeding in different situations. Further investigation is required to ascertain the identity of these advantages but the nature of the food items, their ability to defend themselves against predators and the amount of movement required of a bird to catch prey may all help to determine the flock characteristics. For example, grassland invertebrates are capable of more rapid movement in summer than at other times of year and may therefore be more prone to disturbance. Starlings that attempt to feed in close proximity to one another might, therefore, disturb each others' potential food, making it less readily available and thus depressing the rate of food intake of all flock members. This mutual interference will decrease as the mobility of the prey diminishes, resulting in the closest inter-individual spacings occurring where the food is stationary, as when the birds are feeding on grain. Even in this situation, however, the depressant effect of feeding too close together can be realized (Fig. 10.1).

These conflicting interests of greater feeding efficiency and mutual interference that are associated with flocking must also interact with the advantages that accrue with respect to predator avoidance; here, the law of diminishing returns applies for in large flocks the addition of more birds to provide more eyes will add little to the perceptive abilities of the flock (Lazarus 1979) or even to the other anti-predator attributes of flocking discussed above. Exactly how these factors interact in different feeding situations to produce the 'best' flock size remains to be investigated.

DAY ROOSTS

At most times of year, groups of Starlings can be seen sitting in exposed situations in trees, or on buildings, or other structures (Plate 2). These day roosts may be small, consisting of only two or three birds, or they may contain several hundred. Their diurnal and seasonal occurrence has not been recorded and their function has rarely been discussed, let alone studied. They can be presumed, however, to play an important role in the Starling's life but we can only speculate about their function.

Like other ornithologists, I have paid little attention to the existence of day roosts but my impression is that they occur less frequently during the breeding season than at other times of year. This is not altogether unexpected since the birds' time seems to be more fully occupied with foraging while breeding than during summer, autumn, and even winter. In addition, day roosts seem to be more frequent and also larger in early morning and late evening than during the remainder of the day.

Starlings indulge in several activities in day roosts, including preening, sleeping, singing, and apparently just sitting. When a day roost is disturbed by a predator, for example a Sparrow Hawk, all of the birds take off and fly in a tight, co-ordinated flock (Plate 11) but when not disturbed the roost loses its apparent integrity and individuals commute to nearby feeding areas with no sign of co-ordination whatever. In winter, my observations on wing-tagged birds at Bridgets Experimental Husbandry Farm showed that day-time roosting sites were traditional: individuals regularly returned to the same tree, and often the same section of the same branch, to roost throughout the winter.

These admittedly scant observations suggest that day roosts may have several functions. They provide a means whereby individuals can perform essential activities such as preening in company with others, thereby deriving the kinds of advance warning about predators that have already been discussed with respect to flocking. Those birds that roost in exposed tree-tops are also in a good position to see the whereabouts of feeding flocks and thus have a continuous input of information concerning the availability of food. The birds that appear to be simply sitting may be the vigilant ones or they may be the ones that are about to recommence feeding. The purpose of singing during the day in these roosts is obscure.

In the evening, when day roosts at feeding sites tend to be larger than at other times of the day, singing may help to synchronise departures for the night roost. The singing that occurs prior to departure builds to a climax and then suddenly ceases. This may happen several times but the taking off of some or all of the birds always coincides with one of the sudden silences. We shall see later that similar behaviour precedes departure from much larger night roosts. In addition to being aware of predators and feeding flocks, there is no doubt that the birds in evening tree-top roosts are also looking out for other Starlings that are flying over on their way to the night roost, for birds from the tree-tops commonly join other over-flying flocks. This behaviour may help to synchronize the arrival at the night roost of birds from different day-time feeding areas.

Further discussion of day roosts would be even more speculative than the forgoing and it becomes difficult, in the afternoon when the size of roosting groups increases, to distinguish between 'day roosts' and 'pre-roost assemblies': clearly, the one intergrades into the others. There can be no doubt that day roosts are important to the birds in providing them with security and information and a large area of research awaits the student of Starling behaviour.

NIGHT ROOSTS

Starlings sleep communally at night throughout the year but these roosts are most noticeable in winter when they are at their largest. The kinds of site used for roosting at night have already been discussed in Chapter 3 and the purpose of this section is to consider the behaviour of the birds at roosting time. Roosting behaviour has four components: the assembly of the birds from the surrounding feeding areas; entry into the roost; behaviour inside the roost; and morning dispersal to the feeding areas.

In the evening, birds that are going to roost communally must converge on the roost site from their varying distances within the feeding area served by the roost. This feeding area is very variable in size. In Cornwall, Wynne-Edwards (1929) found that the roost was not always in the centre of its feeding area and in some cases was even at the edge. The greatest distance travelled between feeding site and roost recorded by Wynne-Edwards was 38 km (24 miles) but in most cases feeding areas did not extend more than 24 km (15 miles) from the roost. In North America, however, Hamilton and Gilbert (1969) recorded daily travel distances of up to 80 km (50 miles) from the roost. These are, of course, extremes for each roost and most birds travel much shorter distances each day. We have already seen how individual birds tend to return to the same feeding site each day; this means that soon after adopting a roost for the winter a Starling must decide how far it is to fly each day, a factor which necessitates a certain amount of energy expenditure and which also determines the amount of time that is left for feeding. I shall return to this later when speculating about the function of communal roosting. For the present, it is sufficient to say that if all birds from the catchment area of a roost are to enter the roost at approximately the same time, then those that have farthest to travel must begin to fly towards the roost earlier than those that feed nearby.

Preparation for the flight to roost commences with the cessation of feeding and the occupation of perches in prominent positions, for example in the tops of tall trees or on buildings. The onset of this behaviour probably depends upon some, as yet unknown, aspect of daylight and within the small groups of birds involved the individuals may preen, sing or rest as in daytime roosts. At some stage, however, the singing birds suddenly stop and all or part of the group takes off and heads for the roost. For birds at the periphery of the roost's feeding area the decision to begin the journey must depend upon some external cue or on an internal psychological state or a combination of both. Birds in tree-top assemblies closer to the roost, however, can be stimulated to take off by flocks overhead flying towards the roost; they often fly up and join these flocks, though some may return to their waiting place after a brief flight.

Starlings that are flying to the roost do so normally in a direct line. The only exception to this appears to be when such a direct line would take them over high ground which they prefer to fly round (Wynne-Edwards 1929). By observing the bearings of two flight lines it is possible, by triangulation, to determine fairly precisely the position of the roost. The flocks of birds flying to the roost become larger the closer they get because groups of waiting birds joint those that are over-flying.

Pre-roost assemblies

These large flocks do not generally go straight into the roost. Instead they join other large flocks at what are termed 'pre-roost assembly' areas in Europe or 'staging' areas in North America.

Pre-roost assemblies may involve large flocks of non-feeding birds in trees and bushes, or on buildings, aerials (Plate 2) (in Bradford, Yorkshire, Starlings that pre-roost on the Police Station radio aerial have been known to obliterate the signals), and other suitable structures. More usually, however, pre-roost assemblies involve feeding birds and the largest flocks can literally darken fields (Plate 12). Spencer (1966) found that on short winter days feeding took priority over other activities and was more intense than at other times of year. Short grass, stubble, and germinating winter-sown cereal fields seem to be those especially favoured but the birds' preferences here have not been adequately studied; the kinds of food item eaten are in most cases unknown. Where Starlings pre-roost on winter cereals, however, their effects are readily apparent for the drills are marked by vast numbers of probe holes made by the birds' bills. Plant remains may be scattered all over the surface of the field where the birds have dug up and eaten the remains of the soft grain and discarded the green material. In this feeding situation J.T. Wadsworth (unpublished M.A.F.F. study) found that each bird dug up and ate about three grains per minute. The same field may be used on several consecutive evenings and work in the United States has shown that the birds will stay longer on these fields if an attractive bait is laid. Under natural conditions, however, neither the reasons for selecting particular fields each evening, nor the reasons for changing assembly areas are yet known.

Throughout the assembly period arriving flocks continue to join those already settled and in both feeding and non-feeding assemblies a considerable number of birds sing, those in feeding assemblies doing so on the ground. Preening and bathing are also carried out at this time and if water is not available in the pre-roost assembly area groups of birds will leave the main assembly to visit puddles or pools, only to rejoin the main flock later.

The pre-roost assembly is, therefore, a period of intense activity that precedes, on most evenings, the entry of the birds into the roost site. It enables at least some of the birds to have a last feed of the day and it permits a certain amount of plumage care. In addition, Starlings may, by assembling at places some distance from the roost itself, help to combat predation. The periodic changes of pre-roost assembly area render them less predictable than the roost, so that predators are less likely to be able to take advantage of birds in assemblies. Furthermore, birds that have assembled at a distance from the roost can fly to it *en masse*; as a result, entry into the roost can be rapid, allowing predators that rely on incoming birds the least opportunity to attack. This is important because a traditional roost site is well-known to pre-dators as a good evening feeding area: at a large (> 1 000 000 birds) winter roost in Lincolnshire in January 1975 I saw two Short-eared Owls *Asio flammeus*, two Hen Harriers *Circus cyaneus*, two Kestrels *Falco tinnunculus*, a Rough-legged Buzzard *Buteo lagopus*, a Peregrine *Falco peregrinus*, and a Sparrow Hawk *Accipiter nisus* all attempting to catch Starlings as they entered the roost. The entry of all of the Starlings in a short time minimizes time available to the predators to catch a Starling, and the large number of birds present confers the predator-swamping advan-tages of flocking that were discussed earlier. Wynne-Edwards (1929) even recorded Kestrels and Common Buzzards *Buteo buteo* moving away in the face of large swarms of incoming Starlings.

Entry into the roost

Starlings can enter their roost in different ways and Brodie (1974, 1976) tried to explain this variation in entry behaviour. Brodie identified four categories of flight behaviour over the roost prior to entry and a further four categories of behaviour during the descent into the trees. Such a breakdown seems excessively complicated, however, and my colleague R.W. Summers (personal communica-tion) thinks that only two types of entry are really involved: the birds either undertake aerial manoeuvres before descending to the roost (Plate 12), or they enter it directly, without display, from the flight from the feeding rounds or pre-roost assemblies. The swirl-ing displays, with cloud-like formations of vast numbers of birds flying to and fro in a variety of co-ordinated movements, constitute one of the most impressive sights of bird life. They do not occur every night and Brodie thought that wind strength and direction could influence the birds' behaviour. Both Charman (1965) and Summers (personal communication) have found that on some nights, some birds display on arrival at the roost while others do not and Summers noted that it was the earlier arrivals that tended to display while later flocks went straight into the roost. Thus the influence of weather, especially wind, on the mode of entry on any particular evening seems doubtful, although Brodie did find that the onset of rain during an aerial display caused its cessation.

Of perhaps greater importance is that both Charman (1965) and Summers have found no relationship between the method of entry into the roost and the size of that roost, in terms of the number of birds using it on any particular night. Symonds (1961) had suggested that the manner of entry, and in particular the occurrence or not of aerial display, could be used to estimate the sizes of roosts but Charman's and Summers' findings indicate that this cannot be done on the basis of the birds' behaviour.

During entry into the roost some calling may be involved. The entry of small flocks, especially those that are late to arrive, is often achieved by an erratic, tumbling flight that is accompanied by repeated 'chip' calls. Members of large flocks that stream into the roost, on the other hand, do not generally call and this difference again suggests, as mentioned in Chapter 5, that the 'chip' call expresses some kind of anxiety.

Behaviour in the roost

Once inside the roost there is often considerable activity, involving singing, flying to and fro, and fighting. Charman (1965) thought that only males sang in the roost but, in autumn and early winter at least, this needs confirmation. The nature and function of the song and movements is unknown; the movements and fighting certainly involve contests over roosting space but there are also larger scale movements of flocks of birds. Some of this activity is doubtless connected with the sorting of the birds into an age and sex distribution pattern within the roost.

Many (probably most) roosts are not homogeneous in terms of the distribution of roosting places, such as trees of a particular kind, and this is reflected in a patchy distribution of the birds. In particularly favourable parts of a woodland the birds are densely concentrated but between these areas density is much lower. If bird density were mapped, it would have the appearance of the contours of a hilly part of an Ordnance Survey map. Within each concentration the birds are not distributed randomly for it is becoming apparent that a Starling roost has a definite social structure. Recent work (as yet not completely analysed) by my colleague R. W. Summers has shown that within the centre of some roosts the birds are predominantly heavy, consisting especially of adult males, while peripheral birds tend to be lighter and younger with a higher proportion of females. A similar structure was found in Brown-headed Cowbird *Molothurus ater* roosts in Texas by Good and Johnson (1976), who also found that birds that died during the night were mainly those around the periphery of the roost (Heidi B. Good, personal communication).

Departure

Morning activity commences with singing and once this starts it spreads rapidly through the roosting birds. There is considerable variation in the activity of even neighbouring individuals, for while one bird may be singing intensely the next may be asleep. Shortly before departure there are often movements of flocks, sometimes of hundreds of thousands of birds, across the tree tops or through the trees but these birds settle again. There is also further bickering over space on the branches. The most noticeable feature of morning activity, however, is a steady increase in the volume of the singing as more birds join the chorus.

As departure approaches singing reaches a crescendo and then suddenly cuts out, to be resumed again after a few seconds and building up to another climax and cut-out of sound. This may happen several times but at one of the sudden silences birds begin to leave. They do not all leave and those that do go depart from all parts of the roost, rather than from a local area. Even during this departure, the remaining birds re-commence singing and at a subsequent cut-off of sound more birds leave the roost. While rising from the trees the flight directions of the birds seem haphazard and collisions occur frequently, but above tree-top height flight is more ordered as birds group themselves into flocks flying in particular directions (Plate 13).

This departure of Starlings from their roosts in groups, usually at about three minute intervals, was noticed by Wynne-Edwards in

1929. As radar systems became more sophisticated in the years following World War II, echoes of indeterminate origin were detected. Some echoes ('angels' in radar parlance), first recorded in the mid-1950s (Harper 1959) took the form of expanding concentric rings, each with an origin at the same geographical point, like the ripples after a stone is thrown into a pond (Plate 13). These were called 'ring angels' and Eastwood, Isted and Rider (1962) demonstrated that these echoes were from waves of Starlings departing from their roosts. Once the identity of ring angels had been established, radar became a new tool for the study of Starling roosting behaviour, as it had already become for studying various aspects of bird migration (Eastwood 1967).

The pattern of waves leaving a roost is difficult to observe from the ground but they do show clearly on the plan position indicator of an airfield radar. The echoes do not always appear as perfectly concentric circles since wind speed and direction affects the expanding rings. At wind speeds below six knots departing birds do show as rings but at greater wind speeds the the waves of birds travelling down wind are displaced, giving the rings a more elliptical appearance. In strong winds those birds heading into the air current fly low, sometimes as little as half a metre above the ground, and they cannot be detected by radar. In this case, the angels appear as arcs expanding in a downwind direction. Nevertheless, Eastwood (1967) and his co-workers were able to determine how many waves emerged from a roost, the time interval between successive waves and their speed of departure, in addition to the various seasonal changes in roosting activity that occur. Their observations are the more noteworthy since their radar, based at Bushy Hill, Essex, permitted them to observe roost dispersals at ranges of about 80 km (50 miles) from Bushy Hill; their data are therefore based on records of many roosts.

Figure 10.4 shows the seasonal changes in the number of roosts within the radar detection range of Bushy Hill. The maximum number of occupied roosts was observed in July–August. This number decreased towards the winter and for a period during the breeding season none was recorded. Some of the roosts in late summer are temporary and Eastwood (1967) suggested that these consisted primarily of juveniles that were roosting for the first time. We should expect juveniles to begin roosting earlier than this, however, since most become independent of their parents in late May. Tahon (1980) found that in Belgium the many roosts in

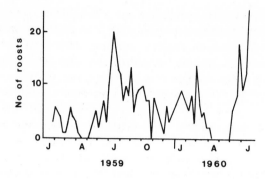

Fig. 10.4. Seasonal change in the number of Starling roosts recorded within the detection range of the radar at Bushy Hill, Essex. (Redrawn from Eastwood *et al.* (1962).)

June, to which juveniles as well as adults resorted, were small, scattered, and mainly of a temporary nature. As summer progressed these small roosts amalgamated into a smaller number of larger ones, and even in these larger roosts the proportion of juveniles was highly variable, ranging from 10 to 78 per cent. The proportion of young birds was not related to the size of those July roosts but the relation between the proportion of juveniles and the permanence of the roosts was not investigated.

The reduction in the numbers of roosts towards winter is also due to amalgamation of smaller into larger ones, a feature recorded by many field workers, but the size of winter roosts in Britain and south-west Europe is, of course, augmented by large numbers of migrants from the north and east. In Britain at least, these migrants concentrate into rural roosts while the growing number of urban roosts consist mainly of British resident birds (Potts 1967). In January, the break-up of large winter roosts into smaller ones commences although some may persist until later. This seasonal patern may, however, be disrupted by unusually severe weather when all of the birds in a large roost may suddenly vacate the site; where they go in such circumstances has not been ascertained. In other roosts, however, severe weather may lead to an increase in roost size (Symonds 1965).

The absence of roosts for a period in April–May (Fig. 10.4) corresponds with the time when most Starlings are breeding. It is known from field observations, however, that at least some breeding males and non-breeding birds roost communally throughout the breeding season. This suggests that the picture obtained from radar records is not strictly accurate, but radar records echoes from birds during their dispersal and the smaller number of birds that depart from breeding season roosts may be inadequate to produce an angel recognisable as a Starling roost on the plan position indicator. This may also explain why the multitude of small roosts found in June by Tahon (1980) were not revealed by Eastwood *et al*'s (1962) radar until some coalescence had occurred in July. The assembly of Starlings prior to roosting in the evening does not have the characteristic pattern of morning wave departure and it is consequently much more difficult to identify roosts from radar observations of evening behaviour.

The other seasonal component of roosting behaviour that could be readily studied by radar was the time of departure of the birds. They do, of course, leave earlier in the summer than in the winter simply because the day begins earlier in the summer. But Wynne-Edwards (1929) had noted that Starlings left their roost before sunrise in December while they left progressively later as spring advanced. Similar seasonal changes in the time of departure relative to sunrise were recorded by Frieswijk and Bresser (1961) in The Netherlands and these authors also observed similar changes in the times of evening arrival, with birds arriving relatively earlier in summer than in winter. These changes in the time of morning departure are clearly demonstrated by Eastwood *et al*'s (1962) data (Fig. 10.5).

Several attempts have been made to relate these events to light intensity; the birds certainly leave later on dull than on bright mornings, suggesting that they make some adjustment to this

Fig. 10.5. Seasonal change in the time of departure of Starlings from their roosts, showing that they left relatively later, in relation to sunrise, in summer than in winter. (Redrawn from Eastwood *et al.* (1962).)

factor. Frieswijk and Bresser (1961) and Eastwood *et al.* (1962) found, however, that Starlings left their roost at a higher light intensity in summer than they did in winter. This has the advantage of allowing the birds more time to feed on short winter days than if they waited until the equivalent light intensities of summer had been attained. Sensible though this varying seasonal response to light intensity seems, it does not fully explain the timing of departure, for by leaving in waves at certain time intervals, it is inevitable that the evacuation of a roost with a large number of waves will be a prolonged process. The morning exodus from some roosts can, in fact, take as long as an hour and the birds that leave in the last wave are departing at a much higher light intensity than that at which the first wave left. This begs the question: do all or even any of the waves depart in response to a given light intensity?

Eastwood *et al.* (1962) recorded 425 time intervals between wave departures and Fig 10.6 shows a preponderance of departures between two and three minutes. The longer itervals in Fig 10.6 tended to occur in July and August when, as we have seen, roosts were smaller than in winter. There appears, therefore, to be a considerable regularity in the time intervals between the departures and it might be possible for one wave, the first, to depart at a critical light intensity for the time of year and for the departure of the other waves to be determined by the regularity of the intervals between successive waves. Wynne-Edwards (1931), however, found that when a roost with four wave departures split into two,

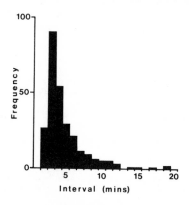

Fig. 10.6. The frequency distribution of time intervals between the departure of waves from Starling roosts recorded on radar. Most waves departed at intervals of three minutes. (Redrawn from Eastwood *et al.* (1962).)

the birds that remained at the original site departed in two waves at times corresponding to the first two waves of the original roost while those that moved to the new site departed in two waves at times corresponding to the third and fourth waves of the original roost. This suggested that each wave was responding to a particular light intensity and, moreover, that each wave consisted of a social group that maintained its characteristics irrespective of where it was roosting. This idea is based on only one set of observations and therefore needs substantiating by more critical measurements of time and light intensity at the departure of different waves. In the evening, Delvingt (1963) and Davis and Lussenhop (1970) found the best relationship between light intensity and time of travel to roost at the birds' feeding areas and suggested that light intensity was an important stimulus to the birds at their initial departure for the roost. As the birds approached, and particularly in the pre-roost assemblies, the correlation between light intensity and initiation of roosting movements was less clear.

Symonds (1961, 1965) suggested that departure of groups at intervals was necessitated by congestion in the roost and Charman (1965) noted that birds moved towards the periphery in order to depart with the minimum of interference from other birds. Although there may be some truth in this, an observer situated in the centre of a roost can see that birds from all parts depart with each wave. Furthermore, if the avoidance of congested air space were the reason for the departure in waves one would expect other species that roost in large assemblages to adopt a similar mode of departure. In Africa, Quelea do indeed depart in waves but many other species, like the Red-winged Blackbird *Agelaius phoeniceus*, Grackle *Quiscalus quiscula*, and Brown headed Cowbird *Molothurus ater*, do not. Again, if wave departure had evolved to minimize congestion we should expect the most waves to emerge from the largest roosts. Charman (1965), however, found no relation between roost size and the number of emergent waves; in fact he found a tendancy for midwinter roosts, which are larger than at other times of year, to produce fewer waves with short inter-wave intervals than when days were longer. He thought that this was an adaptation to maximize the amount of daylight available for feeding.

Yet another feature of wave departure was revealed by Eastwood's radar studies. Wynne-Edwards (1929) had estimated that departing Starlings flew at about 64 km h^{-1} but by recording the rate of expansion of ring angels Eastwood was able to make more accurate measurements. He found that the average air speed was 68 km h $^{-1}$, but that the departure speed was faster in winter than in summer, with speeds of 74 and 59 km h $^{-1}$ respectively.

In summer, Starlings are moulting and this may reduce their flight speed; a more important determinant of flight speed, however, might be body weight, for it is more efficient, in terms of energy expenditure, to fly faster when heavier than when light (Pennycuick 1975). This aerodynamic consideration could explain these seasonal variations in flight speed and it may also explain differences in the flight speeds of the waves that emerge from a roost. Eastwood (1967) found that flight speeds decreased by about 1.8 km h $^{-1}$ in each successive wave that leaves a roost. In 1975 and 1976 I (with the help of a considerable number of colleagues) shot Starlings from each of the only two waves from a small roost near Guildford. The sample was admittedly small, being restricted to about 60 birds (this restriction due to the difficulty of shooting birds that were almost out of range: this means that, furthermore, the sample may have been biased toward the lower flying birds), but the birds in the first wave were significantly heavier than those in the second wave: there were no age or sex differences between the composition of birds shot from the two waves. These findings again follow Pennycuik's (1975) predictions but we clearly have much to learn about the mechanics of wave departure from Starling roosts before we can begin to understand the functional significance of this aspect of behaviour.

The foregoing discussion might have given the impression that each roost has its own exclusive feeding area but this is not the case. Eastwood (1967) found that in some cases the rings from different roosts overlapped, indicating that some feeding areas were shared by two or more roosts. Birds that I had marked at Bridgets Experimental Husbandry Farm continued to feed at the farm when the roost site changed and in the 1976–7 winter, when a change of roost site led to the formation of two roosts, each used by some of the wing-tagged birds, the marked birds from both roosts fed at the farm.

FUNCTIONS OF COMMUNAL ROOSTING

To fly from a roost to a feeding site, feed, and then return to the roost in the evening requires energy. Hamilton, Gilbert, Heppner, and Planck (1967) assumed that the same net benefits accrued if a

Starling fed close to the roost or if it fed further away, and these authors attempted to assess the relative costs and benefits of travelling different distances to feeding areas. They based their calculations of the energetic costs on the work of Brenner (1965) and I have also used some of his data as a base-line; since Hamilton *et al's* (1967) publication there have, however, been a number of studies of the metabolic rates associated with various activities of Starlings and I have been able to recalculate some of the costs associated with communal roosting. My own calculations are, nevertheless, based on many assumptions.

Brenner (1965) found that Starlings roosting alone had metabolic rates of 139 and 74 KJ at 2.4°C and 24–30°C respectively. I have used these values to represent the daily metabolic rates of Starlings roosting in winter and summer, even though the temperature ranges are somewhat extreme for the British climate. A further source of error arises from the weights of the birds used by Brenner to establish these metabolic rates, for while the mean weight of the 24–30°C experimental birds was reasonably realistic (69.4 g) for summer, the mean weight of his 2–4°C experimental birds was only 68.0 g, which is 10–20 g lower than the average weight of a Starling in winter.

Tinbergen (1981) used the value 1.5 BMR (basal metabolic rate) for Starlings that were sitting, preening, and resting and I have assumed the metabolic rates for roosting birds, mentioned above, to be approximately 1.5 BMR. Tinbergen considered that active foraging for leatherjackets required an expenditure of about 5 BMR. During a day's foraging a Starling devotes some time to less demanding activities such as preening and resting, and some to more demanding activities, notably flying, in addition to the time devoted to active foraging. To take account of all of these activities I have assumed that a Starling's energy expenditure, while not flying to or from the roost, averages 5 BMR. Torre-Bueno and Larochelle (1978) calculated that the energetic cost of flight for a Starling was 9.9 BMR and I have used this value to calculate the energy expenditure involved in flying to and from the roost in the evening and morning. Both the 5 BMR energy expenditure during foraging time and the 9.9 BMR expenditure during flights to and from the roost have been assumed to be the same in summer and winter. The time taken to fly different distances was based on the flight speeds given by Eastwood (1967): 32 knots (c. 59 km h^{-1}) and 40 knots (c. 74 km h^{-1}) for summer and winter respectively.

These data have been used to construct Fig. 10.7, showing the energy expenditure involved in flying different distances from the roost and in foraging during the remainder of the day, with the total times available for non-roosting activity being 8 h in winter and 16 h in summer. Figure 10.7 shows that the cost of flying to and from the roost is greater for all flight distances in winter than in summer, and yet, as we saw earlier, with the coalescence of roosts in winter there is a tendency for Starlings to fly further to feed at this time of year than during the remainder of the year. The effect of this on daily energy expenditure is more clearly shown in Fig. 10.8: in summer, a Starling that flies 50 km to its feeding grounds (about the maximum recorded in Britain) uses about 18 per cent of its daytime energy expenditure in the flight, while in winter the same journey utilizes 27 per cent of the energy required for daytime activity. In other words, flying to and from a roost is energetically expensive and considerable savings could be made if the birds roosted on their feeding grounds instead of commuting to night-time assemblages. If the costs of communal roosting are so high, what are the gains to be expected from this behaviour?

The problem has been defined in energetic terms and in Chapter 3 I alluded to the possible energetic benefits of communal roosting. Starlings, and other communally roosting birds, do appear to select roosting sites that confer protection from wind and thereby reduce metabolic losses but whether they derive any benefit from

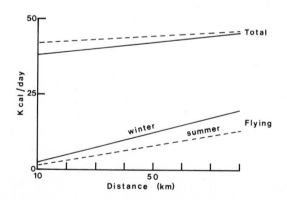

Fig. 10.7. Calculated daily energy expenditure of Starlings that fly different distances from their night roost to their daytime feeding areas, and the energy used in flying to and from the roost. The assumptions made in constructing the graphs for winter and summer are given in the text.

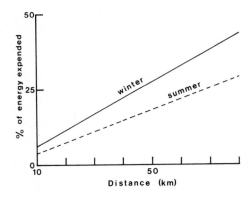

Fig. 10.8. The proportion of daily energy expenditure that is devoted to flying different distances to and from the roost in winter and summer. (Derived from Fig. 10.7).

the heat output of neighbours is moot. At low temperatures (2–4°C), Brenner (1965) found that metabolic rates were lower in groups of four birds than in solitary individuals but these measurements were made in a respiratory chamber: conditions are here very different from those in a winter roost where air flow may remove any benefits of neighbour proximity. The energy saving that might be derived from roosting together certainly seems unlikely to be sufficient to offset the expenditure involved in commuting to and from distant feeding areas. In many parts of the species' range there seem to be alternative sites that confer protection from wind and these may be readily adopted when the original roost is disturbed and may even be the ones used before and after roost coalescence in the winter. Although some roost sites may confer more protection than others, the overflying of apparently suitable woods by birds travelling to a distant wood to join other birds suggests that the reduction of metabolic losses at night is not the ultimate factor responsible for the evolution of communal roosting behaviour.

Nor does it seem likely that the advantages that flocking confers with respect to predation can account for the aggregation of such large numbers of birds at night. I pointed out above that a winter roost can attract predators, although it is highly unlikely that predators are ever present in sufficient numbers to limit the numbers of the prey. This might be taken as an argument that predator swamping works in this situation but I doubt whether one roost of one million Starlings would receive any more protection in this respect than four roosts each accommodating a quarter of a million birds. The erratic and unpredictable flight of Starlings as they enter a roost, and also immediately above the trees as each wave departs in the morning, together with the 'chip chip' calls that may be emitted at these times, does appear to be anti-predator behaviour; this presumably reduces the risk of predation for individuals as they enter and depart the traditional roosting area where predators are anticipated. If Starlings roosted in small groups which changed position regularly but unpredictably, however, predators would be less readily able to locate the aggregations and such anti-predator behaviour would not be so essential. I consider, therefore, that the anti-predator manoeuvres indulged by Starlings entering and emerging from communal roosts are secondary adaptations made necessary by the accumulation of large numbers of birds for some other purpose (Feare *et al.* 1974). This purpose is, I suggest, the obtaining of information concerning the whereabouts of good food sources.

Ward (1965) considered that large communal roosts of Quelea allowed those individuals that had experienced a bad day's feeding, for exampe due to the depletion of a previously abundant food supply, to learn the whereabouts of alternative food supplies from the behaviour of individuals that had fed well. Thus poorly fed birds used the roost as a centre where they could gather information about the distribution of unpredictable food sources. This information centre hypothesis was further amplified by Ward and Zahavi (1973) but the mechanism of the information transfer was not identified. Two stages would have to be involved. First, a poorly-fed bird must be able to recognize those birds that are well-fed and second, the undernourished individual must somehow make use of the better knowledge of the satiated bird. A well-fed Starling might betray its state by body postures or by its behaviour—this is pure speculation—but the time at which information transfer occurs, be it during entry into the roost, in the roost or during the exodus, is quite unknown. It is usually assumed that the poorly-fed birds follow the well-fed birds to their known good patch but evidence of this is difficult to obtain. Information transfer has been demonstrated in some social insects (von Frisch 1950) but since the hypothesis was proposed for 'higher' animals its plausibility has stimulated the publication of a volume of circumstantial evidence that various of its predictions are satisfied (e.g. Krebs 1974). There are also studies, however, that have failed to demonstrate behaviour that conforms with the predictions of the hypothesis (e.g. Mock 1982). The weight of opinion does, nevertheless, follow Ward and Zahavi's attractive proposal but it is surprising that the theory has only once been subjected to laboratory experiment.

The subjects of de Groot's (1980) studies were captive Quelea. He did indeed find that naive birds could learn the whereabouts of food from experienced individuals but he was unable to identify with certainty the mechanisms involved. Some naive birds did follow birds that knew the location of good food supplies, while in other tests the naive birds headed in the direction of the best food before the experienced Quelea. De Groot's findings are nevertheless the best evidence to date that the 'information centre' hypothesis can operate but more critical work, in both the laboratory and field, is required before we can establish that information transfer lies behind the evolution of communal roosting (and colonial breeding and perhaps other assemblages).

The existence of a social structure within Starling roosts and the highly organized departure from these roosts might arguably facilitate information transfer but evidence that undernourished Starlings learn the location of better feeding areas from well-fed birds is still awaited. There is, however, an important point to raise concerning observations that apparently fail to support the Ward and Zahavi hypothesis.

In the 1975–6 winter the Starlings that fed at Bridgets Experimental Husbandry Farm roosted initially in some hill-side scrub 6.5 km to the south of the farm. In early January 1976, the roost split into two, with some birds going to a small plantation 3 km to the north-west of the farm and others to another plantation 6 km to the south-east. The wing-tagged birds that I had previously been watching continued to feed at the farm but some went to one roost and some to the other; these birds were consistent in the roost to which they departed each evening. This suggests that, as Hamilton *et al.* (1967) surmised, the distance that has to be travelled to the roost is relatively unimportant, within certain limits, as long as the birds can guarantee a good feeding area. It suggests further, however, that these wing-tagged individuals had no need for information from their fellows regarding good food supplies and were not using the roost as an information centre. This kind of observation has led some workers to doubt the hypothesis proposed by Ward and Zahavi.

Ward and Zahavi mentioned, but did not stress, an aspect of

their hypothesis that I regard as particularly significant—the 'insurance policy'. We have seen from Tinbergen's (1981) work how important memory and learning are to the Starling's successful foraging during the breeding season. Such acquisition of knowledge of the feeding area can only be accomplished through familiarity with that area and its own peculiarities of prey distribution. My own studies in the winter (Feare 1980) have also demonstrated great fidelity to a feeding area which presumably permits a similar level of learning. With such an outstandingly successful bird, we must assume that most individuals, for most of the time, have little difficulty in obtaining their daily food requirement. So why should Starlings expend energy flying to a communal roost where they might gain information that they do not need?

There are occasions when the good feeding sites suddenly, and unpredictably, become unavailable to the birds. In Britain and in many other parts of the Starling's geographical range this eventuality is probably most commonly brought about by heavy snow and severe frosts. If the birds had no means, other than random searching, of locating new food sources there would be a likelihood that many would starve; but there is little evidence of mass starvation in severe winters (see Chapter 8). There are indications, however, that under such conditions some Starlings undertake 'weather' movements, the birds involved vacating their 'known' area and moving off in search, presumably, of milder climes. The first indication that moving birds might have that they entered a region with available food could be the discovery of flocks of feeding Starlings. By returning to the roost with these flocks, the recent arrivals may gain access to a greater knowledge of the feeding areas available within easy reach of the roost on the following day. It cannot be coincidence that the autumn coalescence of roosts leads to the largest assemblages occurring in December, January and February, which are the times when we expect the most severe winter weather. The reader will note that this piece of discussion has contained an abundance of words like 'if', 'might', and 'could'. Is there any evidence that this kind of system actually operates in Starlings?

There is another time when Starlings need information about local food supplies; this is when the birds arrive in a new area following migration. At such times we would predict that dispersal from roosts would be somehow different from more normal occasions when all birds knew where they were going. I have already described that the roost exodus is a periodic emergence of waves that appear as ring angels on a radar screen. In late October 1980 and early November 1981 I was fortunate to observe, on one day each year, on the plan position indicator at an RAF station in Lincolnshire the departure of Starlings from a large winter roost. From coastal bird-watching forays on previous and following days I knew that Starlings were entering the country across the North Sea with heavy falls of migrants in October 1980. Infuriatingly, I had no access to a camera while watching the plan position indicator and I have therefore had to represent my observations for October 1980 diagrammatically in Fig. 10.9. The first seven waves appeared in typical form but the radar picture suggested that,

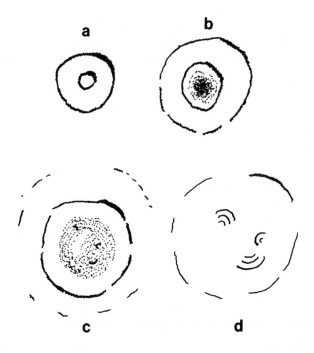

Fig. 10.9. Diagrammatic representation of the departure of Starlings from a large winter roost in Lincolnshire in October 1980, as seen on the plan position indicator (p.p.i.) of the radar of an RAF Station. (a) Waves of Starlings departing 'normally'. (b) After the eighth wave, remaining birds left in a continuous stream, appearing as a cloud on the p.p.i. (c) As the cloud became more dispersed, small wave departures became apparent from secondary sites of dispersal. (d) The secondary dispersal centres showing two or three expanding waves, leaving the dispersal centre at about one-minute intervals.

instead of the remaining birds departing in an eighth and subsequent waves, they all left in a prolonged and continuous exodus. This appeared on the p.p.i. as an expanding 'cloud', of diminishing density, centred on the roost. This cloud vanished before it had extended to the extremities reached by the first seven waves but then miniature wave-formations appeared within the area where the 'cloud' echo had become extinguished. On 3 November 1981 these subsidiary dispersals were seen again but on a smaller scale, and five 'normal' waves emerged from the roost. This picture suggested that many Starlings had left the roost, had settled and had then undergone a secondary dispersal that appeared to take the form of a reorientation.

There is no doubt that roost departure on these two days of active immigration was different from the pattern seen during the winter. My interpretation, that recent immigrants departed after the birds that 'knew' the area and later re-orientated themselves from secondary dispersal centres to discover good feeding areas, indicated by the knowledgable birds, is nevertheless highly speculative. Despite the obvious shortcomings of this information, I have included it to suggest that the 'information centre' hypothesis, which I think is the most plausible explanation for communal roosting in Starlings and other animals, should be subjected to much more direct research; by this I mean that the research should address specific predictions of the hypthesis, rather than attempt to add to the already large volume of circumstantial evidence that the roost 'might' be acting as a information centre. Such research must also take into account the 'insurance policy concept' mentioned above, for it may well be that the requirement for information from roosting neighbours is rare, but when the requirement does arise it is vital to the survival of a large proportion of the population.

ASSOCIATIONS OF STARLINGS WITH OTHER SPECIES

Starlings are commonly to be seen feeding with other species. I am not referring here to the small flocks of Starlings that visit bird tables and there encounter a wide variety of small birds, but to the larger flocks that feed in grass fields with other species that share some of the Starling's ecological characteristics. In Europe, the most frequent associates are Rooks *Corvus frugilegus*, Jackdaws *C. monedula*, Lapwings *Vanellus vanellus*, Golden Plover *Pluvialis apricaria*, and various gulls *Larus* sp., while in North America

American Robins *Turdus migratorius* and blackbirds are frequent companions, especially the Red-winged Blackbird *Agelaius phoeniceus*, the Grackle *Quiscalus quiscula*, and the Brown-headed Cowbird *Molothurus ater*. All of these associates take similar foods in grassland and it is likely that each species can derive information from the others about the location of abundant food and the approach of predators, in other words precisely the same kind of information that Starlings receive from other Starlings. What we do not know is whether the passage of information from species to species is mutual or whether some species are parasitic on others. Williamson and Gray (1975) found that Starlings fed in mixed flocks with other North American species more in winter than at other times of year. These authors also commented, without providing supporting data, that in these mixed flocks Starlings tended to imitate the feeding methods of other species. Imitation involved modifications of the Starling's inter-individual spacing, the duration of their feeding sessions and the rate of foraging (Williamson and Gray did not say whether this meant a change in peck rate, in walking rate, or both).

Starlings also associate with other species in roosts, especially in winter. This does occur in Britain and Europe but when, for example, Starlings, Jackdaws, and thrushes occupy the same wood at night the species tend to segregate into monospecific groups. In North America this does not appear to happen and in roosts, some containing several millions of birds, of Starlings and blackbirds the various species involved seem to be thoroughly inter-mixed. This does, however, require confirmation by identifying nearest neighbour associations within these roosts; this may reveal small monospecific assemblages that are not readily apparent on cursory inspection.

Of greater interest is the behaviour of Starlings during dispersal from these roosts. Red-winged Blackbirds, Grackles, and Brown-headed Cowbirds do not leave their roosts in waves; instead, they depart in a more or less continuous stream. In 1981 I timed the emergence of Starlings as they left a large Kentucky roost but unfortunately there were few Starlings among the mass of black-birds. Those that were present gave no suggestion of a departure in waves but further work along these lines would be rewarding: there may here be yet another facet of the Starling's versatility in its ability to mimic the behaviour of other species.

11 A ROUTE TO SUCCESS

There can be no doubt that the European Starling is an extremely successful bird; it is one of the most numerous birds in the world, it occupies a huge land area, and it is a formidable competitor in contests with other species for nest sites and for some food resources. The most remarkable demonstration of its success has certainly been the colonization of North America, to the extent that one third of the world's population of Starlings has been derived from only 100 birds in the incredibly short period of 90 years. Nicholson (1951), while admitting the success of the species, remarked that 'we know surprisingly little about the reasons behind this success'. In the foregoing chapters of this book I have highlighted a number of facets of the Starling's biology that we now know have contributed to its success and my aim in this chapter is to briefly summarize those features that appear to have played major roles in the success story. This consideration should not be regarded as exhaustive, however, since future research will inevitably propose additional attributes that may well be equally important as those mentioned here.

It is not possible to place the events that have led to the Starling's present success in any chronological sequence, but some fundamental changes must have occurred early in the evolution of our species. One of the earliest transitions may well have been from a largely fruit- and insect-eating arboreal bird, like some of the more primitive forms today, to a more ground dwelling habit. This transition was made possible by the structural alterations of the skull and its musculature, enabling the bird to feed on subterranean organisms using the 'open-bill probing' technique. Once this feeding method had evolved, the food resources in the upper layers of the soil, especially in grasslands, became available to these birds.

Like many of the genus *Sturnus* today, the progenitor of *S. vulgaris* either was, or became, migratory, with a breeding area to the north of the presumed ancestral region in south-east Asia but retreating into this region in the winter. The combination of a northward spring migration to the breeding grounds and the ability to feed by open-bill probing opened up the temperate grasslands to the Starling's exploitation. As the last glaciation, the Würm, retreated the area of temperate grassland expanded, allowing the Starling the opportunity of extending its geographical range into what we now call the Palaearctic. The northward extension of this range would have been limited at the southern boundary of the boreal forests, as it is in much of eastern Europe and western Asia today.

I do not wish to imply here that the European Starling evolved during or after the Würm glaciation: we do not know when it evolved, but if it had evolved earlier during the Pleistocene, the extension of geographical range that resulted in its present distribution could have occurred only after the most recent glacial period.

A further contribution to the species' successful exploitation of the temperate grasslands was probably the Starling's ability, with further climatic amelioration, to curtail its autumn migration so that it remained throughout the year in the temperate zone. The resulting loss of contact with the Oriental region would have permitted a westward extension of range over the Palaearctic. Furthermore, the reduction of migration distances, doubtless to the extent that part of the population became resident, would have allowed these birds to breed earlier than long-distance migrants (Berthold 1968). Early breeding in Starlings enables the rearing of second broods, which raises the possibility of producing a large number of juveniles. In addition, the flexibility of mating systems, involving polygyny, mate change and parasitism, permitted by the extended breeding season, introduces into this large juvenile cohort a genetic diversity that presumably confers adaptability in the face of environmental changes.

One of the ancestral habits that did not change was that of nesting in holes. The retention of this habit, and the consequent ability to lay a large clutch and successfully rear a large brood (Lack 1966), may have helped to put the Starling at a numerical advantage over other birds that feed to a large extent on grassland invertebrates, such as many thrushes and crows (the Jackdaw is the only other grassland-feeding bird in the western Palaearctic that nests in holes).

But the production of a large number of young *per se* is not enough to confer numerical success, for large numbers of them must survive to breed. To do this, they must survive the particularly vulnerable periods of gaining independence from parents and potential food shortage in summer, when soil invertebrates are scarce, and again in winter, when frost and snow can prevent feeding in grassland. We are now, thanks to the work of Joost Tinbergen and Rudi Drent, beginning to appreciate the complexities of Starling feeding behaviour, in grassland during the breeding season, that permit such a successful exploitation of the available food supply. The Starling's ability to diversify its diet, by modifications of behaviour and morphology, undoubtedly help it to overcome periods of potential adversity by making available alternative food supplies, such as soft fruit for juveniles in the summer and seeds for all age groups in winter. The adaptations that permitted the exploitation of localized invertebrate food sources in grassland—including the ability to form flocks, mimicry of neighbours' feeding behaviour, rapidity of learning the whereabouts of localized food, and the fidelity to good feeding sites— were adaptations of equal value in exploiting plant-based foods in other habitats.

These, then, are some of the main adaptations that have helped the Starling in its successful invasion of the temperate grasslands of the Palaearctic. But the Starling could not have achieved its present distribution and abundance without the agencies of an even more successful animal—man. The area of temperate grassland in the western Palaearctic was comparatively small, being restricted to the steppes to the north and east of the Black and Caspian Seas (Fig. 11.1), while most of Europe was dominated by temperate forests (Harlan 1981). The hunter-gatherer tribes of Europe had relatively little impact on the temperate forest but when farming tribes from the near East began to extend their influence westwards, their agricultural practices signalled the end of most of the deciduous forest. Their activities were, in effect, to replace forest with open country, thereby extending the area of grassland or cereals to the Atlantic seaboard. This ecogeographical transition, that occurred over a relatively short historic period, was undoubtedly the main factor that allowed the Starling its major range expansion and its development of an almost commensal existance with Man.

This commensal relationship was facilitated by other adaptations already possessed by Starlings, namely their adaptability in choice of nest hole and their ability to use a wide range of foods. While the early farmers destroyed the forest they left pockets of

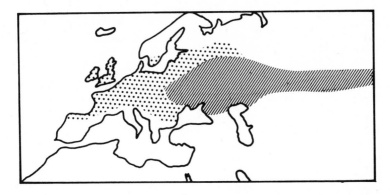

Fig. 11.1. The extent of temperate grassland (hatched) prior to man's encroachment of temperate forest and the area (stippled) over which forest was largely destroyed to create grassland-like ecosystems.

trees in which Starlings could nest but, in addition, they provided yet more nest sites in the form of cavities in the houses and shelters that they built for themselves and their stock. And very close to these structures the farmers provided a superabundance of cultivated foods, many of which the Starling was able to utilize for much of the year. Wherever these farmers replaced forest by agriculture, therefore, they straightaway provided conditions suitable for Starlings and it seems likely that the occupation of western Europe by agricultural man and by Starlings (and by House Sparrows, Summers-Smith 1963) was almost simultaneous.

Man's conversion of temperate forest to grassland was not restricted to Europe but occurred also in north America and in parts of the Southern Hemisphere. In these areas, however, there appear to have been no indigenous species that could so successfully exploit the man-made habitats. This is surprising, for while some species, such as the Red-winged Blackbird, Grackle, and Brown-headed Cowbird in North America, did take advantage of man's agricultural presence, they still left a niche that the Starling could occupy when transported from Europe and released in the Nearctic and southern temperate man-made environments.

The geographical, numerical, and competitive success of the Starling have resulted, therefore, from a variety of factors, some derived from the ancestral starlings, some acquired by the European Starling during its evolution, and some as a result of man's recent evolution. No single factor can be regarded as of over-

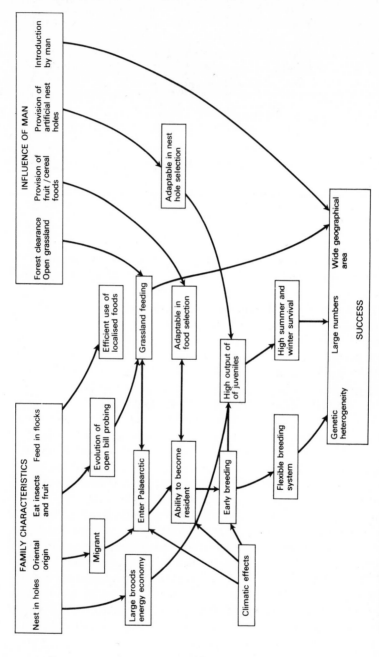

Fig. 11.2. The probable route to the Starling's present success, involving family and specific characters and their interaction with man's influences.

riding importance; instead, the present success of the Starling results from a web of coincidences (Fig. 11.2).

Man and his agriculture have nevertheless clearly been instrumental in opening up a large area of the globe to the Starling and the relationship between these two species has been close. Earlier, I described this relationship as commensal, rather than symbiotic and in Chapter 12 we shall see that the relationship does tend to favour the Starling at man's expense.

12 RELATIONS WITH MAN

In the foregoing chapters we have seen how supremely well the Starling is adapted to life in areas cultivated by man. Many of the features that comprise this adaptive capacity are shared by other species of starling, and this has led several of them into conflict with man. In Africa, the Blue-eared Glossy *Lamprotornis chalbaeus* and the Superb *Spreo superbus* Starlings appear to be responsible for considerable damage to grapes; in this they may well be joined by the Lesser Blue-eared Glossy Starling *Lamprotornis chloropterus*, the Ashy Starling *Cosmopsarus unicolor*, the Red-wing Starling *Onychognathus morio*, and the Wattled Starling *Creatophora cinerea*, but more detailed study is required to verify this. I suspect that the Superb Starling is also responsible for damage to germinating wheat in Tanzania but this again needs confirmation. Doubtless other members of the genera *Lamprotornis* and *Spreo*, and possibly other African starlings, damage crops, especially soft fruit, in their various ranges. In Asia some *Acridotheres* mynahs damage fruit and cereals (Ali and Ripley 1972; La Touche 1925–1934) and species of other genera certainly have the potential for damaging crops, especially fruit.

In the genus *Sturnus*, the Grey Starling *S. cineraceus* is a pest of rice in Japan (Kuroda 1973); the Brahminy Starling *S. pagodarum* eats fruit in Sri Lanka (Henry 1971); the Pied Mynah *S. contra* damages crops in India (Whistler 1963); the Spotless Starling *S. unicolor* eats grapes and other soft fruits in Iberia and north Africa and the Rose-coloured Starling *S. roseus* eats cereals and fruit in Sri Lanka and India (Sema 1976). According to Voous (1960) the Rose-coloured Starling in Asia Minor is called the 'holy bird' in May due to its devouring of large numbers of locusts, while in July it is the 'devil bird' because it eats ripening grapes.

Many agricultural problems with starlings occur outside their normal geographical ranges, however, and result from introductions to new regions by Man. In many instances these introductions were for 'beneficial' reasons, hopefully as agents for the biological control of insect pests; but, as with introductions of many other animals and plants, they often rapidly demonstrated the inadequacy of ecological information about the birds or the lack of foresight of the introducers for, instead of fulfilling useful functions, the birds quickly demonstrated their potential as pests. The histories of these introductions and the ensuing problems have been recently reviewed by Long (1981). The genera of starlings that have been chiefly involved are *Acridotheres* and *Sturnus* and it is due to introductions, of course, that many of the problems associated with the European Starling have arisen.

Within the enormous geographical range of the European Starling a wide variety of cultivated foods is encountered and in many parts of this range the Starling is regarded as a pest for different reasons. Table 12.1 indicates the spectrum of economically valuable foods eaten in damaging quantities in different parts of its range, but it must be pointed out that in some regions Starlings are regarded as beneficial.

Table 12.1. Extent of losses of crops and stock food caused by Starlings. In addition to these crops it is well known that Starlings are capable of inflicting severe damage to a variety of others, including grapes and olives, but these losses do not appear to have been quantified

Crop	Country	Loss	Reference
Cherries	Canada	Up to 100% (but other species also involved)	Brown 1974
	Britain	14–21%, £1296 ha^{-1}	Feare 1980
Apples		20–30% of marketable fruit	Flegg 1982
Wheat	United States	0.4–3.8% plants	Dolbeer *et al.* 1978
	Britain	23–37% of plants, no reduction of yield	Wadsworth unpublished
Barley		29% of plants, no reduction of yield	Feare 1980
Poultry food		£30 000 pa	Murton and Westwood 1977
Cattle food	United States	$84/1000 birds	Besser *et al.* 1968
.	Britain	0–12% of food £0–£222	Feare and Swannack 1978 Feare 1980
		0–15% of food £0–£1000	Feare and Wadsworth 1981
Pig food	Britain	£3.36/week	Smart 1980

BENEFITS OF STARLINGS

The Rose-coloured Starling, which has an enormous capacity for locusts, is thought to be beneficial, though whether it ever exerts any significant control on locust populations and, therefore, reduces the damage caused by them, is doubtful. The Wattled Starling in Africa is also noted for its delectation for locusts. Many of the introductions of the Common Mynah *Acridotheres tristis*, Jungle Mynah *A. fuscus*, and Crested Mynah *A. cristatellus* to islands of the Indian and Pacific oceans were ostensibly to control insect pests (Long 1981) but there has been no assessment of the effectiveness of this control. Reservations must be held for the 'controlling' abilities of these and the European Starling: in parts of the north of its range it is held to be a valuable asset on account of its consumption of invertebrate pests in grassland and, to a lesser extent, in forests. In New Zealand, Starlings are encouraged to breed in sheep-rearing areas by the provision of nestboxes on fence posts (Plate 2), in order that the birds may control population of the Grass Grub *Costelytra zealandica*, an insect pest of grasslands. However, a study by East and Pottinger (1975) has shown that Starlings exert control only under particular conditions of sheep grazing and irrigation, and where Starling populations are high and grass grub infestations localized; such conditions are infrequently encountered. Although sufficiently detailed studies have yet to be undertaken, it seems unlikely that Starlings exert any better control of leatherjackets in Europe. A novel approach currently being investigated by a farmer in Holland might nevertheless have interesting results. He has a cattle yard that is completely enclosed with netting, the purpose of which is to keep Blue-eared Glossy Starlings, bought from a local zoo (one sex only!), within the enclosure to eat flies and maggots.

Starlings can also be regarded as being an asset to man in some other ways. As mentioned in Chapter 1, several species are kept as cage birds, usually on account of their ability to mimic human speech. Through this ability they fulfil the role of entertainers, a role which Rose-coloured Starlings can play in a different way; in India they are shot for sport! (Whistler 1963). In terms of providing benefit we should again recall from Chapter 1 that several species, including the European Starling, are caught for human consumption. Even in England Starlings have been shot in their winter roosts for export to the continent while in Spain some fields are planted with maize especially to act as attractive roosting places. The birds that do roost there are then caught in large numbers and sold in local markets (Parsons 1960).

DAMAGE BY STARLINGS

The main interest in European Starlings, from an economic view-point, must however centre on the damage that they cause.

Although Starlings eat a wide variety of crops and are also involved in other kinds of damage, there are very few estimates of the cost of damage or of the cost of preventive measures. In some situations the cost of damage is very difficult to estimate. For example, how does one quantify the value of branches of plantation trees broken or trees partially killed in rural roosts (Plate 1), or the cost of Starlings roosting on the buildings in city centres and the fouling of pavements that results from their presence? And how is the possible role of Starlings in the spread of disease to be measured?

Diseases

In some instances movements of Starlings from their roosts have been held responsible for outbreaks of disease. Usually, the evidence for this is circumstantial, as is the case with the relation between Starling roosts and outbreaks of transmissible gastro-enteritis (TGE) of pigs—the problem here lies in the difficulties of searching for the virus on or in the bodies of the birds. Gough and Beyer (1980) have found that the virus does replicate in the living cells of the Starling's intenstine and these authors thought that this source of virus, rather than that carried mechanically on the birds' bodies, was most likely to be the significant element in the possible transmission of the disease by birds. Pilchard (1965) has demonstrated that the faeces of Starlings, fed on suspensions of infected pig intestines, can re-infect pigs and Gough and Beyer (1980) confirmed that Starlings can carry sufficient virus to constitute an infective dose for pigs. These results have all been obtained in laboratory experiments, however, and evidence from the field remains circumstantial. In East Anglia many pig farmers and veterinary officers firmly believe that birds are implicated in the transmission of TGE (Pritchard 1982) and the latter are currently assembling data relating to outbreaks in the hope of obtaining statistical evidence. Despite frequent claims to the contrary, it now seems that, in Britain at least, Starlings are unlikely to be involved in the introduction or spread of foot and mouth disease (FMD). Murton (1964), in a detailed analysis of FMD outbreaks, concluded that most outbreaks could be explained on the basis of imported infected meats, or by transport from the Continent into British ports on vehicles or people. Later, Snow (1968) found that, in the 1968 outbreaks, the spread of the disease in one area was dependent on the prevailing wind direction rather than on the local roosting-feeding movements of Starlings. Starlings may eventually prove to be implicated in the transmission of other animal diseases, but there is no good evidence of this at present. Starlings have been found to be infected with various forms of *Salmonella*, with *Yersinia pseudo-tuberculosis*, *Mycobacterium avium* (avian tuberculosis), and *Leptospira laura*, along with several other bacterial diseases. Antibodies to some viruses, such as yellow fever, dengue and influenza group, have been isolated but the relationship between infections of all of these organisms in birds and in domestic stock is unclear (Feare 1980; Keymer 1980). In Britain at least, the indoor rearing of some domestic stock has reduced the chances of birds transmitting, through infection or mechanical transport, diseases like Newcastle disease and duck virus hepatitis whose spread has been blamed on Starlings in the past.

In addition to animal diseases, there are indications that Starlings may be involved in the dissemination of some human diseases. In 1965, Dodge suggested that histoplasmosis (due to a fungus *Histoplasma capsulatum*) infections in school children in the United States resulted from contamination by faeces in a Starling roost and since then more evidence of the relationship between human incidence of histoplasmosis and Starling/blackbird (Icteridae) roosts has been obtained (Tosh, Doto, Beecher, and Chin, 1970). The accumulations of faeces on the floor of a roost provide a growth medium for the fungus; to disperse roosts close to habitation would simply make the birds select another roost site whose guano deposits would then constitute another focus of infection. For this reason, attempts are still made to eliminate the birds in roosts close to conurbations in regions where temperature and humidity are such that the fungus will grow. Also in the United States, antibodies to *Toxoplasma gondii*, a protozoan parasite, have been found in Starlings in an area where antibodies have also been found in stock reared for human food. In Britain, Crewe and Owen (1978) feel that Starlings may be involved in the dissemination of eggs of the human beef tapeworm *Taenia saginata*. However, much more research into the role of Starlings in disease transmission is required before their importance can be assessed.

Crop losses

Starling damage to crops is more tangible and can be more readily measured, but even so there are very few estimates of the cost of damage in different parts of the world. Some of the losses that have been recorded, however, (Table 12.1) are considerable. In Britain, the main areas of damage are to cherries, germinating winter cereals, and to food presented to cattle, again largely in winter. While damage to cherries is due mainly to British-bred juveniles, consumption of cereals and cattle food is mainly by immigrants from continental Europe. Each kind of damage results from an interaction between farm management practices and Starling ecology, and in attempting to alleviate the problems we should study both aspects and, as far as possible, make the most practical and economic adjustment that the results of these studies dictate. This can be illustrated with the three principal kinds of damage that British farmers suffer.

Damage to cherries

During the last half century the area of cherry orchards in Britain has fallen from 7000 to 2400 ha. This decline has resulted from a number of factors, e.g. the large size of mature trees (which leads to high picking costs), diseases, fruit splitting, irregular cropping, and also from bird damage, especially by Starlings (Plates 14 and 15). For the same reasons declines in cherry growing have also occurred in other countries. However, the demand by the British public for cherries has not declined and the unsatisfied part of this demand cannot be made up by imports from continental Europe because imports are prohibited between June and September. This ban is to keep out of the British Isles another cherry pest, the Cherry Fruit Fly *Rhagoletis cerasi*, which reduces yields on the continent. Thus the cherries that are still grown by British farmers can command a high price and any losses to Starlings are financially important to the farmer, and also to the housewife who has to pay more for her fruit.

The scale of a farmer's concern, and of the losses that he can incur, are well illustrated by a study that I made in a 16-ha commercial cherry orchard in 1975. In an attempt to prevent Starlings eating his cherries, this farmer, like many others, tried to make his orchard unpleasant for birds by shooting them (or rather shooting at them to scare them, although some were killed), by making noises with propane bangers, rattles, tin cans, and even a siren mounted on a car which was continuously driven around. In terms of labour, cartridges and other materials used, these attempts to reduce or prevent damage cost the farmer around £2000. Starlings, despite this, consumed about 15 per cent of the cherries and in that year the value of this quantity of fruit was about £20 000. This raises two important questions. Firstly, would the losses of cherries to Starlings have been any greater had the farmer not spent his £2000 on attempted control, and secondly, why were the Starlings not deterred by his expensive actions? In attempting to answer these questions we need to look at both the scheme of management practised in the orchard during the harvesting season, and also at the feeding ecology of the birds during the same season.

In Figure 12.1 I have shown, diagrammatically, the relationship between the number of ripe trees, the number of cherry pickers employed by the farmer, and the number of birds that were feeding in the orchard, as the season progressed. The number of trees bearing ripe fruit increased to a peak in the middle of the

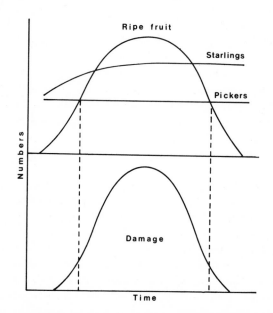

Fig. 12.1. The relations between the quantities of ripe fruit, cherry-pickers, and Starlings in a cherry orchard, and the amount of damage done by the birds. The most serious losses of cherries occurred at the peak of the cherry season when there were too few pickers to collect the fruit from all of the ripening trees.

season and then declined. The number of pickers, the expensive labour force, remained approximately constant throughout. Most of the Starlings that were responsible for the damage were juveniles (this is true of cherry damage by Starlings elsewhere in the world) and at the beginning of the cherry season their numbers increased as juveniles from the late brood gained independence from their parents and joined communal roosts, but thereafter numbers available to feed in the orchard remained more or less constant until the end of the season when the orchard no longer offered attractive food.

The main problem, from the farm management point of view, resulted from the farmers inability, due to high costs, to regulate his labour force according to the number of trees that required picking. Early and late in the season, there were sufficient pickers to harvest each tree as it ripened—although the presence of pickers in a tree did not prevent Starlings from feeding in the same tree, the few birds that did feed were wary and probably fed more slowly than when undisturbed. During the middle of the season, on the other hand, trees ripened so fast that the number of pickers available could not possibly harvest the fruit sufficiently quickly. Large numbers of Starlings were therefore able to feed with no disturbance other than the farmer's attempted scaring. Since the main problem lay in the inadequacy of the picking force, it seems unlikely that the level of damage was significantly reduced by the scaring methods employed. Thus if the number of pickers could have been increased in the middle of the season far fewer cherries would have been available to Starlings and the 15 per cent damage that I recorded would have been considerably reduced. In view of the high value of this damage in 1975, one wonders whether the cost of additional pickers might not have been well worthwhile!

However, while the farmer has economic problems resulting from high labour costs and Starlings, among other factors, Starlings have thier own problems relating directly to their survival. We have seen earlier how juveniles rapidly become independent of their parents and aggregate together in feeding flocks during the day and in communal roosts at night. I have also indicated that these feeding juveniles tend to be arboreal, a feature that predisposes them to discover and eat ripening fruit, and I have tentatively suggested that this arboreal behaviour serves to reduce the chances of competition with more experienced adults for less easily found soil invertebrates. The eating of fruit may also be nutritionally important for juvenile Starlings (Herrera and Jordane, 1981), but this aspect has yet to be investigated. It is important to realize, however, that cherries have evolved alongside birds, the latter being the main agents of seed dispersal. The cherry has therefore evolved a high degree of attractiveness to its avian predator and in areas where this fruit is grown commercially it constitutes an abundant and readily available food supply. In Belgium, Tahon (1980) has shown, through extensive ringing programmes, that juvenile Starlings are attracted to cherry growing areas from breeding colonies up to, and sometimes exceeding, 100 km away. If cherries are so attractive and important to Starlings, it follows that attempts to prevent them from feeding in orchards will be difficult indeed; such attempts would entail forcing the birds to feed on other, probably less abundant and less nutritionally adequate foods, thereby achieving a significant alteration in the bird's way of life and possibly causing a part of the population to starve.

Loss of winter-sown cereals

During the first part of this century Starlings were regarded as a pest on account of their consumption of germinating cereals (Collinge 1924–27). From the mid-1920s onwards, however, there appear to have been no records of Starlings damaging germinating cereals until new reports of this kind of damage began to occur in the late 1960s. Interestingly, this resurgence of damage in Britain has been paralleled by the occurrence of similar damage in the United States (Dolbeer, Stickley, and Woronecki, 1978). We can hardly expect the European and north American populations of Starlings to have coincidentally developed a new trait of behaviour, allowing them to eat growing cereals and, as with the cherry problem, we shall see that this kind of cereal damage results from an interaction between husbandary techniques and bird behaviour.

Starlings dig up recently-emerged plants by probing down beside the shoot; if they can reach the remains of the seed they eat it, either by removing it from the plant in the ground or by digging up the plant and discarding the remains after consuming the grain. A field that has been subjected to this kind of attack has rows of plants peppered with probe holes, 4–6 mm in diameter, and discarded plant remains scattered along the drills (Plate 15). The crops that suffer most are those sown in the autumn; in the early

1970s this restricted damage almost entirely to wheat, but the recent advent of winter barley has led this crop to be equally susceptible to attack. At present, damage to winter barley has received little study (Feare 1980) and the following discussion relates only to winter wheat.

In both Britain and North America the damage is done mainly in the wintering area of migrants and tends to be concentrated near winter roosts (Dolbeer *et al.* 1978). Damage seems to be most severe in fields used as pre-roost assembly areas (Plate 14), where large flocks of birds have a last meal of the day before entering the roost (J. T. Wadsworth, in Feare 1980). During the 20 minutes or so that the pre-roosting flock feeds in a cereal field each individual eats about three grains per minute, so that a flock of 200 000 birds can consume a huge quantity of seeds and in so doing kill a significant proportion of the plants, especially if the flocks return to the same field on several consecutive evenings.

Since the large winter roosts, with which these pre-roost assemblies are associated, do not form in Britain until after the continental immigrants have arrived, the damage does not generally begin until November and it is therefore the later-sown crops that are most vulnerable. In Kentucky and Tennessee (USA), Dolbeer *et al.* (1978) similarly found that this kind of damage to wheat was done mainly by migrants from further north, so that here again the later sown crops suffered most. Later crops generally commence their growth in poorer conditions than early sowings and their rate of development is slower. The late crops are therefore at a disadvantage, with respect to Starling damage, as there is a comparatively long interval between emergence of the shoots and their growth to such an extent that Starlings lose interest.

British farmers, especially those in the east, are additionally faced with other problems with late-sown crops. In particular another pest, an insect called Wheat Bulb Fly *Delia coarctata*, whose larvae live in the shoots of emerging plants and may kill them, can cause severe damage to crops. Now Wheat Bulb Fly tends to attack weaker plants. The lower soil temperatures in late autumn lead to slower plant establishment and this tends to produce weaker plants in the later sown crops and these are therefore more susceptible to the insect pest. Apart from sowing early, which is not always feasible, one method of counteracting the insect is to sow the seed shallowly. This not only enables the plants to establish themselves more quickly than with deeper sowing, but it also promotes a greater effectiveness of insecticide treatments should these become necessary. However, shallow sowing brings the grain within the probing depth of a Starling's bill and it appears to have been a tendency to sow more shallowly in recent years that has led to an upsurge in Starling damage. A farmer who has to sow late and who has a Starling roost close to his fields is certainly faced with a dilemma.

On the other hand, the limited work that has been done has suggested that plant losses are usually insufficient to affect yield, even though on rare occasions farmers feel they should re-drill some fields or parts of them. In a British study, J. T. Wadsworth (in Feare 1980) recorded plant losses, in six fields close to a large Starling roost in Lincolnshire, of between 23 per cent and 37 per cent. He compared the number of ears, grain weights, and total yields in damaged and undamaged (protected by mesh cages) plots and found no significant differences. Dolbeer *et al.* (1978) examined a much larger sample of 218 fields in Tennessee and Kentucky and found that 91 per cent of these fields had lost less than 5 per cent of their plants while one one per cent of the fields had received more than 25 per cent damage. Overall, damage levels in Dolbeer's study averaged 1.5 per cent which is much lower than in Wadsworth's more localized investigation. Dolbeer did not measure yields directly (it would be very difficult with such a large sample of fields) but by extrapolating losses of yield due to reductions in plant density from experiments in which damage was simulated, he estimated that Starlings had been responsible for a loss of 5873 tonnes of wheat in the two states in the 1976–7 winter. Wadsworth's finding that wheat plants can compensate for the losses caused by Starlings contrasts with Dolbeer's experimental results but the ability of cereals to produce tillers (side-shoots) does depend on growing conditions: these were not defined in either study.

In Wadsworth's study we encounter another problem for the scientist, for if the activities of the Starlings have no effect on the ultimate yield of the crop, can we say that any damage has been done? The farmer certainly complains but there seems to be no economic loss. In parts of Britain, however, farmers anticipate Starling attack and sow their seed more densely in an attempt to counteract the damage and higher sowing rates are normally applied with later crops. These resulting high seed densities might, in fact, attract Starlings! But where the expected attack fails to materialize the excessively high sowing rates, and the resultant competition between plants, may reduce yields and cause other problems such as lodging (flattening) of the ripening crop. The situation is, therefore, complicated and it is here worth returning to the history of the problem.

When Collinge (1924–27) reported damage to germinating wheat the drilling machines that were then available were presumably less efficient than those available today, especially in relation to the precision with which the seed could be sown at a pre-determined depth. We do not know what factors led to the dearth of reports of Starling damage between 1930 and 1970 but more precise drilling at a depth that placed the grain out of the Starling's reach may have been an important factor. The recent trend of sowing more shallowly, largely to overcome other problems as mentioned earlier, has once again brought the germinating seed within the probing range of the Starling's bill (Boyce 1979). We can see again, therefore, that this kind of damage (if it is to be regarded as damage) has resulted from a change in husbandry techniques, rather than from a change in the birds themselves.

Consumption of cattle food

The eating of cattle food, or of components of the ration given to cattle, by Starlings is another comparatively recent problem which has stemmed from the intensive feeding of cattle restricted in yards, especially in winter (Plate 14). The problem has been studied primarily in Britain and America but also occurs in France (Gramet 1982). As with the other examples of damage that were discussed above, the factors involved in the predation of cattle food illustrate the complex interaction between farm management and bird ecology and behaviour.

In Britain, problems first arose with the advent of intensive rearing of beef cattle and my colleague, E. N. Wright (1973) demonstrated that cattle that were protected from Starlings grew faster than cattle that had to compete with Starlings for their food. Subsequently, I have estimated the weight and value of cattle food eaten by Starlings at a calf rearing unit over five winters (Table 12.1). That these losses can be serious is self evident. But we can ask why a Starling, which we have seen is primarily a grassland feeder, should feed, sometimes within buildings, on food prepared by man for cattle. Do all Starlings in a local area eat this food, or is

Table 12.2. The amount and value of calf food removed by Starlings from an open-fronted calf yard at Bridgets Experimental Husbandry Farm, Winchester, over five winters

Year	Amount of food taken (tonnes)	% of food given	Value (£)
1974–5	1.5	6	125
1975–6	1.7	8	188
1976–7	2.0	12	222
1977–8	0.8	4	70
1978–9	negligible	—	—

it only a select few? If so, do the same birds return to eat this food each day? These questions are important when we come to consider what steps might be appropriate in attempts to alleviate the problems.

Starlings which were caught in mist nets after feeding in the calf unit contained a higher proportion of males than one normally expects in Starling populations (Feare 1981d). This suggested that males fed preferentially on the food given to the calves. The food was presented to the animals in troughs approximately 2 m long and 25 cm wide, so that the space available for groups of Starlings to feed was limited, even though food was available there for most of the day. In Chapter 9 we saw how male Starlings tended to be dominant over females in restricted feeding areas, and it is possible that the competitive advantage of males over females in this situation excluded the latter from the calves' food. Thus only a section of the total farm population of Starlings was responsible for the damage at this farm and the remaining birds spent most of their feeding time in grass fields.

But did the males (and the few females) that were caught in the calf unit return to feed there every day or did different birds utilize this food source each day? As noted earlier, birds that had been marked with wing tags tended to return from the roost to the same feeding area, be it the calf unit or grass fields (Figs 9.4 and 9.5), day after day and it therefore seems that the birds that feed in the calf unit do indeed represent a particular section of the population that is able to make use of this resource, recently made available by man. However, birds that fed regularly in the calf unit were also seen feeding in grass fields, so that calf food was not their sole diet. What determines the relative proportions of calf food and grassland invertebrates or wild seeds in their diet remains an interesting point for further study, as does the advantage that the dominant birds accrue from eating calf food. Almost certainly, the birds that feed mainly in the calf unit have to spend a much smaller part of their day feeding than those that feed mainly on invertebrates in winter.

The number of Starlings present on this farm varies from year to year as well as during the winter (Feare 1980) and it follows that the number of birds that feed in the calf unit must also vary, but other factors, which as yet we do not understand but which probably involve weather, also contribute to the variation in numbers illustrated in Fig. 12.2. Now when the calves are weaned, they are given a diet of calf starter pellets, which are expensive, but during December or January the diet is changed to one consisting of 25 per cent concentrate pellets and 75 per cent crushed barley: the latter is much cheaper than the pellets and the Starlings select the barley and avoid the pellets (Feare and Swannack 1978). Thus any food that Starlings eat after the calves' diet has been changed will

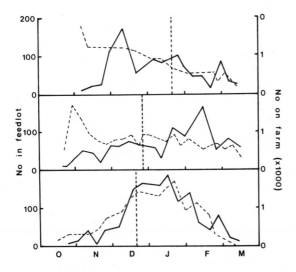

Fig. 12.2. The number of Starlings utilizing the calf feedlot at Bridgets Experimental Husbandry Farm (solid line) and the number estimated on the entire farm (broken line) on approximately weekly counts during the 1975–6, 1976–7, and 1977–8 winters. The vertical dashed line denotes the change in the food given to the calves; calf starter pellets were replaced with a cheaper mixture of concentrate pellets and crushed barley.

have a lower financial value than food eaten before the change. The farmer cannot predict (nor can the ornithologist) when peak numbers of birds will feed in the calf unit but even so he does have an option that will help to alleviate damage: the earlier he changes the diet of the calves, the lower are his chances of losing quantities of expensive pellets.

Since the advent of intensive rearing of beef cattle and calves, another development in animal husbandry has been the intensive rearing of dairy cows on 'complete diets'. A 'complete diet' ration is one that contains all of the nutrients and fibre that a cow needs: the various ingredients are so intimately mixed that the cow is totally unable to select any one of them at the expense of any other. The basic constituent of most rations is silage and the high energy portion is usually provided as barley, which may abe incorporated as whole grains, crushed or ground cereal. While the cows cannot select from the ration, Starlings can and do and they take the barley, thereby altering the energetic value of the complete diet. The removal of this high energy fraction by Starlings is believed to reduce milk yields but this has not been thoroughly investigated; there is no doubt, however, that the quantities of barley removed are economically significant.

Feare and Wadsworth (1981) estimated the amount of barley taken by Starlings from five English farms that were feeding complete diets to dairy cows. At these farms Starlings took between one and fifteen per cent of the barley presented to the cows. The most severe loss occurred at a farm with 140 cows; here, 11.9 tonnes of barley, valued at £1009, were eaten by the birds between October and early February. In a more general survey of 49 farms some other aspects of this kind of damage emerged. Farms were more likely to experience damage if the cows were fed outdoors than if they were fed inside open-ended buildings. They were also more likely to suffer damage if rolled (= crushed), rather than ground, barley constituted the high energy fraction of the diet. When ground barley was presented to the cattle and Starlings nevertheless fed at the farm, the birds consumed less barley than if rolled barley had been given. These findings suggest certain damage prevention measures that might be taken but I shall discuss this later.

The feeding of complete diets to dairy cows had a relatively short period of popularity in Britain and most dairy farmers now prefer other feeding techniques. Dairy cows are, however, still given large quantities of barley, sometimes mixed with silage and sometimes outside in open yards and Starling damage therefore continues. It is interesting to speculate that had ornithologists, with experience of Starling feeding behaviour at intensive beef units, been consulted during discussions of the possible benefits and drawbacks of introducing complete diets for dairy cows, these bird experts might have predicted the damage that was to come. But they were not consulted!

Another problem associated with the Starlings' consumption of cattle food is their fouling of the food, food troughs, and associated structures and of the cows themselves. The main worry of most farmers is the possibility of transmission of disease, which, as I have already discussed, is probably not great. There is no doubt that deposits of Starlings' faeces on animals and in buildings provide unpleasant working conditions for herdsmen. Farmers have also suggested, however, that the presence of bird faeces on the cattle food renders this less palatable to the cows. When Glahn and his colleagues (personal communication) placed cages of Starlings and Red-winged Blackbirds over troughs from which an experimental group of calves was allowed to feed, they found that this group of calves grew faster than a control group whose food was not contaminated with bird droppings. The explanation was that the bird faeces, rich in uric acid, presented the calves with an added supply of nitrogen. Thus it seems that bird droppings might even enhance cattle food, rather than render it unpalatable; this assumes, of course, that the birds do not carry a disease that can be transmitted to cattle. A surprising finding such as this highlights the inadequacy of our basic knowledge of the relationships between our avian pests and the agricultural areas in which they cause problems.

PREVENTION OF DAMAGE

The traditional means of attempting to prevent or reduce damage are to kill or scare the birds involved. In other words, the farmer attempts to reduce the population of birds to the extent that the amount of food that they consume is negligible, or he attempts to make the area where the birds are causing damage unattrative so that they feed elsewhere. We have seen that our knowledge of the economics of Starling damage is at present very limited but our understanding of the cost and effectiveness of the control measures used is even more sketchy. We do know, however, that many traditionally used methods are not effective. For example, we have seen that a commercial cherry farmer spent £2000 in 1975 in attempts to reduce Starling damage but despite this expenditure, the Starlings in his 16 ha orchard consumed cherries worth £20 000. In this particular case, we do not know whether any more damage would have occurred had the £2000 not been spent on prevention measures. Attempts to kill Starlings, even using techniques that inflict very heavy local mortality, such as dynamiting roosts, have also failed to kill sufficient birds to achieve any regulation of their numbers (Tahon 1980). In deciding which methods should be used we must, therefore, examine carefully the relationship between the aspects of husbandry that encourage the damage and the ecology and behaviour of the bird.

Population reduction

Various attempts to prevent Starling damage have been made using techniques designed to kill the birds. In Belgium, summer roosts are destroyed using dynamite to reduce damage in cherry orchards. In Spain, large numbers are trapped both for pest control and for food (Parsons 1960) and in the Mahgreb region of north Africa olives are supposedly protected by spraying roosts with the organophosphorus insecticide fenthion, a chemical widely used in tropical Africa to kill Quelea. In north-western France roosts are sprayed with a chemical developed by the Denver Wildlife Research Center and commonly called DRC-1347 (3-chloro-4-methyl-benzenamine). In the United States a variety of poisons have been developed as roost sprays or as baits: the best known of the latter has the commercial name 'Starlicide' (DRC-1339: 3-chloro-4-methyl-benzenamine hydrochloride) (Besser, Royall, and de Grazio 1967; Royall, De Cino, and Besser 1967; West 1968). In addition, the organochlorine insecticide endrin is used as a contact poison: a wick, through which this chemical can soak, is incorporated into perches specially provided at outdoor cattle feeding areas. An alternative to poisoning, again used in the United States, is to spray winter roosts with a detergent (Lefebvre and Seubert 1970). This destroys the birds' water-proofing properties so that ensuing rain (or water sprayed on to the roost) and cold results in their death due to hypothermia. In Britain, a stupefying agent, alpha-chloralose, has been used experimentally to kill Starlings that were eating cattle food (Feare *et al.* 1981). This is not an exclusive list of the materials that are available, and have been used, to kill Starlings but it shows that man has the capability to kill large numbers of them if he so desires.

The expectation of destroying roosts using explosives, poisons, or detergents was that a long-term reduction of the general Starling population would be achieved. That this expectation was not realised has been clearly shown by Tahon (1980) in Belgium. On average, about one fifth of the estimated half million Starlings that lived in the cherry growing region around St. Trond were killed, using explosives, in each of seven years and yet no reduction in the population in subsequent years was recorded. This failure to reduce the population is not really surprising, for in Chapter 8 we saw that the Starling's average annual mortality is about 50 per cent. Since mortality factors tend to substitute each other rather than be additive, an artificial mortality that is designed to regulate the population, at a lower than 'natural level, must exceed 50 per cent of the birds present. Thus the mortality imposed by the Belgian Ministry of Agriculture was simply not enough to achieve the stated aim of the operation. Furthermore, the level of mortality attained could not be increased because some Starlings roosted in areas, such as on buildings or in plantations, where dynamite could not be used to kill them.

We do not know how successful are the north African operations against their immigrant Starlings in winter but since the killing seems to be repeated each year, there appears to be no overall population reduction. This has certainly been the conclusion reached by American scientists, despite the many kinds of mortality that they have been able to inflict, and in North America attempts to reduce the national population of Starlings have now been discontinued. As the Starling is regarded as an unwelcome introduction by the conservationists in the United States, even the Audubon Societies supported the attempts to reduce Starling numbers. It seems, therefore, that pest control operations aimed at reducing these bird populations to 'tolerable' or 'acceptable' levels are doomed to failure simply because we are unable to impose sufficiently heavy mortality: the Passenger Pigeon *Ectopistes migratorius* must indeed have had some peculiar ecological features to have enabled it to be killed to extinction by hunters (Halliday 1980).

The imposition of locally heavy mortality can, however, confer protection to crops over a short period provided that the immigration of new individuals is limited. This strategy is now used in

Africa against Quelea, earlier attempts to reduce the overall population of this species having been curtailed on account of their expense and failure. The Belgian Ministry of Agriculture's dynamiting operations are worthwhile only when large numbers of Starlings are roosting in the same place. This occurs only during the latter part of the cherry season when there has been some coalescence of the small early summer roosts and the early ripening, and especially valuable, cherries are unprotected by this technique. Tahon (1980) concluded that later ripening cherries did receive some protection as a result of the 20 per cent mortality inflicted on the Starlings, although the protection would have been greater but for the wide-ranging movements, leading to considerable immigration, of juveniles during the summer.

Similar immigration led to the failure of my own attempt to prevent damage at a dairy farm in East Anglia in winter. Half of the Starlings that had been feeding at this farm were killed, over a three day period, using alpha-chloralose but within a week the number of Starlings on the farm returned to the pre-treatment level (Feare *et al.*, 1981). This immigration to fill an artificially created void lends support to the suggestion made in Chapter 9 that there is considerable competition at these cattle feeding areas.

An alternative to a large-scale quick kill is to effect a low but continuous mortality throughout the birds' predation of the crop requiring protection. Endrin-soaked perches and continuous baiting with Starlicide are used to achieve this objective in the United States, but these techniques cannot be legally used in Britain. It is very difficult to assess the effectiveness of these techniques: one rarely finds dead birds and the measurement of the loss of cattle food to birds needs to be fairly sophisticated. The main problem with using poisons that have to be ingested, however, is to find a bait that will attract the target birds, but not other species, away from the often superabundant alternative foods that they would normally eat on the farm. This problem is exacerbated by the tastes of some of the toxic chemicals used, for the detection of these by the birds can lead to the ingestion of sublethal doses that can induce an aversion to the bait. In this case the poison will not have its desired effect of killing the birds and a period of pre-baiting with untreated food is required to accustom them to the bait once more. To overcome bait aversion during large-scale poisoning in pre-roost assemblies, American workers dilute the bait, usually consisting of specially prepared pellets containing

Starlicide, with untreated cracked corn. This also serves an added purpose in maintaining the interest of surviving birds in the baiting station: this nucleus is believed then to attract incoming birds.

The absence of really attractive baits, together with the Starlings' tendency to avoid confined spaces, often renders trapping an inadequate way of catching Starlings in sufficient numbers to reduce populations locally, although large decoy traps have met with some success in the United States. What is clearly needed is a 'super-bait', a bait of extreme attractiveness that will lure Starlings from their natural foods to the newly provided source. By adding various additives, especially animal proteins, to rolled barley I have recently shown experimentally that baits can be made more attractive to Starlings than the untreated barley that they eat in the feedlots. These simple 'super-baits' now need extensive testing in the field.

A further technique to reduce populations is to prevent breeding: Bernis (1960) proposed that people living in the breeding areas of Starlings that winter in Spain should undertake work to reduce the output of young. This is unlikely to happen because in many regions the Starling is regarded as a beneficial bird: such is the esteem in which the species is held in Russia that Polyakova, Ardamatskaya, Ganya, Ezerskas, Marisova, Prinklonskii, and Sema (1978) estimated that there are currently about 22.5 million Starling nestboxes in the USSR! In any case, we do not have the capability to achieve a dramatic reduction in the number of breeding Starlings. Nest destruction is impracticable since most nests are inaccessible and despite intensive search there is still no chemical available that will act as a practicable long-lasting reproduction inhibitor. Even if there were, the practical difficulties of introducing the chemical into Starlings, but not into non-target species, might prove insuperable.

Scarers, frightening agents, and chemical repellents

The aim of these devices is to make the place where Starlings are causing damage less attractive to them so that they move elsewhere to feed. This presupposes, of course, that alternative and adequate food sources are available, which is sometimes not the case when Starlings are eating foods of economic significance to man. The scarcer are these alternatives, the harder it is to drive the birds away from the area of damage. The decision that the bird must make is: should I stay here and risk the danger of predation (this is the threat supposedly presented by scarers) or eat something with a bad taste, or should I move away and face certain starvation. Successful birds, like Starlings, elect to risk predation!

Scarers that are readily available and are widely used involve a range of objects from the traditional scarecrow and suspended polythene bags to more sophisticated devices such as gas bangers. The current industrial trend is to make scarers more and more sophisticated by introducing signals novel to the birds; once the novelty has worn off, however, the new scarer becomes no better than the old. Once this has happened, the presence of a scarer in a field may, in fact, indicate to the birds that good food is to be had there, precisely the opposite of what the farmer intends!

Scarers can be made more effective by incorporating indications to the birds that there is danger. For example, there is no doubt that the best scarer available is a man with a gun, expensive though this scarer may be, for the killing of an occasional bird reinforces the 'threat' of the bang. Other meaningful signals can be incorporated into scarers, however, and the most widely used of these is the tape-recorded distress call which is broadcast through loudspeakers to birds doing damage. This technique is successfully used against Starlings in their roosts; by playing the calls to the birds as they arrive at the roost in the evening on four or five consecutive nights, the roosting population can usually be persuaded to move elsewhere. Protection can thus be afforded to valuable timber plantations or to game coverts but there is no guarantee that the birds will not move into an equally valuable place. Should this happen, neighbouring farmers may well devote considerable time and energy driving roosting Starlings backwards and forwards between alternative roosting sites. Broadcast distress calls are generally less effective at keeping Starlings away from feeding sites although they are used in cherry orchards (Plate 16) and vineyards, especially in Germany. The broadcasting of distress calls is thought to work because such calls are given only when a bird is in some sort of danger; the precise function of the call is not understood but it does seem to indicate to other flock members that all is not well (Chapter 5). My colleague Ian Inglis is currently looking at the possible use of other biologically meaningful signals as scarers and he has found in laboratory experiments that Starlings do respond, by curtailing or delaying feeding, to simulated predators eyes. Whether this kind of signal can be effectively incorporated into practical scarers remains to be seen.

A logical extension of the use of distress calls is to employ a distressed bird as a scarer. Such a technique has been developed in the United States where a chemical, 4-amino-pyridine (commercially called Avitrol), is presented in a bait to flocks of birds. Only one item of bait in every hundred or so actually contains the chemical so that few flock members are affected. Those that are, however, soon begin to fly erratically and emit distress calls until they eventually die, but in the meantime their behaviour frightens other flock members away (Besser, De Grazio, and Guarino 1973). Rowsell, Ritchey, and Cox (1979) have shown that by the time an affected bird begins to exhibit the symptoms of Avitrol poisoning, the bird is technically unconscious but I suspect that it will be hard to convince protectionists of this!

At first sight, the simplest way of reducing crop damage would be to treat or spray the crop with a material that renders the food unpalatable to the marauding birds. This approach is often advocated by farmers, who are so accustomed to spraying chemicals to counteract insect attacks. For birds, however, the problem is that we so far do not know of a chemical that acts reliably as a repellent. Several candidate materials have been investigated and one, methiocarb, is widely sprayed on to fruit, especially cherries, in the United States and in Europe. It acts by inducing sickness in a bird that eats it, after which the bird develops a conditioned aversion to treated fruit (Rogers 1980). Methiocarb is not the 'perfect' repellent and it was, in fact, developed as an insecticide and molluscicide and it is interesting that some other insecticides belonging to this group of compounds, the carbamates, also show bird-repellent properties (Green 1980). These chemicals are highly toxic but their repellent effects, which are extremely variable, depend upon sub-lethal effects on the birds. There is no doubt that in many cases methiocarb does reduce damage but equally there are instances where it has not been possible to detect any bird repellent effect. Its efficiency may well, like that of scarers, be influenced by the availability of alternative foods to which Starlings can be driven.

Farm management

We have seen how the present levels of Starling damage to cherries, winter cereals, and in cattle feeding areas in Britain have resulted from changes in various aspects of plant and animal husbandry. To reverse these changes would remove the threat of damage in these areas of agriculture. This is clearly not a practicable way of overcoming these bird problems for the agricultural developments that have led to these problems have nevertheless brought other advantages for the farmer. Equally, the problems associated with Starlings cannot be overcome by 'getting rid of the birds': although this step may often by advocated by farmers who suffer damage, we have seen that the extermination of Starlings from a given area is not practicable and even if it were it would not make economic sense. If extermination could be achieved, we have no idea of the repercussions that there might be with regard to other animals, especially insect populations, and there are also, of course, ethical arguments for not attempting to eliminate large segments of wild populations of animals. Perhaps husbandry techniques could be modified to reduce the damaging effects of marauding birds; birds are, after all, simply another enivironmental factor with which the farmer must contend.

Consideration of pests in this light is not a new idea and even with insect pests, changes in husbandry techniques are integrated with what have become the accepted forms of insect population control—the spraying of toxic chemicals. Simple changes in agricultural practices can help to maintain the insect numbers at a low level but should dangerous outbreaks occur then the chemicals are applied. This form of integrated pest control makes economic and environmental sense, for the quantity of expensive pesticide that is used is much reduced and the hazard of environmental pollution is similarly diminished. So can simple changes in practice be used to combat bird damage?

When describing the three main kinds of damage suffered by British farmers I intimated that certain developments in management had given rise to problems with Starlings. For example, the winter-wheat farmer who has a traditional large Starling roost on or near his land has a choice of sowing deep to avoid Starling damage, but risking a Wheat Bulb Fly attack, or sowing shallowly to overcome the latter problem while risking Starling damage. He could, of course, sow early and overcome both problems. The idea of timing events in the agricultural calendar so that bird problems are avoided was suggested by Elliott (1979) for Quelea but this technique does rely on the accurate prediction of weather conditions which, in most parts of the Starling's geographical range, is not possible. In the case of winter wheat in Britain, however, the apparent absence of a reduction in yield following Starling attack should sway the farmer in favour of shallow sowing of late crops in order to counteract Wheat Bulb Fly in areas where this insect is prevalent.

Starling activities in cherry orchards have much more serious consequences but the employment of more pickers in the middle of the season would reduce losses considerably. In the example that I quoted earlier, where a grower lost £20 000 of cherries to birds, it would seem that this farmer could have afforded to spend much more on labour in order to increase his share of the harvest. The picking of a 'traditional' cherry tree, which may be around 15 m high, is difficult and time-consuming but a change in husbandry, ostensibly to overcome these picking problems, will undoubtedly hold benefits with respect to Starling damage. For there is an urgent campaign to grow dwarf varieties of cherry tree that will grow to only about 5 m tall, and which can be grown closer together than existing trees. Once these trees are in commercial use, the cherries will be easier and quicker to harvest, thus reducing the chance of bird damage, and small trees will be easier to protect from birds, as we shall see in the last section of this chapter.

Simple changes in food presentation might also help to reduce the amount of food Starlings take from feedlots. We have already seen how an early change from calf starter pellets to a mixture of concentrates and rolled barley can cut the cost of Starling damage at a calf farm (Fig. 12.2) and other possibilities for reducing damage exist. Feare and Wadsworth (1981) found that a farm that incorporated ground barley into the complete diet ration for dairy cows lost less barley than did farms that presented rolled barly. In laboratory experiments, Feare *et al.* (1981) showed that when given a simple choice, Starlings in fact preferred ground to rolled barley, but when these two forms of barley were mixed with silage, as in the cattle rations, this preference was reversed. Obseravation showed that the birds found it more difficult to extract ground barley from the mixture, because the fragments were so small, whereas fragments of rolled barley were easy to see and to pick up sufficiently quickly to fulfil the Starlings' requirements.

Starling exclusion

The changes in husbandry that I have so far discussed have been relatively minor but the farmer can, if he chooses, eliminate some of his problems altogether; naturally, this involves more financial outlay.

The total exclusion of birds from a cherry orchard is admittedly difficult, especially with old, very large (up to 15 m tall) trees but it is nevertheless practised in New Zealand and in parts of Britain (Plate 16). Exclusion is achieved by totally enclosing the orchard with netting and this will become a more feasible proposition when smaller trees, currently being developed, are readily available and growers replace their large older trees. The use of netting has advantages apart from simply keeping out Starlings. For example, if the netting is erected before the trees flower, the wind-stopping properties of the net help to maintain an elevated temperature within the enclosure, thereby reducing the likelihood of frost damage. If bee-hives are placed in the enclosure at flowering time, the warmer climate within allows the bees to be more active and pollinate more flowers than if there were no enclosure. At harvest time, with no worries of bird damage, the farmer can leave his cherries to ripen on the trees a little longer: during this extra ripening period the cherries increase in weight and, since they are sold by weight, this alone can confer financial benefits.

Similarly, where cattle are fed within buildings, some financial outlay can alleviate all the problems of food loss and fouling and also provide benefits such as a warmer environment for the animals, although adequate ventilation must be ensured. In recent experiments a 'curtain' of heavy-duty PVC strips, each strip about 0.25 m wide and with 5 cm gaps between the strips, hanging over openings in the buildings, has proved to be a satisfactory method of keeping the cattle houses free of Starlings (Plate 16). These strips are strong enough to withstand frequent licking by cows, and people and machinery can readily move through them simply by pushing them aside. Although these strips are comparatively expensive they are anticipated to have a life of 5–10 years, which renders their purchase economically worthwhile (Feare and Swannack 1978). Over openings through which animals or machinery rarely pass, cheaper alternative materials, such as wire or plastic netting, can be used to exclude Starlings. Outdoor cattle feeding troughs present a much greater engineering problem, for any covers that are placed over the food to exclude Starlings must not restrict access to the cattle. This is an area where farmer, engineer, and ornithologist must work together.

These examples show that changes in management techniques can be used to reduce Starling damage with economic benefit to the farmer. It would certainly be helpful if agricultural planners and ornithologists could liaise when changes in technique are considered. Some of the problems could then be avoided at an early stage, rather than when some farmers have already suffered heavy losses. This does presuppose, of course, that the ornithologist knows sufficient about the biology of his subject to predict how it will respond under the new circumstances. With a species as adaptable as the Starling, the importance of pure research on its ecology, physiology, and behaviour cannot be underestimated, for all aspects of its biology impinge on the species' ability to exploit the agricultural environment and create problems therein.

REFERENCES

Abdulali, H. (1947). The movements of the Rosy Pastor in India. *J. Bombay Nat. Hist. Soc.* **46**, 704–708
—— (1964). The birds of the Andaman and Nicobar Islands. *J. Bombay Nat. Hist. Soc.* **61**, 483–571.
Ali, S. and Ripley, S. D. (1972). *Handbook of the birds of India and Pakistan.* Vol. 5. Oxford University Press, Oxford.
Al-Joborae, F. F. (1979). The influence of diet on the gut morphology of the Starling (*Sturnus vulgaris*) L.1758. D.Phil. thesis, University of Oxford.
Amadon, D. (1943). The genera of starlings and their relationships. *Am. Mus. Novitates* **1247**, 1–16.
—— (1956). Remarks on the Starlings, Family Sturnidae. *Am. Mus. Novitates* **1803**, 1–41.
—— (1962). Family Sturnidae, Starlings. In *Peters check-list of birds of the world*, (eds. E. Mayr and J. C. Greenway) Vol. 15. Museum of Comparative Zoology, Cambridge.
Anderson, A. (1961). The breeding of the Starling in Aberdeenshire. *Scott. Birds* **70**, 60–74.
Ashmole, N. P. and Tovar, H. (1968). Prolonged parental care in Royal Terns and other birds. *Auk* **85**, 90–100.
Aspock, H., Graefe, G., Kunz, C., and Radda, A. (1972). Antikörper gegen Arboviren in Staren (*Sturnus vulgaris* L.) in Osterreich. *Zentralb. fur Bakteriol.* **221**, 141–2.
Atkinson, R. J. C. (1956). *Stonehenge.* Hamish Hamilton, London.
Bährmann, U. (1964). Über die Mauser des europaischen Stars (*Sturnus vulgaris* L.). *Zool. Abh. Mus. Tierk. Dresden* **27**, 1–9.
Bailey, E. P. (1966). Abundance and activity of Starlings in winter in Northern Utah. *Condor* **68**, 152–162.
Baker, R. R. (1978). *The evolutionary ecology of animal migration.* Hodder & Stoughton, London.
—— and Parker, G. A. (1979). The evolution of bird coloration. *Phil. Trans. R. Soc.* **B287**, 63–130.
Bannerman, D.A. (1953*a*). *The birds of west and edquatorial Africa.* Vol. 2. Oliver & Boyd, Edinburgh.
—— (1953*b*). *The birds of the British Isles.* Oliver & Boyd, Edinburgh.
—— (1966). *Birds of the Atlantic islands*, Vol. 3. Oliver & Boyd, Edinburgh.
Barnard, C. J. (1980). Flock feeding and time budgets in the House Sparrow (*Passer domesticus* L.). *Anim. Behav.* **28**, 295–309.

Beecher, W. J. (1978). Feeding adaptations and evolution in the starlings. *Bull. Chicago Acad. Sci.* **11**, 269–98.

Beklova, M. (1972). Age structure and mortality of the Czechoslovakian populations of *Turdus merula* L. 1758, *Sturnus vulgaris* L. 1758 and *Parus major* L. 1758. *Zool. Listy* **21**, 337–46.

—— (1978). Distance and direction of migration of the Czechoslovak population of *Sturnus vulgaris*. *Folia Zool.* **27**, 25–36.

Bernis, F. (1960). Migracion, problema agricola y captura del Estornino Pinto (*Sturnus vulgaris*). *Ardeola* **6**, 11–109.

Berthold, P. (1968). Die Massenvermehrung des Stars *Sturnus vulgaris* in fortpflanzungs—physiologischer Sicht. *J. Ornithol.* **109**, 11–16.

—— (1971). Experimentelle Untersuchung von Zwillingsarten: Über Fortpflanz Ungsverhalten und Brut von *Sturnus unicolor/vulgaris*—Mischpaaren. *Vogelwelt* **92**, 141–7.

—— (1976). The control and significance of animal and vegetable nutrition in omnivorous song birds. *Arden.* **64**, 140–154.

Besser, J. F., De Grazio, J. W., and Guarino, J. L. (1968). Costs of wintering Starlings and Red-winged Blackbirds at feedlots. *J. Wild. Manage.* **32**, 179–80.

——, ——, —— (1973). Decline of a blackbird population during seven years of baiting with a chemical frightening agent. *Proc. Bird Control Seminar* **6**, 12–14.

——, Royall, W. C. and De Grazio, J. W. (1967). Baiting Starlings with DRC-1339 at a cattle feedlot. *J. Wildl. Manage.* **31**, 48–51.

Bevan, D. (1962). Starling roosts in woodland. *Q. J. For.* **66**, 59–62.

Bickford, A. A., Ellis, G. H. and Moses, H. E. (1966). Epizootiology of tuberculosis in Starlings. *J. Assoc. Vet. Med. Assoc.* **149**, 312–18.

Biebach, H. (1979). Energetic des Brütens biem Star (*Sturnus vulgaris*). *J. Ornithol.* **120**, 121–138.

Blackmore, D. K. and Keymer, I. F. (1969). Cutaneous diseases of wild birds in Britain. *Br. Birds* **62**, 316–31.

Blom, E. (1962). *Mozart*. Dent, London.

Bogucki, Z. (1972). Studies on the activity of Starlings *Sturnus vulgaris*. Linnaeus, 1758, in the breeding season. *Acta Zool. Cracov.* **17**, 97–119.

Bond, J. (1979). *Birds of the West Indies*. Collins, London.

Boyce, D. V. H. (1979). The influence of sowing depth on the removal of grain from winter wheat by Starlings (*Sturnus vulgaris* L.). *J. Plant Pathol.* **28**, 68–71.

Boyd, E. M. (1951). A survey of parasitism of the Starling *Sturnus vulgaris* L. in North America. *J. Parasitol.* **37**, 56–84.

Brand, A. R. and Kellogg, P. P. (1939). Auditory responses of Starlings, English Sparrows and Domestic Pigeons. *Wilson Bull.* **51**, 38–41.

Bray, O. E., Larsen, K. H., and Mott, D. F. (1975). Winter movements and activities of radio-equipped Starlings. *J. Wildl. Manage.* **39**, 795–801.

Brenner, F. J. (1965). Metabolism and survival time of grouped Starlings at various temperatures. *Wilson Bull.* **77**, 388–95.

Brodie, J. (1974). Evening assembly of Starlings at a winter roost. *Scott. Birds* **8**, 63–71.

—— (1976). The flight behaviour of Starlings at a winter roost. *Br. Birds* **69**, 51–60.

Brown, L. H. (1965). Redwinged starlings of Kenya. *J. East Afr. Nat. Hist. Soc.* **25**, 41–56.

Brown, R. G. B. (1974). Bird damage to fruit crops in the Niagara Peninsula. *Can. Wild. Serv. Rep.* **27**, 1–57.

Brownsmith, C. B. (1977). Foraging rates of Starlings in two habitats. *Condor* **79**, 386–7.

Bryant, D. M. and Westerterp, K. (1982). Evidence for individual differences in foraging efficiency amongst breeding birds: a study of House Martins *Delichon urbica* using the doubly labelled water technique. *Ibis* **124**, 187–92.

Bullough, W. S. (1942). On the external morphology of the British and Continental races of the Starling (*Sturnus vulgaris* L.). *Ibis* **6**, 225–39.

Cadbury, C. J. (1980). *Silent death*. Royal Society for the Protection of Birds, Sandy..

Cain, A. J. and Galbraith, I. C. J. (1956). Field notes on birds of the eastern Solomon Islands. *Ibis* **98**, 262–95.

Casals, J., Henderson, B. E., Hoogstraal, H., Johnson, K. M. and Shelokov, A. (1970). A review of Soviet viral haemorrhagic fevers, 1969. *J. Infect. Dis.* **122**, 437–53.

Chapman, F. M. (1895). *Handbook of birds of eastern north America.* Appleton, New York.

Charman, K. (1965). Studies on the communal roosting of Starlings (*Sturnus vulgaris* L.) Ph.D. thesis, University of Durham.

Cheke, R. A., Hassall, M. and Peirce, M. A. (1976). Blood parasites of British birds and notes on their seasonal occurrence at two rural sites in England. *J. Wildl. Dis.* **12**, 133–38.

Clergeau, P. (1982). Attractivité et utilisation du milieu chez des Etourneaux en alimentation. *Oecol. Applic.* **3**, 307–20.

Coleman, J. D. (1974). The use of artificial nest sites erected for Starlings in Canterbury, New Zealand. *N. Z. J. Zool.* **1**, 349–54.

—— (1977). The foods and feeding of Starlings in Canterbury. *Proc. N. Z. Ecol. Soc.* **24**, 94–109.

—— and Robson, A. B. (1975). Variations in body weight, fat-free weights and fat deposition of Starlings in New Zealand. *Proc. N. Z. Ecol. Soc.* **22**, 7–13.

Collinge, W. E. (1924–1927). *The food of some British wild birds.* Published by the author, York.

Collins, V. B. and de Vos, A. (1966). A nesting study of the Starling near Guelph, Ontario. *Auk* **83**, 626–36.

Coombs, C. J. F. (1978). *The crows*. Batsford, London.

Cooper, C. L. and Crites, J. L. (1976). Additional check list of the helminths of the Starling (*Sturnus vulgaris* L.). *Amer. Midl. Nat.* **95**, 191–94.

Coulson, J C. (1960). A study of the mortality of the Starling based on ringing recoveries *J. Anim. Ecol.* **29**, 251–71.

—— (1972). The significance of the pair-bond in the kittiwake. *Proc. XV. Int. Ornithol. Congr.*, pp. 424–433.

Crewe, B. and Owen, R. (1978). 750 000 eggs a day—£750,000 a year. *New Scientist*, **80**, 344–6.

Crossner, K. A. (1977). Natural selection and clutch size in the European Starling. *Ecology* **58**, 885–92.

Davies, N. B. (1976). Parental care and the transition to independent feeding in the young Spotted Flycatcher *Muscicapa striata*. *Behaviour* **59**, 280–295.

Davis, D. E. (1950). The growth of Starling, *Sturnus vulgaris*, populations. *Auk* **67**, 460–5.

—— (1959). The sex and age structure of roosting Starlings. *Ecology* **40**, 136–9.

Davis, G. J. (1970). Seasonal changes in flocking behavior of Starlings as correlated with gonadal development. *Wilson Bull.* **82**, 391–9.

—— and Lussenhop, J. F. (1970). Roosting of Starlings (*Sturnus vulgaris*): a function of light and time. *Anim. Behav.* **18**, 362–5.

Dawson, A. and Goldsmith, R. (1982). Prolactin and gonadotrophin secretion in wild Starlings (*Sturnus vulgaris*) during the annual cycle and in relation to nesting, incubation and rearing young. *Gen. Comp. Endocrinol.* **48**, 213–221.

Dehaven, R. W. and Guarino, J. L. (1970). Breeding of Starlings using nest boxes at Denver, Colorado. *Colorado Field Ornithol.* **8**, 1–10.

Deignan, H. G. (1945). The Birds of northern Thailand. *US Nat. Mus. Bull.* **186**, 1–615.

Delacour, J. and Mayr, E. (1946). *Birds of the Philippines*. Macmillan, New York.

Delvingt, W. (1961). Les dortoirs d'Etourneaux *Sturnus vulgaris* L. de Belgique en 1959–1960. *Le Gerfaut* **51**, 1–27.

—— (1962a). Die Beziehungen zwichen Brutgröße and Jungengewicht biem Star. *J. Ornithol.* **103**, 260–5.

—— (1962b). L'Etourneau en Belgique: Longevité, pontes. *Le Gerfaut* **52**, 586–601.

—— (1963). Rhythme quotidien des activites de l'Etourneau, *Sturnus vulgaris* L., au dortoir. *Le Gerfaut* **53**, 489–507.

Dement'ev, G. P. and Gladkov, N. A. (1960). *Birds of the Soviet Union* Vol. 5, Israel Program for Scientific Translations, Jerusalem.

Dobinson, H. M. and Richards, A. J. (1964). The effects of the severe winter of 1962/63 on birds in Britain. *Br. Birds* **57**, 373–434.

Dodge, H. J. (1965). The association of a bird-roosting site with infection of schoolchildren by *Histoplasma capsulatum*. *Am. J. Pub. Health*. **55**, 1203–11.

Dolbeer, R. A. and Stehn, R. A. (1979). Population trends of blackbirds and Starlings in north America, 1966–76. *United States Department of the Interior, Fish and Wildlife Service, Special Scientific Report No. 214*, pp. 1–99.

——, Stickley, A. R., and Woronecki, P. P. (1978). Starling, *Sturnus vulgaris*, damage to sprouting wheat in Tennessee and Kentucky, U.S.A. *Prot. Ecol.* **1**, 159–69.

Dorst, J. (1962). *The migrations of birds*. Heinemann, London.

Douglas, N. (1928). *Birds and beasts of the Greek anthology*. Chapman & Hall, London.

Drent, R. H. and Swiestra, P. (1977). Goose flocks and food finding: field experiments with Barnacle Geese in winter. *Wildfowl* **28**, 15–20.

Duncan, J. S., Reid, H. W., Moss, R., Phillips, J. D. P., and Watson, A. (1978). Ticks, louping ill and Red Grouse on moors in Speyside, Scotland. *J. Wildl. Manage.* **42**, 500–5.

Dunnet, G. M. (1955). The breeding of the Starling *Sturnus vulgaris* in relation to its food supply. *Ibis* **97**, 619–62.

—— (1956). The autumn and winter mortality of Starlings in relation to their food supply. *Ibis* **98**, 220–30.

—— and Patterson, I. J. (1968). The Rook problem in north-east Scotland. In *The problems of birds as pests* (eds. R. K. Murton and E. N. Wright). Academic Press, London.

Dyer, M. E. and Ward, P. (1977). Management of pest situations. In *Granivorous birds in ecosystems* (eds. J. Pinowski and S. C. Kendeigh). Cambridge University Press, Cambridge.

East, R. and Pottinger, R. P., (1975). Starling (*Sturnus vulgaris* L.) predation on Grass Grub (*Costelytra zealandica* (White) Melolonthinea) populations in Canterbury. *N.Z. J. Agric. Res.* **18**, 417–52.

Eastwood, E. (1967). *Radar ornithology*. Methuen, London.

——, Isted, G. A. and Rider, G. C. (1962). Radar ring angels and the roosting behaviour of Starlings. *Proc. R. Soc. Lond.* **B156**, 242–67.

Ebling, F. J. P., Goldsmith, A. R. and Follett, B. K. (1982). Plasma prolactin and luteinizing hormone during photoperiodically induced testicular growth and regression in Starlings (*Sturnus vulgaris*). *Gen. Comp. Endocrinol.* **48**, 485–90.

Edwards, C. A. and Lofty, J. R. (1972). *Biology of earthworms*. Chapman & Hall, London.

Eiserer, L. A. (1980). Effects of grass length and mowing on foraging behaviour of the American Robin (*Turdus migratorius*). *Auk* **97**, 576–80.

Elgar, M. A. and Catterall, C. P. (1981). Flocking and predator surveillance in House Sparrows: test of an hypothesis. *Anim. Behav.* **29**, 868–72.

Elliott, C. C. H. (1979). The harvest time method as a means of avoiding Quelea damage to irrigated rice in Chad/Cameroun. *J. Appl. Ecol.* **16**, 23–35.

Ellis, C. R. (1966). Agonistic behaviour in the male Starling. *Wilson Bull.* **78**, 208–24.

Emlen, S. T. (1975). Migration: orientation and navigation. In *Avian biology*. (eds. D. S. Farner and J. R. King) Vol. 5. Academic Press, New York.

Etchecopar, R. D. and Hue, F. (1967). *The birds of north Africa*. Oliver & Boyd, Edinburgh.

Evans, P. G. H. (1980). Population genetics of the European Starling *Sturnus vulgaris*. D. Phil. thesis, University of Oxford.

Faddoul, G. P., Fellows, G. W. and Baird, J. (1968). Erysipelothrix infection in Starlings. *Avian Dis.* **12**, 61–6.

Falla, R. A., Sibson, R. B., and Turbott, E. G. (1979). *Birds of New Zealand*. Collins, London.

Falls, J. B. (1969). Functions of territorial song in the White-throated Sparrow. In *Bird vocalizations* (ed. R. A. Hinde). University Press, Cambridge.

Fankhauser, D. P. (1971). Annual adult survival rates of blackbirds and Starlings. *Bird-Banding* **42**, 36–42.

Feare, C. J. (1975). Post-fledging parental care in Crested and Sooty Terns. *Condor* **77**, 368–70.

—— (1976a). Communal roosting in the Mynah *Acridotheres tristis*. *J. Bombay Nat. Hist. Soc.* **73**, 525–7.

—— (1976b). The breeding of the Sooty Tern *Sterna fuscata* in the Seychelles, and the effects of experimental removal of its eggs. *J. Zool. Lond.* **179**, 317–60.

—— (1980). The economics of Starling damage. In *Bird problems in agriculture* (eds E. N. Wright, I. R. Inglis, and C. J. Feare) British Crop Protection Council, Croydon.

—— (1981a). Breeding schedules and feeding strategies of Seychelles seabirds. *Ostrich* **52**, 179–86.

—— (1981b). Zum Rückgang des Stars (*Sturnus vulgaris*) in Skandinavien: Bestandsdezimierung in Überwinterungsgebieten? *J. Ornithol.* **122**, 435–6.

—— (1981c). The relevance of 'natural' habitats to Starling damage. In *Pests, pathogens, and vegetation* (ed. J. M. Thresh). Pitmans, London.

—— (1981d). Local movement of Starlings in winter. *Proc. XVIII Int. Ornithol. Congr.* **2**, 1331–6.

—— and Burnham, S. E. (1978). Lack of nest site tenacity and mate fidelity in the Starling. *Bird Study* **25**, 189–91.

—— and Constantine, D. A. T. (1980). Starling eggs with spots. *Bird Study* **27**, 119–20.

——, Dunnet, G. M., and Patterson, I. J. (1974). Ecological studies of the Rook (*Corvus frugilegus* L.) in north-east Scotland: food intake and feeding behaviour. *J. Appl. Ecol.* **11**, 867–96.

—— and Inglis, I. R. (1979). The effects of reduction of feeding space on the behaviour of captive Starlings *Sturnus vulgaris*. *Ornis Scand.* **10**, 42–7.

——, Isaacson, A. J., Sheppard, P. A. and Hogan, J. M. (1981). Attempts to reduce Starling damage at dairy farms. *Prot. Ecol.* **3**, 173–81.

——, Spencer, P. L., and Constantine, D.A. T. (1982). Time of egg-laying of Starlings *Sturnus vulgaris*. *Ibis* **124**, 174–8.

—— and Swannack, K. P. (1978). Starling damage and its prevention at an open-fronted calf yard. *Anim. Prod.* **26**, 259–65.

—— and Wadsworth, J. T. (1981). Starling damage on farms using the complete diet system of feeding dairy cows. *Anim. Prod.* **32**, 179–83.

Fischer, K. and Stephan, B. (1974). Eine pleistozäne Avifauna aus der Ghal Dalam-Höhle, Malta. *Z. geol. Wiss. Berl.* **2**, 515–23.

Flegg, J. J. M. (1982). Bird damage to ripening fruit. *Ann. Rep. East Malling Res. Stn.* 1981, pp. 109–11.

Flux, J. E. C. and Flux, M. M. (1981). Population dynamics and age-structure of Starlings (*Sturnus vulgaris*) in New Zealand. *N.Z. J. Ecol.* **4**, 65–72.

Follett, B. K. and Davies, D. T. (1979). The endocrine control of ovulation in birds. In *Animal reproduction* (ed. H. Hawk). Allanheld Osmun, Montclair, New Jersey.

Ford, E. B. (1964). *Ecological genetics*. Methuen, London.

Francis, W. J. (1976). Micrometeorology of a blackbird roosts. *J. Wild. Manage* **40**, 132–16.

Freeland, W. J. (1981). Parasitism and behavioural dominance among male mice. *Science N.Y.* **213**, 461–42.

Frisch, K. von (1950). *Bees. Their vision, chemical senses and language.* Cornell University Press, New York.

Frieswijk, J. J. and Bresser, H. (1961). Het vertrek van Spreeuwen van de sociale slaapplaats. *Levende Natuur* **64**, 102–12.

Frings, H. and Cook, B. (1964). The upper frequency limits of hearing in the European Starling. *Condor* **66**, 56–60.

Gallagher, H. (1978). *De Spreeuw.* Spectrum, Utrecht.

Garnham, P. C. C. (1966). *Malaria parasites and haemosporidia.* Blackwell, Oxford.

Geikie, A. (1912). *The love of nature among the Romans.* John Murray, London.

Good, H. B. and Johnson, D. M. (1976). Experimental tree trimming to control an urban winter blackbird roost. *Proc. Bird Control Seminar* 7, 54–6.

Goodacre, M. J. (1959). The origin of winter visitors to the British Isles. 4. Starling (*Sturnus vulgaris*). *Bird Study* 6, 180–92.

Gough, P. M. and Beyer, J. W. (1980). Study of the relationship between birds and T. G. E. Unpublished Research Report, Veterinary Medical Research Institute, Iowa State University.

Gramet, P. (1982). L'Etourneau Sansonnet, *Sturnus vulgaris* en France: les problèmes agronimiques posés et les recherches en cours. *Séance de l'Academie d'agriculture de France*, février 1982, pp. 261–72.

Green, R. (1980). Food selection by Skylarks : the effect of a pesticide on grazing preferences. in *Bird problems in agriculture* (eds. E. N. Wright, I. R. Inglis, and C. J. Feare). British Crop Protection Council, Croydon.

Gromadzka, J. and Gromadzki, M. (1978). Sklad pokarmu pisklat szpaka, *Sturnus vulgaris* L., na Zulawach Wislanych. *Acta Ornithol.* 16, 335–64.

—— and Luniak, M. (1978). Pokarm pistklat szpaka, *Sturnus vulgaris* L., w Warszawie. *Acta Ornithol.* 16, 275–85.

Gromadzki, M. (1969). Composition of food of the Starling *Sturnus vulgaris* L., in agrocenoses. *Ekol. Polska* 17, 287–311.

—— (1978). Abundance of the Starling, *Sturnus vulgaris* L. in the breeding season in the vicinity of Gdańsk. *Acta Ornithol.* 16, 325–34.

—— (1979). Food requirement and effect of Starling, *Sturnus vulgaris* L. on agriculture in Zulawy Wislane. *Acta Ornithol.* 16, 467–92.

—— (1980). Reproduction of the Starling *Sturnus vulgaris* in Zulawy Wislane, North Poland. *Acta Ornithol*, 17, 195–224.

—— and Kania, W. (1976). Bird-ringing results in Poland. Migrations of the Starlings, *Sturnus vulgaris* L. *Acta Ornithol*, 15, 279–312.

Groot, P. de (1980). Information transfer in a socially roosting weaver bird (*Quelea quelea;* Ploceinae): an experimental study. *Anim. Behav.* 28, 1249–54.

Grue, C. E., Powell, G. V. N. and McChesney, M. J. (1982). Care of nestlings by wild female Starlings exposed to an organophosphate pesticide. *J. Appl. Ecol.* 19, 327–35.

Gruys-Casimir, E. M. (1965). On the influence of environmental factors on the autumn migration of Chaffinch and Starling: a field study. *Arch. Neerl. Zool.* 16, 175–279.

Gwinner, E. (1975*a*). Circadian and circannual rhythms in birds. In *Avian biology* (eds. D. S. Farner and J. R. King). Vol. 5. Academic Press, New York.

—— (1975*b*). Effects of social stimuli on the circannual rhythm of gonadal function in the European Starling (*Sturnus vulgaris*). *Z. Tierpsychol.* 38, 34–43.

—— (1977). Photoperiodic synchronization of circannual rhythms in the European Starling (*Sturnus vulgaris*). *Naturwissenschaften* **64**, 44–5.

—— (1978). Effects of pinealectomy on circadian locomotor activity rhythms in European Starlings, *Sturnus vulgaris*. *J. Comp. Physiol.* **126**, 123–9.

Gyllin, R., Källander, H. and Sylven, M. (1977). The microclimate explanation of town centre roosts of Jackdaws *Corvus monedula*. *Ibis* **119**, 358–61.

Hailman, J. P. (1958). Notes on pre-copulatory display in the Starling. *Wilson Bull.* **70**, 199–201.

Hair, J. D. and Forrester, D. J. (1970). The helminth parasites of the Starling. (*Sturnus vulgaris* L.): a checklist and analysis. *Am. Midl. Nat.* **83**, 555–564.

Halliday, T. R. (1980). The extinction of the Passenger Pigeon *Ectopistes migratorius* and its relevance to contemporary conservation. *Biol. Conserv.* **17**, 157–62.

Hamilton, G. A., Hunter, K., Ritchie, A. S., Ruthven, A. D., Brown, P. W. and Stanley, P. I. (1976). Poisoning of wild geese by carbophenothion-treated winter wheat. *Pestic. Sci.* **7**, 175–83.

Hamilton, W. J. and Gilbert, W. M. (1969). Starling dispersal from a winter roost. *Ecology* **50**, 886–98.

——, ——, Heppner, F. H., and Planck, R. (1967). Starling roost dispersal and a hypothetical mechanism regulating rhythmical and animal movement to and from dispersal centers. *Ecology* **48**, 825–33.

Haneda, K. and Ushiyama, H. (1967). Life history of the Red-cheeked Myna (*Sturnia philippensis*). *Jpn. J. Ecol.* **17**, 49–57 (In Japanese).

Harlan, J. R. (1981). Ecological settings for the emergence of agriculture. In *Pests, pathogens and vegetation*. (ed. J. M. Thresh). Pitmans, London.

Harper, W. G. (1959). Roosting movements of birds and migration departure from roosts as seen by radar. *Ibis* **101**, 201–8.

Harris, M. A. and Lemon, R. E. (1976). Responses of male Song Sparrows *Melospiza melodia* to neighbouring and non-neighbouring individuals. *Ibis* **118**, 421–4.

Hartby, E. (1969). The calls of the Starling (*Sturnus vulgaris*). *Dansk. Ornithol. Foren. Tidsskr.* **62**, 205–230.

Haslett, T. M. and Schneider, W. J. (1978). Occurrence and attempted transmission of *Toxoplasma gondii* in European Starlings (*Sturnus vulgaris*). *J. Wildl. Dis.* **14**, 173–5.

Hausberger, M. and Guyomarc'h, J. C. (1981). Contribution à l'etude des vocalisations territoriales sifflees chez l'étourneau sansonnet *Sturnus vulgaris* en Bretagne. *Biol. Behav.* **6**, 79–98.

Havlin, J. and Folk, C. (1965). Potrava a vyznam spacka obecneho, *Sturnus vulgaris* L. *Zool. Listy* **14**, 193–208.

Henry, G. M. (1971). *A guide to the birds of Ceylon*. Oxford University Press, Oxford.

Herrera, C. M. and Jordane, P. (1981). *Prunus mahaleb* and birds: the high-efficiency seed dispersal system of a temperate fruiting tree. *Ecol. Monogr.* **51**, 203–18.

Heuls, T. R. (1981). Cooperative breeding in the Golden-breasted Starling *Cosmopsarus regius*. *Ibis* **123**, 539–42.

Hilton, F. K. (1961). Relationships of testicular cholesterol to hormonal activity and behaviour in the Starling. *Proc. Soc. Exp. Biol. Med.* **107**, 653–65.

Hirvela, J. (1977). Kottaraisen, *Sturnus vulgaris*, pesivästä kannasta limingassa 1967–1976. *Aureola* **2**, 73–5.

Hodson, N. L. and Snow, D. W. (1965). The road deaths enquiry, 1960–61. *Bird Study* **12**, 90–9.

Hofer, R. and Schiemer, F. (1981). Proteolytic activity in the digestive tract of several species of fish with different feeding habits. *Oecologia, Berl.* **48**, 342–5.

Hoffman, K. (1959). Die Richtungsorientierung von Staren unter der Mitternachtssonne. *Z. vergl. Physiol.* **41**, 471–80.

Holyoak, D. (1971). Movements and mortality of Corvidae. *Bird Study* **18**, 97–106.

Hoogstraal, H. (1972). Birds as tick hosts and as reservoirs and disseminators of tickborne infectious agents. *Wiadomosci Parazytologiczne* **18**, 703–6.

Howard, R. D. (1974). The influence of sexual selection and interspecific competition in Mockingbird song (*Mimus polyglottis*). *Evolution* **23**, 428–8.

Hudec, K. and Folk, C. (1961). Postnatálrt vyvoj spacka obecného v prirozenych podmtnkách. *Zool. Listy* **24**, 305–30.

Imms, A. D. (1947). *Insect natural history*. Collins, London.

Inglis, G. M. (1947). The starlings and mynas of Bengal with special reference to north Bengal. *J. Bombay Nat. Hist. Soc.* **22**, 3–5.

Inglis, I. R. and Isaacson, A. J. (1978). The responses of Dark-bellied Brent Geese to models of geese in various postures. *Anim. Behav.* **26**, 953–8.

Jablonski, B. (1976). Estimation of birds abundance in large areas. *Acta Ornithol.* **16**, 23–76.

Jakubiec, Z. (1972). Przyroda rezerwatu Muszkowicki Las Bukowy w województwie wroclawskim: Ptaki. *Ochrona Przyrody* **17**, 135–52.

Jennings, T. and Evans, S. M. (1980). Influence of position in the flock and flock size on vigilance in the Starling, *Sturnus vulgaris*. *Anim. Behav.* **28**, 634–5.

Jones, M. M. (1980*a*). Diurnal variation in the distribution of lipid in the pectoralis muscle of the House Sparrow (*Passer domesticus*). *J. Zool. Lond.* **191**, 475–86.

—— (1980*b*). Nocturnal loss of muscle protein from House Sparrows (*Passer domesticus*). *J. Zool. Lond.* **192**, 33–9.

Jones, P. J. (1976). The utilization of calcareous grit by laying *Quelea quelea*. *Ibis* **118**, 575–6.

—— and Ward, P. (1976). The level of reserve protein as the proximate factor controlling the timing of breeding and clutch size in the Red-billed Quelea *Quelea quelea*. *Ibis* **118**, 546–74.

Kalela, O. (1949). Changes in geographic ranges in the avifauna of northern and central Europe in relation to recent changes in climate. *Bird Banding* **20**, 77–103.

Kalmbach, E. R. (1922). A comparison of the food habits of British and American Starlings. *Auk* **34**, 189–95.

—— (1928). The European Starling in the United States. *Farmers Bull.* **1571**, 1–26.

—— (1932). Winter Starling roosts of Washington. *Wilson Bull.* **44**, 65–75.

—— and Gabrielsen, I. N. (1921). Economic value of the Starling in the United States. *U.S. Dept. Agric. Bull.* **868**, 1–66.

Kazakov, B. A. (1979). Wintering of Starlings in Ciscaucasia. *Ornitologiya* **14**, 214–16. (In Russian).

Keeton, W. T. (1981). Avian orientation and navigation: new developments in an old mystery. *Acta XVII Congr. Int. Ornithol.* **1**, 137–57.

Kelty, M. P. and Lustick, S. I. (1977). Energetics of the Starling (*Sturnus vulgaris*) in a pine woods. *Ecology* **58**, 1181–5.

Kendeigh, S. C., Dol'nik, V. R., and Gavrilov, V. M. (1977). Avian energetics. In *Granivorous birds in ecoseptems*. (eds. J. Pinowski and S.C. Kendeigh). Cambridge University Press, Cambridge.

Kessel, B. (1953*a*). Distribution and migration of the European Starling in North America. *Condor* **55**, 49–67.

—— (1953*b*). Second broods in the European Starling in north America. *Auk* **70**, 479–83.

—— (1957). A study of the breeding biology of the European Starling (*Sturnus vulgaris* L.) in north America. *Am. Mid. Nat.* **58**, 257–331.

Kettle, P. (1977). A study of Phthiraptera (chiefly Amblycera and Ischnacera) with particular reference to the evolution and host–parasite relations of the order. Ph.D. Thesis, University of London.

Keymer, I. F. (1980). Discussion of Starlings as agricultural pests. In *Bird problems in agriculture* (eds. E. N. Wright, I. R. Inglis, and C. J. Feare). British Crop Protection Council, Croydon.

—— (1982*a*). Parasitic diseases. In *Diseases of cage and aviary birds*. (ed. M. L. Petrak). 2nd edn. Lea & Febiger, Philadelphia.

—— (1982*b*). Mycoses. In *Diseases of cage and aviary birds*. (ed. M. L. Petrak, 2nd edn. Lea & Febiger, Philadelphia.

King, B., Woodcock, M. and Dickinson, E. C. (1975). *Birds of south-east Asia*. Collins, London.

Kluyver, H. N. (1933). Bijdrage tot de biologie en de ecologie van de Spreeuw gedurende zija voortplantingstijd. *Versl. meded. Plantenkd. Dienst* **69**, 1–145.

Korpimäki, E. (1978). Breeding biology of the Starling, *Sturnus vulgaris*, in western Finland. *Ornithol. Fenn.* **55**, 93–104.

Kramer, G. (1951). Eine neue Methode zur Erforschung der Zugorientierung und die bisher damit erzielten Ergebnisse. *Proc. X. Int. Ornithol. Congr.*, pp. 269–80.

—— (1952). Experiments on bird orientation. *Ibis* **94**, 265–85.

Krebs, J. R. (1974). Colonial nesting and social feeding as strategies for exploiting food resources in the Great Blue Heron (*Ardea herodias*). *Behaviour* **51**, 99–134.

—— (1977). The significance of song repertoires: the Beau Geste hypothesis. *Anim. Behav.* **25**, 475–78.

Kroodsma, D. (1976). Reproductive development in a female songbird: differential stimulation by quality of male song. *Science N.Y.* **192**, 574–5.

Kuroda, N. (1973). Fluctuation of winter roosting flock of *Sturnus cineraceus* at Koshigaya and the roost change to Omatsu in summer. *Misc. Rep. Yamashina Inst. Ornithol.* **7**, 34–55. (In Japanese).

Lack, D. (1943). *The life of the Robin.* Witherby, London.

—— (1948). Natural selection and family size in the Starling. *Evolution* **2**, 95–110.

—— (1960). The height of bird migration. *Br. Birds* **53**, 5–10.

—— (1963). An undiscovered species of Swift. *Bird Notes* **30**, 258–60.

—— (1966). *Population studies of birds.* Oxford University Press, Oxford.

—— (1968). *Ecological adaptations for breeding in birds.* Methuen, London.

—— and Schifferti, A. (1948). Die Lebensdauer des Stares. *Ornithol. Beob.* **3**, 107–14.

Lancaster, J. E. and Alexander, D. J. (1975). Newcastle disease virus and spread. *Can. Dept. Agric. Monogr.* **11**, 1–79.

Landolt, M. and Kocan, R. M. (11976). Transmission of avian pox from Starlings to Rothschild's Mynahs. *J. Wildl. Dis.* **12**, 353–6.

La Touche, J. D. D. (1925–1934). *A handbook of the birds of eastern China.* Taylor & Francis, London.

Lazarus, J. (1979). Flock size and behaviour in captive Red-billed Weaver (*Quelea quelea*); implications for social facilitation and the functions of flocking. *Behaviour* **71**, 127–45.

Lebreton, J. D. and Landry, P. (1977). Premiers résultats sur la mortalité des Étourneaux français et ses implications sur la dynamique des populations. *EPPO Pubns. Ser. B. No.* **84**, 55.

Lefebvre, P. W. and Seubert, J. L. (1970). Surfactants as blackbird stressing agents. *Proc. Vert. Pest Conf.* **4**, 156–61.

Lindsay, A. A. (1939). Food of the Starling in central New York State. *Wilson Bull.* **51**, 176–82.

Lipkind, M. A., Weisman, Y., Shihmanter, E. and Shohman, D. (1979). The first isolation of animal influenza virus in Israel. *Vet. Rec.* **105**, 510–11.

Liversidge, R. (1962). The spread of the European Starling in the eastern Cape, *Ostrich*, 13–16.

Lloyd, J. A. (1965). Effects of environmental stimuli on the development of the incubation patch in the European Starling (*Sturnus vulgaris*). *Physiol. Zool.* **38**, 121–8.

Long, J. L. (1981). *Introduced birds of the world*. David & Charles, London.

Luniak, M. (1977). Liczebnose i produktywnose legow szpaka *Sturnus vulgaris* L, w Warszawie. *Acta Ornithol.* **16**, 241–74.

MacArthur, R. H. and Wilson, E. O. (1967). *The theory of island biogeography*. Princeton University Press, Princeton, NJ.

MacGillivray, W. (1840). *A manual of British ornithology*. Vol. 2. Scott, Webster & Geary, London.

Mackworth-Praed, C. W. and Grant, C. H. B. (1955). *Birds of eastern and north-eastern Africa*. Vol. 2. Longmans, Green, London.

—— (1963). *Birds of the southern third of Africa*. Vol. 2. Longmans, Green, London.

—— (1970). *Birds of west-central and western Africa*. Longmans Green, London.

MacLean, S. F. (1974). Lemming bones as a source of calcium for arctic sandpipers (*Calidris* spp.). *Ibis* **116**, 552–7.

Mal'kov, G. B., Dargol'ts, V. G., and Voronin, Y.K. (1966). Mass parasitism by adult *Ixodes persculatus* P. Sch. ticks on adult gallinacious and passeriform birds in tick borne encephalitis foci. *Tezisy Dokl. I. Akarol. Soveshch.* p. 127 (In Russian)

Manson-Bahr, P. E. C. (1953). The European Starling in Fiji. *Ibis* **95**, 699–700.

Marien, D. (1950). Notes on some Asiatic Sturnidae (Birds). *J. Bombay Nat. Hist. Soc.* **49**, 471–87.

Markov, G. C. (1940). Seasonal and annual variations in parasite-fauna of Starlings in connection with changes in meteorological factors. *Zool. Zhurn.* **19**, 741–9.

Marples, B. J. (1934). The winter Starling roosts of Great Britain, 1932–1933. *J. Anim. Ecol.* **3**, 187–203.

Marples, G., (1936). Behaviour of Starlings at nesting site. *Br. Birds* **30**, 14–21.

Martin, E. W. (1914). *The birds of the Latin poets*. Stanford University Press, Stanford.

Matthews, G. V. T. (1953). *Bird navigation*. Cambridge University Press, Cambridge.

McClure, H. E. (1974). *Migration and survival of the birds of Asia.* SEATO Medical Project, Bangkok.

McGregor, P. K., Krebs, J. R., and Perrins, C. M. (1981). Song repertoires and lifetime reproductive success in the Great Tit (*Parus major*) *Am. Nat.* **118**, 149–59.

Medway, Lord and Wells, D. R. (1976). *The birds of the Malay Peninsula.* Vol. 5. Witherby, London.

Meinertzhagen, R. (1954). *Birds of Arabia.* Oliver & Boyd, Edinburgh.

Merkel, F. W. (1978). Sozialverhalten von individuell markierten Staren—*Sturnus vulgaris*—in einer kleinen Nistkastenkolonie (I. Mitteilung). *Luscinia* **43**, 163–81.

—— (1980). Sozialverhalten von individuell markierten Staren—*Sturnus vulgaris*—in einer kleinen Nistkastenkolonie (3. Mitteilung). *Luscinia* **44**, 133–58.

Mertens, J. A. L. (1969). The influence of brood size on the energy metabolism and water loss of nestling Great Tits *Parus major major Ibis* **111**, 11–16.

Mettrick, D. F. (1960). Helminth parasites of Hertfordshire birds. IV Survey results. *J. Helminthol* **34**, 267–76.

Meyer, A. B. and Wigglesworth, L. W. (1898). *The birds of Celebes and neighbouring islands.* Friedlander & Sohn, Berlin.

Mock, D. (in press) Falsifiability and the information centre hypothesis.

Morley, A. (1941). The behaviour of a group of resident British Starlings (*Sturnus vulgaris*) from October to March. *Naturalist* **88**, 55–61.

Mueren, E. van der (1980). Intraspecific aggression in a group of caged Starlings, *Sturnus vulgaris.* Le Gerfaut **70**, 455–70.

Murton, R. K. (1964). Do birds transmit foot-and-mouth disease? *Ibis* **106**, 289–98.

—— (1965). *The Woodpigeon.* Collins, London.

—— and Westwood, N. J. (1977). *Avian breeding cycles.* Oxford University Press, Oxford.

Nankinov, D. N. (1978). Nomadic movements of the Starling, *Sturnus vulgaris* L. in post-breeding period. *Acta Ornithol.* **16**, 309–13. (In Russian)

Nelson, J. B. (1980). *The Gannet.* Poyser, Berkhampstead.

Newton, I. (1972). *Finches.* Collins, London.

—— and Marquiss, M. (1982). Food, predation and breeding season in Sparrowhawks (*Accipiter nisus*). *J. Zool., Lond.* **197**, 221–40.

Nicholson, E. M. (1951). *Birds and Man.* Collins, London.

Noordwijk, A. J. van, Balen, J. H. van, and Scharloo, W. (1980). Heritability of ecologically important traits in the Great Tit. *Ardea* **68**, 193–203.

Numerov, A. D. (1978). Cases of abnormal egg laying by Starlings (*Sturnus vulgaris* L). *Proc. Oka State Reserve* **14**, 356–57 (In Russian).

Oddie, W. (1980). *Bill Oddie's little black bird book.* Eyre Methuen, London.

Oelke, H. (1967). Siedlungsdichte und Brutplatzwahl des Stares (*Sturnus vulgaris*) in der norddeutschen Kulturlandschaft. *Orn. Mitt.* **19**, 31–4.

Ojanen, M., Orell, M., and Merila, E (1978). Population decrease of Starlings in northern Finland. *Ornithol. Fenn.* **55**, 38–9.

Orell, M. and Ojanen, M. (1980). Zur Abnahme des Stars (*Sturnus vulgaris*) in Skandinavien. *J. Ornithol.* **121**, 397–401.

Owen, R. W. and Pemberton, R. T. (1962). Helminth infection of the Starling (*Sturnus vulgaris* L.) in northern England. *Proc. zool. Soc. Lond.* **139**, 557–87.

Parmelee, A. (1959). *All the birds of the Bible.* Lutterworth Press, London.

Parslow, J. (1968). Changes in status among breeding birds in Britain and Ireland. *Br. Birds* **61**, 49–64.

Parsons, J. (1972). Egg size, laying date and incubation period in the Herring Gull. *Ibis* **114**, 536–41.

Parsons, J. J. (1960). Sobre la caza a gran escala del Estornino Pinto (*Sturnus vulgaris*) en España. *Ardeola* **6**, 235–41.

Patterson, I. J. (1965). Timing and spacing of broods in the Black-headed Gull *Larus ridibundus*. *Ibis* **107**, 433–59.

——, Dunnet, G. M., and Fordham, R. A. (1971). Ecological studies of the Rook (*Corvus frugilegus* L.) in north-east Scotland. Dispersion. *J. appl. Ecol.* **8**, 803–21.

Pennycuik, C. J. (1975). Mechanics of flight. In *Avian Biology* (ed. D. S. Farner and J. R. King) Vol. 5. Academic Press, New York.

Perdeck, A. C. (1958). Two types of orientation in migrating Starlings, *Sturnus vulgaris* L., and Chaffinches, *Fringilla coelebs* L., as revealed by displacement experiments. *Ardea* **46**, 1–37.

—— (1964). An experiment on the ending of autumn migration in Starlings. *Ardea* **52**, 133–9.

—— (1967a). The Starling as a passage migrant in Holland. *Bird Study* **14**, 129–52.

—— (1967b). Orientation of Starlings after displacement to Spain. *Ardea* **55**, 194–202.

—— (1974). An experiment on the orientation of juvenile Starlings during spring migration. *Ardea* **62**, 190–5.

Perrins, C. M. (1970). The timing of birds' breeding seasons. *Ibis* **112**, 242–55.

—— (1979). *British Tits.* Collins, London.

—— and Jones, P. J. (1974). The inheritance of clutch-size in the Great-tit (*Parus major* L.). *Condor* **76**, 225–9.

Pilchard, E. I. (1965). Experimental transmission of Transmissible Gastroenteritis virus by Starlings. *Am. J. Vet. Res.* **26**, 1177–9.

Polyakova, A. D., Ardamatskaya, T. B., Ganya, I. M., Ezerskas, L. I., Marisova, I. V., Priklonskii, S. G., and Sema, A. M. (1978). Population density of Starlings in the USSR. *Proc. Oka State Reserve* **14**, 315–27. (In Russia.)

Potts, G. R. (1967). Urban Starling roosts in the British Isles. *Bird Study* **14**, 35–42.

Powell, G. V. N. (1974). Experimental analysis of the social value of flocking by Starlings (*Sturnus vulgaris*) in relation to predation and foraging. *Anim. Behav.* **22**, 501–5.

Power, H. W., Litovich, E., and Lombardo, M. P. (1981). Male Starlings delay incubation to avoid being cuckolded. *Auk* **98**, 386–9.

Powlesland, R. G. (1977). Effects of the haematophagous mite *Ornithonyssus bursa* on nestling Starlings in New Zealand. *N.Z. J. Zool.* **4**, 85–94.

Pritchard, G. (1982). Observations on clinical aspects of Transmissible Gastroenteritis of pigs in Norfolk and Suffolk, 1980–81. *Vet. Rec.* **110**, 465–9.

Rand, A. L. (1936). The distribution and habits of Madagascar birds. *Bull. Am. Mus. Nat. Hist.* **72**, 143–499.

Ratcliffe, D. A. (1981). *The Peregrine.* Poyser, Berkhampstead.

Ricklefs, R. E. (1979*a*). Patterns of growth in birds. V. A comparative study of development in the Starling, Common Tern, and Japanese Quail. *Auk* **96**, 10–30.

—— (1979*b*). Adaptation, constraint and compromise in avian postnatal development. *Biol. Rev.* **54**, 269–90.

—— and Peters, S. (1979). Intraspecific variation in the growth rate of nestling European Starlings. *Bird-Banding* **50**, 338–48.

Risser, A. C. (1975). Experimental modification of reproductive performance by density in captive Starlings. *Condor* **77**, 125–32.

Rochard, J. B. A. and Horton, N. (1980). Birds killed by aircraft in the United Kingdom, 1966–76. *Bird Study* **27**, 227–34.

Rogers, J. G. (1980). Conditioned taste aversion: its role in bird damage control. In *Bird problems in agriculture.* (eds. E. N. Wright, I. R. Inglis, and C. J. Feare). British Crop Protection Council, Croydon.

Rohwer, S. (1975). The social significance of avian winter plumage variability. *Evolution* **29**, 593–610.

Rothschild, M. and Clay, T. (1952). *Fleas flukes and cuckoos.* Collins, London.

Rowley, I. (1976). Cooperative breeding in Australian birds. *Proc. XVI Ornithol. Congr.* pp. 657–666.

Rowsell, H. C., Ritchey, J. and Cox, F. (1978–9). Assessment of humaneness of vertebrate pesticides. *Proc. Can. Assoc. Lab. Anim. Sci.* 1979, 236–49.

Royall, W. C. (1966). Breeding of the Starling in central Arizona. *Condor* **68**, 196–205.

——, DeCino, T. J., and Besser, J. F. (1967). Reduction of a Starling population at a Turkey farm. *Poultry Sci.* **46**, 1494–5.

Royama, T. (1966). Factors governing feeding rate, food requirement and brood size of nestling Great Tits *Parus major*. *Ibis* **108**, 313–47.

Russell, D. N. (1971). Food habits of the Starling in eastern Texas. *Condor* **73**, 369–72.

Rydzewski, W. (1960) A tentative analysis of the migrational populations of Starling (*Sturnus vulgaris*). *Proc. XII Int. Ornithol Congr.* **2**, 641–4.

Saurola, P. (1978). Mita rengastusaineisto kertoo kottaraisesta? *Lintumies* **13**, 90–8.

Savory, C. J. and Gentle, M. J. (1976). Effects of dietary dilution with fibre on the food intake and gut dimensions of Japanese Quail. *Br. Poultry Sci.* **17**, 561–70.

Schneider, W. (1972). *Der Star*. Verlag, Wittenberg Lutherstadt.

Schwab, R. (1971). Circannual testicular periodicity in the European Starling in the absence of photoperiodic change. In *Biochronometry* (ed M. Menaker). National Academy of Sciences, Washington, DC.

Searcy, W. A., McArthur, P. D., Peters, S. S., and Marler, P. (1981). Response of male Song and Swamp Sparrows to neighbor, stranger and self songs. *Behaviour* **77**, 152–63

Seastedt, T. R. and MacLean, S. F. (1977). Calcium supplements in the diet of nestling Lapland Longspurs (*Calcarius lapponicus*) near Barrow, Alaska. *Ibis* **119**, 531–3

Sema, A. M. (1976). Starling damage in vineyards of south-east Kazakhstan and analysis of acoustic repulsion results. *Ornitologiya* **12**, 160–5. (In Russian)

Sema, A. M. (1978). The biology of the Starling in south-east Kazakhstan. *Trud. Inst. Zool. Alma-Ata (Ser. Zool.)* **38**, 42–57 (In Russian).

Sharrock, J. T. R. (1976). *The atlas of breeding birds in Britain and Ireland.*. British Trust for Ornithlogy, Tring

Shcherbinina, O. K. (1971). Bird hosts of *Hyalomma plumbeum* (Panzer) ticks in Turkmenia. *Izv. Akad. Nauk, Turkmen. SSR* **5**, 54–57 (In Russian).

Shi–Chun, L., XI-Yuo, L., Yao-Kuang, T. and Yao-Hoa, S. (1975). On feeding habits of the Rose-coloured Starling (*Sturnus roseus*) and its effects on locust—population density. *Acta Zool. Sinica* **21**, 71–7 (In Chinese).

Sibley, C. G. and Ahlquist, J. E. (1974). The relationships of the African sugarbirds (*Promerops*). *Ostrich* **45**, 22–30.

Sidenko, V. P., Semenov, B. F., Stepanovskaya, L. D., Daraseva, P. S., Sochinsky, V. A., Polyakov, E. M., Gretov, V. S., and Solomko, R. M. (1972). Seasonal migrations of wild birds inhabiting biotopes of the southern Ukraine littoral and their associations with arboviruses. *Mater. Simp Itogi 6. Simp. Izuch, Virus. Ekol Syazan, Ptits. (Omsk, December 1971)* pp. 130–8 (In Russian).

Silva, E. T. (1949). Nest records of the Song Thrush. *Br. Birds* **42**, 97–111.

Simms, E. (1978). *British Thrushes*. Collins, London

Simpson, S. M. and Follett, B. K. (1981). Pineal and hypothalamic pacemakers: their role in regulating circadian rhythmicity in Japanese Quail. *J. Comp. Physiol.* **144**, 381–9.

Singer, N., Weissman, Y., Yom–Tov, Y., and Marder, U. (1977). Isolation of *Salmonella hessarek* from Starlings (*Sturnus vulgaris*). *Avian Dis.* **21**, 117–9.

Smart, P. M. (1980). Starling (*Sturnus vulgaris* L.) damage and its control at an open air piggery in north-east Scotland. Unpublished BSc thesis, University of Aberdeen

Smythies, B. E. (1953). *The birds of Burma*. Oliver & Boyd, Edinburgh.

Snow, D. W. (1956). The annual mortality of the Blue Tit in different parts of its range. *Br. Birds* **49**, 174–7.

—— (1958). *A study of Blackbirds*. Methuen, London

—— (1968). Birds and the 1967–8 foot-and-mouth epidemic. *Bird Study* **15**, 184–90

Spaans, A. L. (1977). Are Starlings faithful to their individual winter quarters? *Ardea* **65**, 83–7

Spencer, K. G. (1966). Some notes on the roosting behaviour of Starlings *Naturalist* **898**, 73–80

Spencer, R. and Hudson, R. (1980). Report on bird-ringing for 1979. *Ringing and Migration* **3**, 65–108

Steinbacher, J. (1960). Die tragödie der Stare von Tunisien. *Gefiederte Welt* **8**, 148–50

Studer-Thiersch, A. (1969). Das Zugverhalten schweizerischer Stare *Sturnus vulgaris* nach Ringfunden. *Ornithol. Beob.* **66**, 105–44

Summers-Smith, J. D. (1963). *The House Sparrow*. Collins, London

Suthers, H. B. (1978). Analysis of a resident flock of Starlings. *Bird-Banding* **49**, 35–46

Svensson, S. (1964). Weight variations in young Starlings (*Sturnus vulgaris*). Ottenby Bird Station Report No. 39. *Var Fagelv.* **23**, 43–56

Swingland, I. R. (1977). The social and spatial organization of winter communal roosting in Rooks (*Corvus frugilegus*). *J. Zool., Lond.* **182**, 509–28

Symonds, A. E. J. (1961). The counting of Starlings at country roosts. *Bird Study* **8**, 185–93

—— (1965). The rate of build-up and evacuation of country Starling roosts and the effect of severe winter conditions on these procedures. *Bird Study* **12**, 8–16

Szijj, J. (1957). A seregely taplalkozasbiologiaja es mezogazdasag: jelentosege. *Aquila* **63**, 71–101

Tahon, J. (1978). L'Etourneau sansonnet (*Sturnus vulgaris*). Biologie, dortoirs, protection des cultures. *E.P.P.O. Pubns. Ser. B.* No. **84**, 83–153.

—— (1980). Attempts to control starlings at roosts using explosives. In *Bird problems in agriculture* (eds. E. N. Wright., I. R. Inglis, and C. J. Feare) British Crop Protection Council, Croydon.

Taitt, M. J. (1973). Winter food and feeding requirements of the Starling. *Bird Study* **20**, 226–36.

Taylor, R. G. (1953). Starlings in Jamaica. *Ibis* **95**, 700–701.

Tchernov, E. (1962). Palaeolithic avifauna in Palestine, *Bull. Res. Council Israel* **11**, 95–131.

Temple, S. A. (1974). Plasma testosterone titers during the annual reproductive cycle of Starlings (*Sturnus vulgaris*). *Gen. Comp. Endocrinol.* **22**, 470–9

Tenovuo, R. and Lemmetyinen, R. (1970). On the breeding ecology of the Starling *Sturnus vulgaris* in the archipelago of South Western Finland. *Ornithol. Fenn.* **47**, 159–66.

Thompson, R. D., Grant, C. V., Pearson, E. W., and Corner, G. W. (1968). Cardiac response of Starlings to sound: effects of lighting and grouping. *Am. J. Physiol.* **214**, 41–4.

Thomson, A. L. (1964). *A new dictionary of birds*. Nelson, London.

Tinbergen, J. M. (1976). How Starlings (*Sturnus vulgaris* L.) apportion their foraging time in a virtual single prey situation on a meadow. *Ardea* **64**, 155–70.

—— (1981). Foraging decisions in Starlings (*Sturnus vulgaris* L.). *Ardea* **69**, 1–67.

—— and Drent, R. H. (1980). The Starling as a successful forager. In *Bird problems in agriculture* (eds. E. N. Wright., I. R. Inglis, and C. J. Feare) British Crop Protection Council, Croydon.

Tinbergen, N. (1953). *The Herring Gull's world*. Collins, London.

Tomaliojc, L. (1974). Charakterystyka ilościowa legowej; zimowej awifauny lasow okolic Legnicy (Ślask Dolny). *Acta Ornithol.* **14**, 59–97.

Tomaliojc, L. and Profus, P. (1977). Comparative analysis of breeding bird communities in two parks of Wroclaw and in an adjacent *Querco-Carpinetum* forest. *Acta Ornithol.* **16**, 117–77.

Torre-Bueno, J. R. and Larochelle, J. (1978). The metabolic cost of flight in unrestrained birds. *J. exp. Biol.* **75**, 223–9.

Tosh, F. E., Doto, I. L., Beecher, S. B., and Chin, T. D. Y. (1970) Relationship of Starling-blackbird roosts and endemic histoplasmosis. *Am. Rev. Resp. Dis.* **101**, 283–8.

Tucker, V. A. (1970). Energetic cost of locomotion in animals. *Comp Biochem. Physiol.* **34**, 841–6.

Turek, F. W., McMillan, J. P., and Menaker, M. (1976). Melatonin: effects on the circadian locomotor rhythm of sparrows. *Science N. Y.* **194**, 1441–3.

Vaurie, C. (1962). *The birds of the Palaearctic fauna. Passeriformes.* Witherby, London.

Verheyen, R. F., (1969). Le choix du nichoir chez l'Etourneau (*Sturnus vulgaris*). Le Gerfaut **59**, 239–59.

—— (1970). Description et signification des poursuites sexuelles des Etourneaux (*Sturnus v. vulgaris* L.) *Le Gerfaut* **60**, 41–8.

—— (1980). Breeding strategies of the Starling. In *Bird problems in agriculture.* (eds E. N. Wright., I. R. Inglis., and C. J. Feare) British Crop Protection Council, Croydon.

Voous, K. H. (1960). *Atlas of European birds.* Nelson, London.

Wallraff, H. G. and Hund, K. (1982). Homeing experiments with Starlings (*Sturnus vulgaris*) subjected to olfactory nerve section. In *Avian navigation* (ed. F. Papi and H. G. Wallraff). Springer Verlag, Berlin.

Walsberg, G. E. and King, J. R. (1980). The thermoregulatory significance of the winter roost-sites selected by robins in eastern Washington. *Wilson Bull.* **92**, 33–9.

Ward, P. (1965). Feeding ecology of the Black-faced Dioch *Quelea quelea* in Nigeria. *Ibis* **107**, 173–214.

—— (1977). Fat and protein reserves of Starlings. *Institute of Terrestrial Ecology Ann. Rep.* pp. 54–6.

—— and Zahavi, A. (1973). The importance of certain assemblages as 'information centres' for food-finding. *Ibis* **115**, 517–34.

West. R. R. (1968). Reduction of a winter Starling population by baiting its pre-roosting areas. *J. Wildl. Manage.* **32**, 637–40.

Westerterp, K. (1973). The energy budget of the nestling Starling *Sturnus vulgaris*, a field study. *Ardea* **61**, 137–58.

—— Gortmaker, W., and Wigngaarden, H. (1982). An energetic optimum in brood-raising in the Starling *Sturnus vulgaris*: an experimental study. *Ardea* **70**, 153–62.

Whistler, H. (1963). *Popular handbook of Indian birds.* Oliver & Boyd, Edinburgh.

White, G. (1789). The natural history and antiquities of Selborne. B. White, London.

Williamson, F. S. L. (1968). The ecology of pox virus disease in the Starling *Sturnus vulgaris* L. Ph.D. thesis, Johns Hopkins University.

Williamson, K. (1961). Sequence of post-nuptial moult in the Starling. *Bird Migration* **2**, 43–5.

—— (1968). A breeding bird survey of Queen Wood in the Chilterns, Oxon. *Q. J. Forestry* **42**, 118–31.

Williamson, P. and Gray, L. (1975). Foraging behaviour of the Starling (*Sturnus vulgaris*) in Maryland. *Condor* **77**, 84–9.

Wilson, P. R. (1979). The Starling: a potential brood parasite? *Notornis* **26**, 96–7.

Wright, E. N. (1973). Experiments to control Starling damage at intensive animal husbandry units. *E.P.P.O. Bull.*, No. **9**, 85–9.

Wynne-Edwards, V. C. (1929). The behaviour of Starlings in winter. *Br. Birds* **23**, 138–53 and 170–80.

—— (1931). The behaviour of Starlings in winter. II. Observations at Somerset, 1929–1930. *Br. Birds* **24**, 346–53.

—— (1962). *Animal dispersion in relation to social behaviour*. Oliver & Boyd, Edinburgh.

Yom-Tov, Y. (1975). Synchronization of breeding and intraspecific interference in the Carrion Crow. *Auk* **92**, 778–85.

Yom-Tov, Y. (1979). The disadvantage of low positions in colonial roosts: an experiment to test the effects of droppings on plumage quality. *Ibis* **121**, 331–3.

—— Dunnet, G. M., and Anderson, A. (1974). Intraspecific nest parasitism in the Starling, *Sturnus vulgaris*. *Ibis* **116**, 87–90.

—— Imber, A., and Otterman, J. (1977). The microclimate of winter roosts of the Starling *Sturnus vulgaris*. *Ibis* **119**, 366–8.

Zeleny, L. (1969). Starlings versus native cavity-nesting birds. *Atlantic Nat.* **24**, 158–61.

Index

Page numbers in **bold type** are main areas of discussion